The New Environmental Regulation

The New Environmental Regulation

Daniel J. Fiorino

The MIT Press
Cambridge, Massachusetts
London, England

This book was set in Sabon by SPI Publisher Services and was printed on recycled paper and bound in the United States of America.

Library of Congress Cataloging-in-Publication Data

Fiorino, Daniel J.
The new environmental regulation / Daniel J. Fiorino.
    p. cm.
Includes bibliographical references and index.
ISBN 0-262-06256-9—ISBN 978-0-262-06256-5 (alk. paper)—ISBN 0-262-56218-9—ISBN 978-0-262-56218-8 (pbk. : alk. paper)
1. Environmental law—United States. 2. Environmental policy—United States. 3. Environmental protection—United States. I. Title.

KF3775.F56   2005
344.7304'6—dc22

                                                              2006044444

10 9 8 7 6 5 4

To Tillie Fiorino

Contents

Preface

In *The Morality of Law*, Lon Fuller wrote that "the capacity to devise institutions and procedures adequate to its problems is perhaps the chief mark of a civilized society."[1] Under this standard, the United States could be judged as being highly civilized when it comes to protecting the environment. It has created an elaborate set of laws for responding to a range of problems. Most are administered by a highly capable and technically sophisticated national regulatory agency. Often these capacities are matched by those of the states; most states are as capable as and some are more innovative than the federal government. Although they are not perfect, there are ample procedures for participation and for conducting and evaluating scientific analysis. In response, American industry has created an impressive institutional capacity for complying with this array of laws and for doing much more.

The argument made here, however, is that the United States has been slipping in its capacity to devise institutions and procedures that are adequate to a new era of environmental problem solving. What worked reasonably well in the past will not work so well in the future. It is true there is more than ample evidence that to a large degree a regulatory approach has worked, especially for the problems it originally was designed to address. The air, water, and land are much better off than they would have been without the extensive system of environmental controls this country has put into place since 1970. That proposition is taken as being almost indisputable in this book. However, nothing lasts forever, in public policy as in life in general. The times are changing, and regulation should change with them. Regulation as we know it is due, not just for a tune-up but for a more basic overhaul that will make it more relevant and effective in a new era of environmental problem solving.

The theme of this book is that it is time for a transition from an old to a new regulation. The "old" regulation was very much a product of its times. It reflected a mid-twentieth-century belief in government's ability to solve complex problems and displayed a recognition that industry would not act to reduce air and water pollution without a substantial kick in the pants from government. When the federal government did respond to the growing concern about environmental quality in the 1970s, it drew from a well-established set of strategies and tools that were entirely consistent with our experience and political culture. It relied heavily on bureaucratic, top-down intervention through a system of rules. It assumed that only government coercion would lead to the needed changes in industry behavior. Formal, adversarial relationships were built into the system to ensure that government would be insulated from industry influence. Given the times and the state of mind in both government and industry, this was not a bad model for a first stage of environmental problem solving.

At its core, this response was similar to actions taken and institutions created in most other industrial democracies. It was not based on any particular understanding of a business perspective or the internal dynamics of firms. In this sense, the old regulation was based on a series of fairly crude assumptions about what motivated behavior and how to change it. It assumed that the interests of society in environmental protection and those of industry in realizing profits were at odds. Although entirely understandable as a place to start, these assumptions now appear to be increasingly outdated.

The "new" regulation will build upon the foundations of the old, but will recognize the changes that are occurring in environmental problems, the economy, and society more generally. This new regulation will differ from the old in several respects. It will be based more on performance than on a narrow definition of compliance. It will allow regulated firms, especially the better performers, more flexibility in determining how to achieve environmental goals. It will aim to complement the way that business decisions are made in the private sector rather than just imposing more legal obligations on firms. It will recognize the internal dynamics of decision making within firms and, most important, take into account differences in the willingness and capabilities of different firms to meet their environmental obligations. The new regulation will go beyond the conventional rules-and-deterrence approach and rely on a more diverse set of policy instruments and strategies, including market incentives and information about performance. The new regulation will not replace what exists now, but would modify it in many ways.

As the discussion here documents, some initial steps in this transition to a new regulation are already under way. My purpose is to bring together a great deal of thinking and experience and, in doing so, set out a view of where we should be going as we try to move this transition along. It will not be an easy transition, to be sure, given the state of the environmental debate and of national politics in general. The notion that there should be a different kind of regulation typically has been lost in the political debates over whether there should be more or less regulation along lines of the old model. Environmental politics at the national level are as polarized as most other areas of domestic policy, if not more. Still, over time, the U.S. policy system has shown that it can change. The idea here is that learning why we need to change, what changes already are occurring, and in what directions we should be going will help in moving toward a new regulation.

Many people have helped to make this a better book than it otherwise might have been. Bob Durant, Peter May, and Aseem Prakash offered valuable comments on the entire manuscript, as did three anonymous referees with the MIT Press. Students in my course on strategic management for sustainability at the Johns Hopkins University's Washington Center have helped me test many of the ideas and arguments over the past few years. I am also indebted to the people from the Greening of Industry Network who first made me aware of the changes that are occurring and the need for public policy to change with it. I want to thank Clay Morgan, senior acquisitions editor for environmental studies at the MIT Press, for his interest in this book and his guidance in bringing it to publication. Thanks also to senior editor Katherine Almeida of the MIT Press for her skill and patience in improving the quality of the manuscript. Thanks also to Joanne, Matthew, and Jacob Fiorino for their support and encouragement while I was thinking about and writing this book.

I want to acknowledge with sadness two former professors who died in 2005. Larry E. Esterly of Youngstown State University was not only an outstanding teacher but also a mentor throughout my undergraduate years. My interest in and commitment to the study of political science is largely a result of his influence. He taught me about intellectual discipline and lucid analysis. For four decades, Francis E. Rourke of the Johns Hopkins University was a model of astute, graceful, and self-effacing scholarship and teaching to his students. The clarity of his writing and thinking and the quality of his insights into American bureaucracy and public policy influenced many students who have since taught, written about, or practiced in the field, including myself. These teachers are a loss not only to their family, friends, and students but also to the political science community generally.

This book is aimed principally at students, practitioners, and scholars who want to learn more about environmental regulation and how it should be changing. For students, it should be especially useful in courses on environmental policy, regulation, organizational change and innovation, and public policy generally. It is designed to be used by either undergraduate or graduate students. For practitioners, the goal is to provide an accessible and reasonably concise guide to the core characteristics of environmental regulation in the United States and the need to adapt it to a new phase of environmental problem solving. It should be especially useful to those working in regulatory agencies at all levels of government or who deal with regulatory issues in some other role or setting. For scholars, the aim is to bring together a wide range of important and timely research, thought, and experience into one volume. The book offers a critique of the current regulatory system and sets out a conceptual basis for thinking about how to change it in the context of a new era of governance. The hope is that each of these audiences will benefit from reading this book.

The New Environmental Regulation

1

Environmental Regulation—Past and Future

With updated understanding and better information, there is reason to be optimistic that action in the 2000s will be based not on the fears of the 1970s, but the needs of the next century.[1]

Imagine a picture of environmental regulation in the last decade of the twentieth century: Some more than thirty years old in their basic design, the national laws that authorized federal agencies to create regulations to protect air, water, and other environmental resources have transformed the private sector. The nation spends more than $200 billion annually to carry out these laws.[2] One of the world's most powerful regulatory agencies implements them, in a close but sometimes strained cooperation with its counterparts in the states. Some 15,000 pages of federal regulations alone translate legislation into detailed instructions for the millions of entities that fall within their reach. An elaborate system of reporting, inspections, and penalties exists to make people follow the rules. Many regulated firms use well-trained and highly professional experts to see to compliance as well as to manage the firm's broader effects on the environment.

All of this has cost a great deal of money, to be sure. Since the early 1970s, the United States has spent some $3–4 trillion (in 2004 dollars) on environmental protection related to pollution, mostly to meet the requirements of federal regulations.[3] The scope and stringency of environmental regulations have been the subject of almost constant political controversy. Still, most observers agree that the nation has received a return on its investment. Several kinds of air pollution have decreased or stayed the same, despite economic expansion, population growth, and increased driving. Water pollution, mostly from large industrial sources, has gone down. Many harmful chemicals have been removed from commerce. An impressive infrastructure for environmental management is in place. The United States is recognized around the world for its technical prowess. It is not unreasonable, as Greg Easterbrook has, to call environmental protection one of the major domestic policy successes of the second half of the twentieth century.[4]

And yet there was a widely shared sense of dissatisfaction with environmental regulation as it existed at the time. Of course, there have always been critics of the regulatory system. They argued that regulation is too costly, delivers too few benefits, relies on faulty science, and intrudes too far into the operations of the marketplace. These complaints, often with good foundation, have always been part of the landscape. However, in the 1990s another stream of criticism became more visible. This came from the traditional defenders, not the usual critics, of environmental programs. Their criticisms were aimed, not just at the costs and intrusiveness of regulation, but at its effectiveness. More and more, people were asking: "Is environmental regulation as currently designed sufficient for meeting the challenges of the coming decades?" Increasingly, the answer was "no." A chorus of critics, among them many thoughtful advocates of environmental values, have concluded that the current regulatory system will have to change if long-term environmental goals are to be achieved. The issues raised by these "revisionist" critics define the focus of this book.[5]

The revisionist criticisms of a regulatory approach cover many aspects of its design and performance. One criticism, for example, is that the resulting high levels of conflict and adversarial relations hamper our ability to innovate. Distrust among government, business, and environmental groups increases the transaction costs of regulation (i.e., reporting, record-keeping, and permitting processes) and diverts efforts away from desirable environmental results. Another criticism is that the design of the regulatory system, in which different problems are addressed through distinct laws, organizations, and strategies, leads to more expensive and less effective solutions than would be achieved under a more integrated approach. Many critics also have faulted the emphasis on legal compliance, which encourages businesses to meet the legal standard but offers no incentive for them to exceed the standard. There is even evidence that the current regulatory system, which stresses compliance with technology-based rules over improved environmental performance, is a barrier to innovation over the long term.[6] These issues are examined later in this chapter and in chapter 3.

This book explores these and other criticisms of the current regulatory system. Its purpose is to present a critique of what may be termed the "old" environmental regulation that has existed from about 1970 to the present as well as to set out the elements of a new one. The book does not deny the benefits that the old regulation has brought, which have been substantial. It accepts that regulation in some form was and will continue to be a necessary step in our evolving efforts to protect the environment in the face of economic development, urbanization, and population growth. Regulation was a step all industrial nations took to address environmental issues in the second half of the past century.

This book takes the argument one step further. Although the old regulation served well us in the past, it is time for a new approach. The problems are changing, patterns of governance are evolving, the economy is more dynamic, and new factors influence businesses. Put simply, the old regulation is like a suit we have outgrown. It is beginning to fray around the edges and look slightly out of style. As many of the critics discussed in this book argue, it is time for a newer, updated suit of clothes, in the form of a new approach to environmental regulation.

This new regulation will differ from the current version in key respects. It will be based more on performance than on a narrow definition of compliance. It will allow regulated firms, especially the better performers, more flexibility in determining how to achieve performance goals. It will aim to complement the way that business decisions are made in the private sector rather than just impose more legal obligations on firms. It will recognize the internal dynamics of decision making within firms and, most important, take into account differences in the willingness and capabilities of firms to meet their environmental obligations. The new regulation will go beyond the conventional rules-and-deterrence approach and rely on a more diverse set of policy instruments and strategies, including market incentives and information about performance. The new regulatory approach will not replace what exists now, but will modify it in many ways.

How Did We Get to Where We Are Today?

Forty years ago, when there was limited experience in environmental management, it seemed clear that government intervention in some form was the only means of getting industry to account for the costs of the environmental damage it created. Pollution charges were based on the theoretical estimates of a handful of resource economists. In a political culture hostile to federal involvement in land use and lifestyle choices, an extensive program of government planning was impractical. Direct regulation was a logical choice as the core of a national environmental strategy. It was a strategy that nearly every other industrial society adopted in the late 1960s and 1970s, when they began to respond to the growing awareness of environmental problems and to society's demands that government do something about them.[7]

At first, nearly all of U.S. industry resisted. Eventually, however, after public support for environmental values became evident, most companies complied, and many began to see business efficiencies and opportunities in sound and progressive environmental management. At the same time, in the mid-1980s, U.S. policy makers began to recognize limits in their approach. Consider some of them: There appeared to be far more conflict than cooperation; regulators could not keep up with the pace of change as they tried to define the best available technologies; defining problems by environmental medium impeded efforts to achieve better overall results; technology-based regulation appeared to exchange short-term gain for long-term innovation; environmental protection probably cost much more than it should; and the government often directed resources to low-risk activities while ignoring higher ones.[8]

Countries such as the Netherlands, Sweden, Norway, and the United Kingdom began to address these problems by using integrated regulatory and permitting policies, cooperative initiatives between government and industry, and financial and other incentives.[9] Instead of adapting its regulatory approach to the future, however, the U.S. political system in the 1980s looked more to the past. The Reagan administration launched a major assault on environmental programs. A Democratic Congress responded by increasing the scope and stringency of regulation, especially for hazardous waste. It became an environmental arms race. The more the Reagan and later the Bush administrations tried to roll back regulation, the more specific and demanding were the regulatory laws coming out of Congress. The political struggles between the pro- and antiregulators dominated environmental policy debates through the 1980s and well into the 1990s.[10]

Still, in these years there were successes in improving regulation. The growing use of mediation promoted the search for a middle ground in previously intractable disputes. The Environmental Protection Agency (EPA) began to incorporate formal negotiations into its rule-making procedures. Market incentives, such as emissions trading in the air quality program, were adopted as a means of giving firms a degree of flexibility in deciding how to reduce pollution. The EPA and state agencies experimented with cross-media strategies that, their proponents hoped, would be more effective and less costly than the medium-based strategies of the past. Forward-thinking people developed approaches that prevented rather than simply controlled pollution. By the end of the 1980s, government and industry alike appreciated the value of partnerships and information disclosure as tools for protecting the environment.

Through the 1990s, many groups continued to call for change. They urged more cooperation, more emphasis on performance, less legalism, a better climate for innovation, more policy integration, and increased flexibility. They pointed to trends in Europe and elsewhere as models. The EPA and its state counterparts began efforts to "reinvent" regulatory programs. These included several high-profile initiatives designed to build in flexibility for achieving better environmental results, account for differences among sectors, and reward companies for doing better than required by law. Still, by 2000, regulation looked pretty much as it had in 1990 because few of these ideas were incorporated into laws and institutions, especially at the federal level. Political conflict, pervasive mistrust, and the sheer complexity of environmental laws and programs thwarted efforts to build a new regulation. While other countries adapted their regulatory systems to the demands of a changing world, the United States retained a system that was essentially the same as that adopted in the 1970s.

The Old Environmental Regulation

Regulation as it existed in the United States at the end of the twentieth century conformed to a particular set of ideas. Often called a command-and-control model, but termed here a rules-and-deterrence model, it was based on fairly simple notions about industry's motivations and government's capacities.

Regarding industry, the old regulation was based on the assumption of a zero sum. This is the idea that the private economic interests of the business community inherently conflict with the broader economic interests of society. In this view, firms are seen as "amoral calculators" who will assert their own narrow interests over society's at every turn. Given this incompatibility of private and public interests, and the commitment of industry to economic gain above all other values, the view was that only the blunt hand of legalistic and deterrence-based regulation could be effective in changing industry behavior.

The old approach to regulation was based on questionable assumptions about government as well. A primary one was that government had the cognitive capacity to determine not only what society's environmental goals should be but how, in some detail, they should be achieved. Consider, as examples, new source performance standards under the Clean Air Act or effluent guidelines under the Clean Water Act, both of which establish emission and discharge limits for categories of facilities.[11] The EPA is directed to set emission and discharge limits that reflect the best available technologies that are economically feasible for each industry category, then to update the limits every four or five years. Although EPA has developed procedures for consulting with industry, this approach still assumes a high and unrealistic degree of government omniscience in a complex regulatory setting. In practice, it has been nearly impossible for regulators to keep up with the schedule for updating technologies as directed by Congress.

The old approach to regulation is a classic expression of bureaucratic rationality, as Max Weber defines the term. It aims to control behavior through a system of rules that prescribe uniform standards for diverse circumstances. It relies on a hierarchical model of control. Government sets requirements that regulated firms must follow. Anyone failing to meet the requirements faces penalties, in the form of fines, public censure, and even criminal sanctions. Deterrence is the primary motivational strategy.

Like Weber's model of bureaucracy, this form of environmental regulation relies heavily on technical experts—scientists, economists, lawyers, and administrative experts of many kinds. It reflects the notion that the problems of modern society may be solved through the neutral application of technical expertise. The old regulatory system is also founded on specialization and division of labor. Problems are broken into compartments, such as air, water, and waste, and then further into categories based on type of source (stationary or fixed), action (remedy or prevent), or resource (wetlands or streams), to name a few. A core idea behind this approach is that if one applies enough experts, organized into well-defined groups of specialists, to a given problem, their efforts will eventually yield a solution. Rules, hierarchy, control, deterrence, expertise, and specialization are the hallmarks of the old regulation.

As this model was applied and developed over the past forty years, events and a certain internal logic reinforced its basic tendencies. Regulation became more prescriptive, in the sense of specifying exactly what was to be done and how, as industry tried to carve loopholes in the rules and agencies responded by trying to close them. Transaction costs, such as those associated with reporting and permitting, increased. Eager to maintain high levels of enforcement actions to demonstrate their vigilance, agencies often adopted an adversarial approach to regulated firms. In turn, industry responded with confrontational tactics. The strategy of applying uniform rules to diverse situations often led to unreasonable outcomes.[12] By the early 1990s, recognition of the deficiencies in regulation had reached a critical point. Environmental regulation had long been criticized for being too intrusive, slowing growth, and delivering more costs than benefits. These critics pointed to the unwanted by-products of regulation, especially its economic impacts. They called for more economic and risk analysis, better ways of setting priorities, and more selective regulatory interventions in the economy.

In the 1990s, however, a second stream of criticism of environmental regulation emerged when many of its usual defenders became critics. For these revisionist critics, the main problem was not the economic impacts or other by-products of regulation (although these were still issues), but the conclusion that regulation as designed and practiced in the United States was not up to the task. The revisionist critique went like this: A rules-and-deterrence strategy had been an appropriate initial response to a new set of problems, related to environmental pollution, in which government had intervened forcefully to change behavior. That strategy had shown success, but was becoming increasingly less effective as new problems emerged, social and economic relationships changed, and experience was gained about what worked and when. The old strategy had generated distrust, created barriers to communication and innovation, and built a system full of transaction costs.

These criticisms came from many quarters. In announcing a 1995 initiative, Streamlining Environmental Regulation, for example, President Clinton observed that regulation "can be inflexible, resulting in costly actions that defy common sense by requiring greater costs for smaller returns. This approach can discourage technological innovation that can lower the costs of regulation or achieve environmental benefits *beyond* compliance."[13] Dissatisfaction with the old regulatory approach forged interesting alliances. There was a time when it would have been difficult to find anything that a leading environmentalist and a senior executive from a multinational chemical company could agree on. Yet in 1995, Jonathan Lash, president of the World Resources Institute, and David T. Buzzelli, vice president of Dow Chemical, coauthored a powerful statement on the weaknesses in regulation. Although there had been progress, they argued, it had come at a cost. Regulation was rigid and overly specific. Rules imposed administrative burdens that contributed little to environmental quality. Inflexible rules spelled out in detail what firms had to do and gave them little leeway in deciding how to do it. Companies understandably would ask: "Why spend to voluntarily eliminate the sources of pollution if you still have to endure the same long permitting process, continue the same wasteful recordkeeping and use the same end-of-pipe controls as before?"[14]

In three reports commissioned by Congress, the National Academy of Public Administration (NAPA) set out the most comprehensive version of this revisionist critique in the 1990s.[15] Many of the criticisms related to the inflexibility of the existing regulation, its high transaction costs, the neglect of many key aspects of environmental performance, and the lack of incentives for doing better than compliance. The last report concluded bluntly that the "current environmental protection system cannot deliver the healthy and sustaining world that Americans want."[16] This panel further determined that the environmental statutes "and the system they support are not keeping up with changing technology, changing public attitudes, or changing global relationships."[17]

Another notable exercise in this revisionist criticism was led by former EPA administrator William Ruckelshaus. In the Enterprise for the Environment (E4E) initiative, Ruckelshaus brought his considerable experience and prestige to the task of achieving a consensus among influential groups on the need for incremental, but eventually fundamental, changes in environmental policy. The group agreed on several weaknesses in the current system, including adversarial relationships, inflexibility, and high transaction costs. It endorsed twelve broad principles for a new approach that included flexibility, a focus on results, collaboration, integration, stewardship, and continuous improvement. When the group tried to recommend more specific policy reforms, however, the consensus broke down.[18]

The diagnosis of these critics was essentially sound. By the late 1990s, there was a consensus regarding the general deficiencies in the old regulatory system and the broad principles that should guide the design of a new one. Still, when it was time to move to the next level of detail and build something new, these efforts foundered, as the E4E experience demonstrates.

Within the federal government, the response to the calls for change was typically, and perhaps necessarily, incremental. Reinvention at EPA focused less on designing a new regulatory approach and more on fine-tuning the old one. Indeed, much of what was touted as reinvention in the 1990s may fairly be described as marginal. There was some reduced reporting, more public access, broad stakeholder consultation, slightly faster permitting, plainer language, and the like.[19] Although there is little that is wrong and much that is right about such reforms, they hardly constitute fundamental change. As argued in chapter 5, however, pervasive distrust, a lack of political consensus, and inflexibility in the laws made it difficult to do more.

State governments tried to respond to the calls for change as well. In addition to the usual steps to reduce transaction costs and expedite processes, many states undertook efforts to shift from an old to a new regulation. New Jersey, Oregon, and Wisconsin, to name a few, launched "alternative path" or "performance track" programs to reward facilities that complied consistently and did more than the regulations required. States like South Carolina, Virginia, and Michigan created environmental excellence programs that recognized the better firms and facilities. New Jersey experimented with more integrated ways of permitting. Massachusetts created an Environmental Results Program that engaged small businesses through assistance rather than deterrence-based strategies. In retrospect, the 1990s may be seen as an active period of regulatory experimentation at federal and state levels (discussed in chapters 5 and 6). At least at the federal level, however, this experimentation stopped short of more basic institutional change.

Although there is much to be learned from reforms in the United States, important lessons may be drawn from other countries as well. In particular, the Netherlands provides an example of an environmental policy system that may offer a blueprint for a new regulatory approach. Although there are major cultural and institutional differences between the United States and countries like the Netherlands, their experience provides useful examples and lessons to guide the design of a new approach and will be drawn upon later in this book.

Why Change?

The heart of the revisionist critique was that something that had worked reasonably well in the past was not going to work as well in the future. Why, if the old regulation had provided at least some degree of success in the past, was it necessary to do more than fine-tune at the margins? There are at least five reasons why, by the end of the 1990s, it became necessary to rethink environmental regulation. They involve changes in problems, in the institutional landscape, in economic relationships, in the motivations and behavior of much of industry, and in the lessons that were learned through experience.

New and Emerging Problems

old environmental issues

The old regulation had been designed to respond to what is often termed a first generation of environmental problems. These were caused by large, identifiable sources, such as power plants, petrochemical facilities, auto and steel plants, and sewage treatment operations. The task was to subject these large, point sources of pollution to control through required technologies, to monitor compliance, and to take legal action if they failed to comply.

Over time, however, new and emerging problems required different responses from policy makers. As releases from point sources in manufacturing declined, pollution from scattered, diffuse, and nonpoint sources became more significant. By the late 1980s, for example, nonpoint sources accounted for a larger share of impaired water quality than point sources.[20] Similarly, as serious problems from large sources were brought under control, policy makers turned their attention to smaller ones. To meet the national ambient air standards for ozone in urban areas like Los Angeles and Houston, regulators have looked beyond major industrial plants to control such sources as bakeries, dry cleaners, auto repair shops, and gas stations.[21]

new environmental issues

In addition, new problems emerged on the national and international policy agendas. To the older issues of industrial pollution, that first generation of environmental problems, were added newer ones, such as indoor air pollution, depletion of stratospheric ozone, global warming, habitat loss, and losses in biodiversity. Often referred to as second- and third-generation problems, these became sources of concern after many of the earlier issues had been addressed. A growing awareness of threats to ecological values also influenced the agenda in the 1980s. The environmental "problem" itself was redefined, to include use of resources (such as energy, materials, water), preservation of habitat, and intergenerational equity and justice.

Policy makers in the United States certainly have appreciated the mismatch between the "problem stream" of the 1970s and that of the early 2000s. In responding to health risks from residential radon, for example, they used a strategy of risk communication rather than the typical rules-and-deterrence approach. To deal with nonpoint sources of water pollution, they made changes in farm programs (for example, encouraging the use of buffer areas around a stream) and promoted best management practices to reduce stormwater runoff. As discussed in chapter 2, the U.S. system for environmental regulation has adapted to changes in problems over time. Still, many aspects of the old system do not match up well with a newer generation of problems. In this mismatch lies one of the more compelling reasons for designing a new one.

The Institutional Landscape

Institutionally, the world of environmental protection was less complex than it is today. In the 1970s, it consisted of government, industry, and the national advocacy groups. Government was represented most prominently by regulatory agencies, backed by strict pollution control laws. The industry consisted mostly of large manufacturing interests, who fought pollution control regulations as they were developed and conformed only reluctantly once they were adopted. National groups—the Natural Resources Defense Council (NRDC), the Sierra Club, the Environmental Defense Fund (EDF), Friends of the Earth, and the like—used litigation, lobbying, and the communications media to focus attention on the environment and pressure government and industry to respond. Other nongovernmental organizations (NGOs) were few. Local and community activist groups were rare or short lived. Business groups worked to mobilize opposition to environmental protection, not to determine how they could do better. Associations of environmental professionals were organized along narrow, disciplinary lines to reflect the bureaucratic fragmentation characteristic of the existing environmental laws and agencies.

By the end of the century, the institutional landscape had changed dramatically. For one thing, a variety of bridge-building organizations had formed to moderate conflict among government, industry, and environmental activists. An example is the Coalition for Environmentally Responsible Economies (CERES), which encourages companies to adopt a set of environmental principles and commit to reporting annually on their environmental and social performance. CERES was an outgrowth of the socially responsible investment community, which in itself has influenced the institutional landscape that surrounds environmental protection. Although the precise influence of socially responsible investment still is uncertain, it adds one more factor to the mix. The Social Investment Forum reported that socially responsible portfolios—those that screen companies for performance on environmental and other social factors—accounted for over 11 per cent of total investment assets under U.S. management in 2003.[22]

Today there is a far greater array of advocacy groups than existed in 1970. Many community groups now are active locally. Spurred partly by the environmental justice movement, but formed for other reasons as well, these groups also have been active in mobilizing local and regional interests for "bottom-up" problem solving to protect or restore watersheds, ecosystems, and other resources. At a national level, property rights and other conservative interests have been organized to offset the influence of the more established environmental activist groups.[23]

Within industry, many organizations now exist to improve the ability, not only to control or prevent pollution, but also to promote more advanced ideas of stewardship and sustainability. Among them are the World Business Council for Sustainable Development (WBCSD), the Global Environmental Management Initiative (GEMI), and Business for Social Responsibility (BSR). Similarly, state agencies now are represented better at national policy levels, especially since the Environmental Council of the States (ECOS) was formed in the 1990s. Simply put, there are many more ways to share information and organize for collective action as well as to work differently with government and nongovernmental organizations.

Perhaps the most important factor shaping the institutional landscape for environmental protection is that it has become information rich. We may fairly say that information about environmental performance and conditions exists today that could not have been imagined in the 1970s. This trend began with the Toxics Release Inventory (TRI) and state-level community right-to-know laws in the late 1980s, which compelled many industrial firms to report publicly on potentially harmful chemicals released by or stored at their facilities. As more information became available, community and other advocacy groups began to disseminate it as a way to place pressure on firms. With a growing public demand for information, many firms began to issue their own performance reports. Although many early reports were high on image and short on measurable performance data, the quality and usefulness of information from many firms has improved considerably. Finally, the rapid growth of the Internet through the 1990s and into the 2000s made this information more accessible to the public.

Economic Relationships

The old regulation was designed for large, pollution-intensive manufacturing facilities that made similar products in large quantities. Examples are commodity chemicals, electrical power generation, and steel. Relationships with customers and suppliers were relatively stable, at least compared with those today. Although there were global aspects to their activities, the strategies and operations of even large firms usually were more national than international. The phenomenon of globalization as we understand it was not yet part of the lexicon.

The changes in economic relationships between 1970 and 2005 are striking. One obvious change is that business is far more global. A product may be designed in Texas, contain parts made in the Philippines or China, be assembled in Taiwan, and sold around the world. Production has become more "networked" and "deconstructed," as David Rejeski and James Salzman describe it. "From a policy standpoint," they add, "these emerging networks may require very different strategies than those applied to the hierarchies or markets where most environmental policy traditionally has focused."[24] Multinational corporations yield influence that extends well beyond any one country's borders. Mergers and acquisitions recombine major elements to create new global business entities. Markets, investments, competition, ethical standards, labor practices—all the elements of business are far more global than even three decades ago.

Global competition and the growth of technology industries have increased the pace of change in industry. The saying in the computer industry is that there are "the quick or the dead." Firms either respond to the demand for innovation and change or they do not survive. Products in the semiconductor and specialty tape industries sometimes are obsolete within six to nine months. Changes in the auto sector have compressed the process for developing new vehicles from five years to less than eighteen months.[25] For these reasons, companies like Intel argue that the cumbersome and unpredictable permitting processes that are characteristic of the old regulation cannot allow them to respond to the rapid pace of change in their industry.[26] Indeed, a primary motive for Intel's participation in EPA's Project XL initiative (discussed in chapter 5) was to achieve more flexible permits that would allow them to adapt to customer demands more quickly.

Another economic change is growth in the service and knowledge sectors relative to manufacturing. Between 1960 and 1999, the share of U.S. gross domestic product (GDP) and of total employment attributed to manufacturing in the United States fell by roughly half.[27] The service sector now accounts for some three-fourths of the nation's GDP and four-fifths of employment.[28] In a regulatory system designed to control pollution from manufacturing, this shift will have profound consequences for the kinds of strategies that government will need to employ for environmental protection.

This combination of global interdependence, fluid relationships, and rapid rates of change stretch the capacities of the old regulatory approach, which was designed for less dynamic economies. Many decisions and actions that influence environmental quality are made outside of the national borders of those who are affected. The environmental impacts of the service and knowledge sectors cannot be managed effectively with only a rules-and-deterrence-based regime. A system based on bureaucratic rationality cannot keep pace with the dynamism and fluidity of modern economic relationships. In sum, government is using a modern strategy of bureaucratic rationality in what may be seen, increasingly, as a postmodern economy.

The Motivations and Behavior of Industry

In large part because of the other changes discussed here, the motivations and behavior of industry differ from what they were in the 1970s. These changes are considered in detail in chapter 4, but are worth introducing here. The earlier discussion noted that the assumption of a zero sum— the notion that environmental and economic goals pose inevitable conflict—influenced the design of the old regulation. At a macro level, this meant that any investments made in the environment were seen to involve losses in economic competitiveness and growth. At a micro level, it meant that firms would always be assumed to pursue actions that maximized their profits, whatever the environmental effects. Only the legal hammer of regulation would force industry to act responsibly.

Although there still are areas in which environmental and economic goals may conflict, there is ample evidence today that the assumed zero sum may at times be a potential win-win. At a macro level, studies demonstrate that environmental quality and economic progress may go hand in hand. At the micro level of the firm, evidence of the economic payoff from responsible and innovative environmental policies is accumulating at an impressive rate.[29] The reasons for this possible win-win include the search for operating efficiency, the need to reduce future liabilities, the reactions of customers and investors, and an interest in forestalling more stringent regulation. What is clear is that there are economic and social forces other than government rules that influence industry behavior in ways that are largely unaccounted for in the old regulation. Among many firms, especially large and visible ones, a greening process is under way.

It is certainly true that this greening of industry still applies to only a subset of regulated firms. Most, especially in the small and medium size ranges, have probably been unaffected by this trend. Nor does it mean that regulatory pressures from government are not essential. Many studies confirm that regulation is still the most important influence on environmental behavior by firms. It is also true, however, that many firms and facilities are doing far more than is required by law. They are committing to eco-efficiency goals, defining standards for suppliers, reporting publicly on measures of progress, informing communities, redesigning products to reduce environmental impacts, and even designing closed-loop manufacturing processes that cut their releases to zero. A new regulation should not only recognize greening among leading firms, it should also create conditions and incentives that will encourage greening behavior by them and others. This is a premise underlying the plan for a new environmental regulation that is set out in this book.

The Benefits of Experience

Another compelling reason for moving from an old to a new regulation is that we have learned a great deal about how to design better environmental policies. Regulation by rules and deterrence was a reasonable first response to environmental issues. It also was a blunt instrument, as Kathryn Harrison's image of "the donkey and the two-by-four" aptly suggests.[30] Since 1970, however, policy makers have learned how to use a more diverse range of instruments, to devise new kinds of institutional relationships, and to fine-tune the mechanisms available for achieving their policy goals.

Three brief examples illustrate the learning that has occurred: the growth of market incentives, the use of information as a policy tool, and the interest in building more collaborative relationships with industry. They are considered briefly here and discussed in more detail in the later chapters.

The first truly national pollution control statutes (the Clean Air Act of 1970 and the Federal Water Pollution Control Act of 1972) relied on technology-based standards. In itself, this was evidence of policy learning, because a previous approach based only on ambient targets and technical assistance had proven difficult to implement. Beginning in the late 1970s, however, there was more interest in building flexibility into the technology approach, especially if it meant getting equal or better environmental results at the same or less cost. Over the next two decades, market incentives were gradually but steadily incorporated into environmental laws and regulations, mostly in air quality. These include the bubble policy, emissions trading, and trading of acid rain allowances. There was some progress in using them in water quality programs as well. In the typically incremental style of U.S. policy making, market incentives have been studied, evaluated, and gradually woven into the regulatory system over the past three decades.

The use of information to complement regulation dates to the spread of community right-to-know laws in the 1980s, including the federal Toxics Release Inventory adopted in 1986. Of course, information had long been used as a means of educating people about risks and influencing their behavior; product labels and risk notifications are examples. Here was a different way of using information, however. Laws like the

TRI required industries to report on chemicals they stored at or released from their facilities. These disclosures placed pressure on many firms to lower their releases and present a better public image. Since then, mandatory disclosures have been built into many pollution control and prevention programs. Although their precise effects are unclear, these disclosure rules appear to have made many firms more systematic in managing their activities and more aggressive in seeking pollution reductions. Through experience and evaluation, policy makers are learning how to use information disclosure as a policy tool that complements existing regulatory strategies.[31]

A third example is collaborative relationships with industry. As discussed in the next two chapters, the design of the old regulation was almost inevitably adversarial. Conflict managed through procedural formality was built into the system. Over time, however, policy makers have tried to reduce this conflict and introduce more opportunities for collaboration. An early example of this collaboration was the use of regulatory negotiation in the 1980s, followed by "policy dialogues" and similar mechanisms.[32] The increase in government–industry voluntary programs over the past decade has reinforced this trend. Stakeholder participation was considered to be essential in the reinvention initiatives of the 1990s, to the extent that it sometimes compromised EPA's ability to achieve results. Still, the idea that government, industry, and other societal interests may communicate effectively in ways that improve environmental performance is now widely accepted. The challenge in designing a new regulation is to allow for collaboration while still pressing industry to set stringent environmental goals and holding firms accountable for achieving them.

The New Environmental Regulation

What the revisionist critics discussed earlier were calling for was a new approach to environmental regulation. They realized, without putting it in these terms, that the Weberian model of bureaucratic rationality, with its American gloss of adversarial legalism, was increasingly less appropriate. This old model based on bureaucratic rationality may be seen as a distinctly modern approach to problem solving. In contrast, the proposed new environmental regulation is more of a postmodern approach to solving problems. The last two chapters of the book develop the idea of the new regulation in more detail. For now, it is worth introducing two concepts that will help in grounding the discussion conceptually and comparing the ideal types of the old and the new environmental regulation later on.

The first concept is that of reflexive law. The existing regulatory system is based largely on what Gunther Teubner terms substantive law, which is the law of the regulatory state. Governments use substantive law to intervene in private social and economic arrangements and promote collective goals, such as safety, environmental quality, and equity. It differs from the more traditional formal law, such as contracts and torts, by which government defines relationships among private actors in order to structure social and economic arrangements. Reflexive law is a third stage, after formal and substantive law. It has social purposes, like substantive law, but achieves them differently. The aim of a reflexive legal strategy is to create incentives and procedures that induce people to continually assess their actions (hence the "reflexivity") and adjust them to society's goals, for example, by creating less pollution, using fewer resources, or protecting endangered species.[33]

Although the old regulation relies largely on substantive law, the United States and other nations have gradually been incorporating elements of a reflexive legal strategy into their regulatory systems. Chapter 6 presents market incentives, information disclosure, and management systems as examples. A general characteristic of a new environmental regulation, however, should be even more reliance on reflexive law.

In addition to relying on a different legal strategy, the new regulation would involve different forms of governance. The second concept worth introducing here is that of social-political governance, which recognizes the need for new patterns of interaction among government and other actors.[34] This is a pattern of governance in which lines between public and private are blurred as the boundaries between them become fluid and permeable. Government acts less *on* other actors in a hierarchical relationship as it does *with* them in a more collaborative and communicative way; governing consists less of the state exerting control over others in society and more of an interaction among them. There is more shared responsibility and trust. The process of governing is seen as "the creation of learning processes within the interested actors or society in general."[35] This notion of recasting environmental regulation as a more effective learning system is developed further in the final chapters of this book.

Social-political governance may be seen as new phase of governance. In particular, it reflects an awareness of the limits of a traditional, hierarchical, state-centered model. The limitations of the old environmental regulation may be seen as a subset of a more general need for different patterns of governance in other areas of public policy as well.[36] The changes in environmental problems, institutional landscape, economic relationships, and industry behavior illustrate the dynamism and complexity to which a new regulatory system must be able to respond.

At a theoretical level, the argument in this book is that the changes that have been described here require a shift from an old to a new approach to environmental regulation. The old approach is essentially modern in its design. It relies on a strategy of bureaucratic rationality to define and organize problems. Issues are broken down into small parts to make them manageable. Modern regulation assumes that scientific and technical expertise is sufficient to solve complex problems. Hierarchy—defined as the exercise of control by higher over subordinate levels—is the appropriate organizational design for achieving social goals. Law, backed by the coercive authority of government, is seen to be the principal way to influence behavior. Most of these elements will still characterize the new regulation, but it would be different in many respects.

A new regulation would reflect the characteristics of social-political governance; government will steer more than it will row. Law will be used less to tell people exactly what to do (which assumes that lawmakers and implementers always know best) than to create conditions that induce them to do what should be done. There thus is a use of reflexive as well as substantive law. Relationships among government, business, and other actors will be as much horizontal as vertical. Although coercion through law would still be used to apply pressure, collaboration will be seen as a legitimate and effective way to achieve results. The new approach would stress results and performance over means and conformance.

Government will focus on the "what" of policy but leave the "how" to others as much as possible.

At this point it is important to stress what the new regulation is *not.* It is not an abdication of the role of the state, but offers a different role for the state. It does not reject deterrence and enforcement, but it does focus these regulatory sticks on those who most deserve them. It does not aim to roll back environmental performance standards, but to achieve better results and promote innovation. It is not an antiregulatory strategy but a new strategy that would be adaptable, reflexive, collaborative, and performance based. It would be less rigid, prescriptive, adversarial, and compliance oriented than what has been used in the United States until now.

The Plan of the Book

This is not meant to be a comprehensive assessment of U.S. environmental policy. It does not deal with many regulatory issues, such as how to set priorities, the role of risk assessment in decision making, or the use of cost-benefit analysis. It avoids detailed discussion of many pressing environmental problems, among them land use, suburban sprawl, or local and regional ecosystem management. Nor does it specifically address the many aspects of environmental protection that are decided outside of the regulatory context, especially the use of taxes and other incentives to influence consumption decisions. These are all important issues but are beyond the scope of this book.

The focus here is on one aspect of environmental policy: How do we design and implement policies that will sufficiently influence behavior in the business sector to achieve our environmental goals? It further concentrates on regulation as a strategy—the assumptions behind it, the design of regulatory instruments, the relationships among actors, the incentives regulation offers or fails to offer, the effects on technology innovation, and the ways of measuring results, among others.

This book examines trends in the public and private sectors that are changing the social and economic context for regulation. It brings together much thinking and experience about strategies that maintain government pressure for responsible environmental performance, but allow regulated firms more flexibility and choice in deciding how to respond to that pressure. It argues that a regulation based on some element of deterrence is necessary, but that alone and poorly designed, such a one-dimensional strategy may discourage innovation, undermine relationships, and impede progress. This book maintains that the more we can view regulation as an extended learning process and less as a political struggle among largely incompatible interests, the more likely we will be able to achieve the desired environmental results, over time, in economically and socially acceptable ways.

It deliberately avoids discussion of the provocative but elusive goal of "sustainability." Rather, the goal is what in the international context is often termed cleaner production. This is broader than the notion of compliance and even of environmental performance as it has been applied just to manufacturing. As defined by the United Nations Environment Programme (UNEP) more than a decade ago, cleaner production "means the continuous application of an integrated preventive environmental strategy to processes and products to reduce risks to humans and the environment." With respect to production processes, the term includes "conserving raw materials and energy, eliminating toxic raw materials, and reducing the quantity and toxicity of all emissions and wastes before they leave a process." For products, it means "reducing impacts along the entire life cycle of the product, from raw material extraction to ultimate disposal of the product."[37] Put simply, the goal of a new environmental regulation strategy should be cleaner production. More broadly, our aim should be to integrate economic and environmental goals through the "ecological modernization" that is discussed in the book's final chapters.

The next chapter presents a brief discussion and history of the old regulation. The American approach to environmental protection reflects important characteristics of our political and legal culture as well as the political circumstances of the 1960s. We should not be surprised that regulation in the United States is so adversarial, for example, because conflict was designed into the system, largely as a way to protect regulatory agencies from undue influence by industry. Nor should we surprised that statutes and strategies are fragmented. Environmental regulation in the United States is the product of an incremental approach to policy.

Regulatory policies emerged piecemeal as problems were recognized and coalitions were created to address them. In a brief history, the chapter explores the themes and controversies of the past forty years.

Chapter 3 evaluates the old regulation. The central flaw in its design has been that it confused government pressure for needed results—a critical element of any system of environmental protection—with the perceived need for government to dictate how to achieve those results. It also defined environmental problems too narrowly, stressed compliance over the broader concept of performance, built a system that was loaded with transaction costs, and made other mistakes one would expect to make in responding quickly and comprehensively to a new and pressing bundle of complex issues. We have achieved much with the old regulation, but the challenges of new environmental problems and the demands of a more dynamic world require a different approach.

Chapter 4 turns to industry. The changes in attitudes and behavior of many business firms between 1970 and 2005 are striking. For many of them, government regulation is no longer the sole or even primary influence on their environmental performance. They see opportunities for greater efficiency, fewer liabilities, better reputation, improved community and employee relations, and enhanced market share, among others, as a reward for innovative and responsible environmental practices. This chapter examines and assesses this trend, often termed a greening of industry, and its implications for regulatory policy. A core element in the new regulatory approach is that it will recognize and take advantage of the changes that are occurring within the business community. Even for firms that are not seen to be leaders in this greening trend—certainly the bulk of the business sector at this point—the old regulation may pose barriers to environmental progress.

The chapter presents a generally positive view of part of industry, particularly of the large firms that are taking a comprehensive approach to limiting their effects on the environment. This view is inconsistent with much of the writing on environmental politics, especially that of a decade ago or more, which typically presented industry as largely hostile to improved environmental protection. This book, as well as much of more recent writing in the field, accepts that the changes occurring in large firms are real and worthy of study. The argument here is that if we can understand what motivates the environmentally progressive firms, we will be better able to influence the behavior of others. Still, the book is consistent throughout in arguing that a normative framework of government rules is essential for any system of environmental regulation to succeed, even for high-performing firms. This is not to say that the better firms should not be treated differently by regulators, or that we should not change how we apply the rules or measure success. The discussion recognizes that there are bad actors out there and sometimes government coercion is the only way of dealing with them.

Chapter 5 examines government's response to the calls for change. The story here is mixed. Regulatory agencies, as one might expect, have been reluctant to cede control. This has especially been the case with enforcement officials, typically backed up by environmental advocacy groups. They wave the threat of a regulatory rollback as a reason for keeping the existing legal barriers secure. The continual cycles of conflict and stalemate in Congress have closed legislative change as an avenue for reform. During the 1990s, EPA launched many initiatives to "reinvent" regulation. Although these enjoyed varied success, in part because of the lack of statutory authority for change, they offer many lessons and practical building blocks for the new regulation. At the state level, many similar programs, some carried out with statutory authority, incorporated elements of a new regulation as well. The chapter evaluates government's efforts and draws several lessons from them.

Chapter 6 presents reference points for more "lesson drawing." It begins with the social science literature on reflexive law, social-political governance, and policy learning. Each strand in the literature offers sources of ideas on a conceptual foundation for a new regulation. The chapter then turns to three kinds of practical experience, all of which reflect themes from the literature: innovations in the American states, trends in community-based problem solving, and sector-based planning in the Netherlands. This sets the stage for a discussion of the new regulation that is presented in the final chapter.

Chapter 7 offers an outline for a new system of environmental regulation. It describes a system that will be by no means free of conflict, difficult tradeoffs, or bothersome transaction costs. A new regulation will maintain pressure on industry to continually improve its environmental performance while allowing firms as much discretion as is politically and administratively possible. It will aim to create a climate of cooperation, predictability, and trust among government, industry, and others. Chapter 7 considers the assumptions, conditions, and mechanisms that would characterize a new environmental regulation and discusses changes that will need to occur in laws and institutions if we are to move from the old to the new.

The final chapter also looks at the political prospects for a new regulation and a strategy for achieving it. Despite the opportunity to improve both environmental and economic performance, the conditions for any near-term, comprehensive change in the United States are not favorable. Indeed, if we are to build a new regulation, it is more likely to be in a series of small steps over time than in dramatic statutory or policy changes that might occur in the next decade or so. Rather than just muddling through, however, we should follow a strategy that reflects a more systematic understanding of the conceptual basis for change and an appreciation of the learning opportunities that are available. This "mixed scanning" strategy offers an incremental but conceptually focused path toward a new regulation.

It could be that environmental regulation in the United States will gradually evolve in the directions set out in this book. As this discussion suggests, policies in this country may be moving—slowly and fitfully— toward a new regulatory system. The argument here is that we can promote this evolution toward a new regulation by recognizing explicitly what is not working well, identifying the more promising trends that are under way, and working more systematically to achieve change. The purpose of this book is to help speed up the process of change and to chart a course toward a new regulation in the next few decades.

Before we can build a new system of regulation, however, we need to be able to understand the one that exists now and to consider why it looks the way that it does. That is the focus of the next chapter.

2

How Did We Get Here? Explaining
Environmental Regulation

The process was one of ratcheting ever more stringent provisions with more federal control and more detailed requirements for both polluters and EPA.[1]

This chapter describes and explains the old environmental regulation—the system of institutions, rules, and relationships that has constituted this country's strategy for addressing environmental issues over the past four decades. The mold for this system was cast in a series of choices made in the late 1960s and early 1970s. Although this system has changed incrementally over the past three decades, it retains its defining characteristics. Other nations started in ways very similar to that of the United States. While they have adapted their regulatory systems to changing problems and circumstances, the United States for the most part has not.

The U.S. environmental strategy has by no means been a failure. In fact, in many respects it has been a major success. This country was long viewed as a leader in environmental protection. It boasts a high concentration of scientific, technical, and analytic expertise. It has built an impressive legal framework that other countries have tried to emulate. Environmental managers from around the world come here to learn about monitoring, testing, and technology. At national and state levels, we have developed a formidable set of institutions and relationships for acting on environmental issues. And it arguably has achieved results. As chapter 3 discusses in more detail, regulation has accomplished much of what it was originally designed to achieve.

In broad outline, the United States and other western, industrial democracies reacted to the emergence of pollution problems in similar ways. Industries had no incentive to reduce pollution on their own, so governments stepped in and made them reduce it. They did this through legal coercion. In the late 1960s and early 1970s, governments passed laws, created administrative agencies, issued rules, and exacted penalties. It was a blunt, controversial, but generally effective strategy that eventually changed industry behavior. This chapter explains why regulation looks the way that it does in the United States and describes how it has evolved in the past four decades. The premise is that understanding how we got to where we are today will give us a better idea of where we should be going in the future.

Why Does Environmental Regulation Look the Way It Does?

If we compare environmental regulation in this country with regulation elsewhere, we will see similarities in the basic strategy and approach but differences in style and specific designs. These differences not only affect how regulations are designed and implemented but also how the regulatory system responds to new policy tools, such as voluntary agreements, and to new concepts on which environmental strategies may be based, such as sustainable development. A substantial literature has examined the differences between the United States and other nations and their consequences. A brief look at these differences helps to set the stage for the discussion of environmental regulation in the rest of the chapter.

One frequently cited difference is that the relationships between government and industry reflect more cooperation and consensus as well as higher levels of trust in Sweden, Great Britain, New Zealand, Canada, or Japan than they do here.[2] In the United States, fears of agency capture by industry and a heavy reliance on rules and procedures keep government and industry at arms' length. Strict, action-forcing environmental laws place pressure on firms for expensive, short-term solutions, which provokes industry in turn to resist those pressures through litigation.[3] High transaction costs, which in themselves are a reflection of distrust, create uncertainty and delay for regulated firms, regardless of the stringency of the standards themselves.

Regulation in the United States tends to focus much more on legal compliance and less on overall environmental performance than elsewhere,

where governments have set goals and designed policies to achieve them. The Netherlands is the most commonly cited example; its system of national goals and negotiated agreements for reaching them is discussed in chapter 6. However, countries like Sweden, Norway, and Great Britain have adopted more goal-oriented approaches as well.[4] Because of the emphasis on compliance in the United States, regulated firms have little incentive to do better than meet the legal minimums. In turn, agencies spend their time finding and punishing nonconformance rather than working with industries to find better ways to achieve results. Compared with those in Japan, Robert Kagan writes, "the parallel U.S. regulatory programs are significantly more legalistic, adversarial, and punitive."[5] This intensive focus on legal compliance, Bardach and Kagan have noted, diverts the efforts of all sides to "pointless and dispiriting legal routines and conflicts."[6]

Regulation in the United States tends to be narrower in scope than in other countries, with an emphasis on manufacturing processes and specific categories of pollution, and little or no attention to the many other factors that affect environmental quality. An example is the focus on controlling pollution rather than influencing decisions about processes, raw materials, or products that determine environmental impacts. Regulation in the United States tends to isolate specific aspects of production processes and attempt to control them stringently, which means that some aspects of business are regulated tightly, although sometimes not cost-effectively, while others are ignored. Other countries and several American states have recently made more progress in preventing pollution at its source and considering such issues as product life cycles, packaging waste, and industrial energy efficiency.[7]

Environmental regulation here also is more prescriptive than elsewhere, in the sense of requiring specific actions, with little discretion left to the regulated firm. There also is a greater reliance on action-forcing laws and technology standards. These contrasts are illustrated nicely in a 1974 book that used a hare and tortoise analogy to compare air quality regulation in the United States and Sweden. While the United States (the hare) codified ambitious goals in statutes that drove industry to adopt new technologies under the threat of sanctions, Sweden (the tortoise) used a more collaborative process that stressed results but worked with industry in deciding how to achieve them.[8] In the end, air quality results were about the same. Similar results have been found in other comparative analyses of environmental regulation.[9] For example, one study of a multinational firm with operations in the United States and Japan found that the standards in both countries were similar, despite generally higher pollution abatement expenditures in the United States. The higher costs observed in the United States thus were due in large part, not to more stringent standards, but to the higher regulatory transaction costs. The American subsidiary of the firm "faced a more demanding and potentially punitive legal regime than its Japanese counterpart. It spent more time and money on lawyers, fines, legal conflict, and simply keeping up with regulatory requirements."[10] Because agencies in different countries share information about technologies, best practices, and other issues, they tend to be in about the same place in their standards at about the same time. What differs is the style used in getting there.

U.S. regulation also relies more heavily on legal deterrence as means of changing behavior than do most other countries. It is assumed that industry will act in ways that are contrary to society's interests unless it is threatened with punishment. In the past, and even now for "bad apples" in industry, deterrence is a necessary and appropriate strategy. Furthermore, a great deal of research has established that having basic rules of the game, backed by the coercive powers of the state, is necessary for keeping firms in line and not giving competitive advantages to irresponsible ones.[11] However, the emphasis on deterrence and moral culpability that characterizes the U.S. is less evident elsewhere, and it is increasingly less appropriate for the more compliant and responsible firms, as later chapters argue.

Like most other countries, the initial U.S. response to environmental problems in the early 1970s was somewhat fragmented, in the sense of dividing environmental problems into categories that made them more amenable to bureaucratic solutions. However, while other countries have taken steps to integrate their environmental programs, the United States still relies on a fragmented approach. Separate laws define EPA's responsibilities in each environmental medium. A variety of congressional oversight subcommittees monitor actions under those laws. The EPA and most state agencies reflect this fragmentation in their internal design, with separate offices for each medium. With some recent but rare exceptions, as indicated earlier, environmental agencies in the United States break down their core regulatory functions, such as permitting and compliance, by environmental medium (i.e., air, water, or waste) and program area. Although such integration is always difficult, most other countries have taken steps to modify their laws, agencies, and administrative processes to allow a more integrated regulatory approach.[12]

These differences in regulatory institutions and style affect relationships outside of conventional legal frameworks. Voluntary agreements are examined in chapter 5 as a way to achieve environmental goals and as a possible building block in a new regulation. Yet, as Magali Delmas and Ann Terlak observe, differences among countries affect their ability to use voluntary agreements successfully.[13] With its administrative and institutional fragmentation, adversarial tradition, active congressional oversight, and open access for third parties to affect policy making (especially through the courts), the United States is a challenging setting for using voluntary agreements. These factors, combined with the limited regulatory discretion in the legal framework, make it difficult for agencies to meet commitments made under voluntary agreements. These factors certainly came into play in EPA's Project XL experience, discussed in chapter 5. Delmas and Terlak conclude that a country like the Netherlands is more hospitable to use of voluntary agreements. There, "a culture of consent and cooperation among all parties contrasts with the often hostile relationship between regulators, business, and NGOs in the U.S."[14]

Another way of looking at the contrasts between the United States and other countries is in their responses to the international movement toward sustainable development as a foundation for environmental policy. In an analysis of ten high-consumption societies, including some members of the European Union, William Lafferty and James Meadowcroft classify three of them as "enthusiastic" in their response to sustainable development (the Netherlands, Norway, and Sweden); six as "cautiously supportive" (Australia, Canada, Germany, the European Union, Japan, and the United Kingdom); and one as "disinterested" (the United States). They attribute the more than tepid United States response to several factors. One is that it is less open and supportive in relations with international institutions.

More significantly, however, they trace the United States response to characteristics of the political culture and relationships among key actors in society. The United States, "with its individualist, polarized, and highly litigious society, is far removed from a 'social-democratic' or 'consensual' political culture."[15] They state the point more directly elsewhere, observing that the United States "remains largely frozen in the conservationist, regulation/compliance, industry-versus-environmentalists, and pollution clean-up patterns that took shape either prior to or during the 1970s."[16]

This brief listing of differences between the United States and other nations reveals potential weaknesses in the regulatory system. The next chapter explores these in more detail. For now, the contrasts suggest the defining characteristics of regulation. The questions taken up are why is the United States different from Sweden, the Netherlands, Japan, or other nations and why does U.S. environmental regulation look the way it does and not like something else? The next section suggests eight reasons for why regulation in the United States looks the way it does. Four relate to basic characteristics of American political institutions and culture. The others relate to trends or conditions that prevailed in the late 1960s and early 1970s.

Explaining Environmental Regulation: Institutions and Culture

Any policy system is the product of national institutions and culture.[17] Whether the topic is social welfare in Sweden, energy in France, transportation in Great Britain, or environment in the United States, such factors as the structure of the government (e.g., presidential or parliamentary), the lines between the public and private sectors, the roles of interest groups, and attitudes toward government make a difference. Even when countries have much in common, policies for addressing any given problem will differ in form and content. Four such factors have been especially important in influencing the design and evolution of environmental regulation in the United States.

A Constitutional System that Fragments Power   The designers of the U.S. constitutional system were concerned about too much power being concentrated in any one person or institution, so they deliberately divided power among branches and levels of government. For example, the president may veto laws passed by Congress, but Congress may override that veto. The fact that the president and Congress are elected separately, and not together as they would be in a parliamentary system, with its fusion rather than separation of powers, creates the prospect of divided party control of the two branches. The creation of an independent judiciary and the tradition of judicial review laid the groundwork for the federal courts to play an active role in public policy making. The constitutional division of authority between national and state governments added to this dispersion of power.

These features of the constitutional system laid the foundation for fragmented environmental policy.[18] They increased the potential for conflict between the president and Congress, especially when the two branches are controlled by different parties, as they have been for most of the time since 1970. With power so fragmented, it is difficult to create a consensus for legislative change, except when there is a sense of crisis that compels action. Contrast this arrangement with a parliamentary system, such as that in the Netherlands or Great Britain, where a fusion of legislative and executive power makes consensus on national goals and strategies more likely. In addition, interest groups are in a better position to block change to protect their interests in a more pluralist political system such as that in the United States.

A Tendency Toward Incremental Policy Making   Partly as a result of this constitutional system, and for other reasons related to political culture, policy is usually changed incrementally. There have been exceptions, especially during periods of national crisis, like the 1930s. However, policy change more typically occurs in small steps, as a series of marginal adjustments to the status quo.[19] When change occurs, it is piecemeal, as a response to a perceived need for action. Policy makers build closely on what already exists. As a general rule, policy making in an incremental system is reactive, pragmatic, and specific rather than anticipatory, visionary, and comprehensive.[20]

Environmental regulation in the United States reflects these incremental tendencies. It emerged as a series of specific responses to perceived environmental problems as they came up on the policy agenda. It is no accident that regulators must work through separate laws for air, water, chemicals, pesticides, and other problems, nor that each of these laws varies in such dimensions as evaluation of risks, level of technology controls, balancing of economic versus environmental factors, division of state and federal authority, and other issues. As issues rose on the agenda, they were met with a response that reflected whatever political coalition could be assembled at the time. It usually takes some visible issue that will draw attention, such as a major oil spill, to mobilize the necessary coalition for action. And once the mold is cast, as it was in the late 1960s and early 1970s, it is difficult, without a major event to focus public attention, to introduce major change. Indeed, despite the many reauthorizations of environmental statutes that have occurred in the past forty years, the basic regulatory approach in the United States has not changed significantly.

Belief in a Limited State   The reliance on regulation as a core strategy, and in particular the United States version of regulation, is revealing in itself. As a strategy, regulation allows government to intervene in economic or social arrangements and attempt to correct a problem without fundamentally changing those arrangements. It is what John Dryzek, in his book on environmental discourses, calls a problem-solving approach to environmental protection. This approach recognizes the existence of environmental problems, but treats them "as tractable within the basic framework of the political economy of industrial society, as belonging in a well-defined box of their own."[21] This contrasts with a more comprehensive policy approach in which environmental considerations are integrated into the economic structure of society, a discourse Dryzek and others call ecological modernization. One of the reasons that the U.S. response to the concept of sustainable development has been one of disinterest, Lafferty and Meadowcroft conclude, is this strong belief in limiting the role of government in social and economic affairs.

A regulatory strategy allows policy makers to respond to environmental problems through a series of selective, targeted interventions in private economic activity, mostly manufacturing. These interventions have usually taken the form of commands to different classes of firms directing that they make changes in existing technologies or behavior. This is one reason government efforts to promote pollution prevention in the United States have been so difficult. It is much easier to target pollution at the point of release than to intervene in the decisions about processes and raw materials that produce those releases in the first place.

Regulation is the environmental strategy that is consistent with the belief in a limited state. It allows government to intervene in private behavior with respect to a goal, but in a way that disturbs economic and social relationships as little as possible. This is not necessarily a weakness, given the political culture in the United States, but it does help to explain why environmental policies here look the way they do. While governments in Europe and elsewhere have moved to more comprehensive approaches to the environment through forms of sustainability planning and by integrating environmental goals with other social and economic goals, the United States has had difficulty in moving beyond its more limited rules-and-deterrence approach.[22]

Reliance on Rules and Litigation for Solving Problems   A central aspect of the American political culture is captured in Alexis de Tocqueville's statement that "There is hardly a political question in the United States which does not sooner or later turn into a judicial one."[23] The tendency toward using rules, procedures, and litigation is even more pronounced now than it was in de Tocqueville's time. As Congress and state legislatures enacted more regulatory laws over the past century, in part because of the rights revolution discussed in the next section, a larger number and broader range of social and economic relationships have been brought into the legal arena, thus requiring judicial resolution.

Our national legal style has influenced our approach to social problems, including regulation. It is not just the amount of law that distinguishes the United States, according to Robert Kagan, but the unique legal style that characterizes the American approach to public policy.[24] Across a range of policy issues, Kagan writes, the United States uses more complex legal rules, more adversarial procedures, more punitive legal sanctions, and more judicial interventions into administrative decisions. The result is a style of relationships and decision making that Kagan terms adversarial legalism.

Adversarial legalism is apparent in several aspects of regulation. Important regulations typically end up in a court challenge from industry or environmentalists, and often both. Rule-making processes, which are the primary engine of developing policy once regulatory laws are enacted, consist of a tactical set of preparations for litigation more than a search for solutions. Regulated firms are reluctant to seek help from government agencies because they may reveal or draw attention to violations that lead to punishment. This adversarial legalism is a major barrier to developing the cooperation and dialogue between industry and government that David Wallace and others see as being essential to innovation.[25]

Explaining Environmental Regulation: A Product of the Times

So far, this discussion has suggested characteristics or tendencies that are fairly deep seated in American political institutions and culture. Other explanations may be found in the circumstances that existed at the time, when the current system was created, or that are specific to environmental regulation.

The Rights Revolution Environmental regulation should be seen in the larger context of social and governmental changes that occurred throughout the twentieth century, especially what Cass Sunstein calls the rights revolution.[26] For much of American history, a right was seen as protection *against* government action, such as the right to free speech versus government censorship. Beginning in the 1930s, and again in the 1960s, there was an expansion in the belief that there are rights *to* government protection. In this concept of positive or programmatic rights, government is obligated to guarantee rights to something, such as clean air, a safe workplace, or equal access to education and housing.

This conception of environmental protection as a positive right rather than a problem to be solved has had several implications.[27] For one thing, it has contributed to the legalization of environmental issues because the judicial branch is usually where issues of rights are settled. For another, it has frustrated efforts to view environmental protection as an adaptive, learning, process. Instead, environmental issues are often framed in either/or terms that are more suited to resolution though adversarial combat than through dialogue and cooperation. Again, this is not necessarily a weakness because it has helped to strengthen environmental protections legally, but it does help in explaining the design and style of regulation in the United States.

The Theory of Regulatory Capture   An influential theory in the 1960s was that agencies will be captured by the very industry they were established to regulate. Looking at the histories of agencies like the Interstate Commerce Commission and Civil Aeronautics Board, Marver Bernstein argued that regulatory agencies move through a life cycle.[28] When first created, an agency is backed by political coalitions that support strong regulation for the public good. As these coalitions fade and public attention turns to other issues, the agency becomes increasingly dependent on the regulated industry for political support because the industry has the largest stake in the agency's actions and is organized to influence them. The agency moves through a life cycle, from the youthful enthusiasm of the aggressive regulator, to a mature phase of balancing industry preferences against the public good, to a final stage of organizational senility in which it exists only to serve the interests of the industry. Once captured, the agency places industry's interests over those of society.

Based on this capture theory, environmental advocates argued in the 1960s and 1970s that agencies like EPA should be designed to maintain a strict separation between government and industry, to avoid a close relationship. They should be closely monitored and work through well-defined procedures. They should limit contacts with industry in order to maintain a high degree of autonomy, in perception as well as in fact. The more distant and adversarial the relationships between government and industry, it was thought, the better. It was assumed that such relationships would reduce the chances for agency capture.

Whatever relevance capture theory had for economic regulatory agencies (and this has been debated), it does not necessarily apply well to health and safety issues, such as the environment or occupational health. The latter issues are more salient for the public, and there are countervailing forces, such as environmental activist groups, that historically did not exist in economic regulation. Still, concerns about agency capture have had a major influence on the design of regulatory laws, processes, and relationships with industry. They are the source of much of the adversarial legalism that characterizes relationships among government, industry, and environmentalists.

Suspicions About Corporate Values and Motives   Environmental regulation in the United States was influenced by attitudes toward corporations and business, especially among environmental activists. The environmental movement was part of a broader "postmaterialist" tendency in American society and in many other industrial countries to question the undesirable by-products of economic growth and the attitudes and behavior that had produced it.[29] Among activists especially, this included a suspicion about the values of people in business and the capitalist system in which they operated.

Suspicions about corporate values and motives led to two views that David Spence argues underlie environmental regulation.[30] The first is the view that given an opportunity, industry will pollute because it is in the economic interest of firms. In this view, industry is made up entirely of amoral calculators who will do what they can to maximize profits, whatever the broader effects on society.[31] Because spending money to control pollution typically was seen as a direct tradeoff with economic success, firms would invest only what the government required to control pollution. Their interests were seen to be opposed, almost inevitably, to those of society.

The second view is that polluting is morally wrong. To many environmental advocates, pollution at any level was a moral transgression, not a problem to be solved, like poverty or traffic congestion. If polluters are morally culpable, then they should be treated as if they are criminals. We deter criminal behavior with a deterrence strategy. It follows logically, then, that environmental regulation should be based on a strategy of deterrence, rather than on one of mutual learning or adaptive problem solving. Society does not provide technical assistance to, collaborate with, or pursue joint initiatives with criminals, so why should it engage in such activities with industrial polluters? To be sure, these views have changed significantly, especially since the rise of the pollution prevention movement in the mid-1980s, but nonetheless they have been a major influence on the government–industry relationship and the style of United States regulation.

A Belief in Bureaucratic Rationality This is the view that social and economic problems can be solved through the application of technical expertise, hierarchy, uniform rules, and neutral competence. It is a foundation of modern public administration as well as of economic and social regulation.[32]

Writing early in the twentieth century, social theorist Max Weber described bureaucracy as the most efficient form of social organization in an increasingly complex and interdependent world. In presenting bureaucracy as an ideal type of social organization, Weber described a system based on a division of labor, specialization by subject matter, technical and administrative expertise, predictable rules that are applied uniformly, staffing by politically neutral career officials, defined procedures, and a hierarchy in which upper levels in organizations control the behavior of lower ones.

Environmental regulation fits this model exactly.[33] Congress passes laws and oversees their implementation by agencies, which in turn prescribe rules and oversee the behavior of regulated firms. Agencies are highly specialized, with engineers, biologists, chemists, toxicologists, lawyers, economists, and statisticians, among others, in their ranks. Elaborate rules, applied as uniformly as possible, define the technology, monitoring, and other requirements that regulated entities must meet.

Regulation, American style, is an excellent illustration of bureaucratic rationality. It was consistent with a tradition of government intervention that drew on the strengths of the political system and culture: a highly developed legal system, technical expertise, and a corps of politically neutral professional administrators. Historically, regulation founded on bureaucratic rationality was how this country had handled deficiencies in private markets. From the economic excesses of the railroads in the late 1800s, to the crusades against adulterated food in the early 1900s, to the pursuit of occupational safety in the 1960s, regulation was the strategy of choice.[34] As environmental issues rose on the policy agenda in the 1960s, other approaches were rarely considered. As John Dryzek has written: "It was simply taken for granted that this was how any such issues should be handled."[35]

These eight characteristics have reinforced each other over the years. The prevalence of capture theory and suspicions of corporate motives have promoted adversarialism and mistrust. The belief in a limited state and workings of an incremental policy system perpetuated reliance on bureaucratic solutions that fragment policies. Conceiving of environmental issues as a matter of rights rather than a process of learning freezes policy making in cycles of litigation and legislative prescriptions. Each side, when it can marshal support, struggles to codify its own preferences in law and regulation so the other side is less able to change policy when it has the upper hand.[36] The effects of these characteristics become more apparent in the following section, which gives a brief history of environmental regulation.

A Brief History of Environmental Regulation

The characteristics described here are not the whole story, but they go a long way toward explaining the form environmental regulation has taken. Long- and short-term factors combined to produce a system that is founded on bureaucratic rationalism, is highly adversarial and prescriptive, is fragmented in approach, and is mired in mistrust. These influences produced a regulatory system that offered some considerable success in the past but is poorly suited to the changes in problems, institutions, economic relationships, and industry behavior that are associated with a dynamic and changing world.

Having considered why regulation has taken the form it has in the United States, we now look at environmental regulation over the past four decades. This history may be seen in terms of John Kingdon's concepts of the politics, policy, and problem streams, which have been adapted slightly for this discussion.[37] The politics stream consists of elected officials and their staffs, as well as those whose primary purpose is to influence them (such as lobbyists). It is the most visible of the streams and is influenced by the patterns in and demands of electoral competition. The policy stream includes the networks of policy analysts, experts, researchers, and others who contribute ideas, analysis, and advice in a policy area. The problem stream describes the issues and conditions that are seen to require a governmental response—air and water pollution, habitat loss, climate change, and so on. It includes not only the problems themselves but the ways they are framed by society for discussion and resolution.

While the problem stream has changed dramatically since 1970, and the policy stream has struggled to adapt to this as well as to changes in the economy and society, the politics stream has remained locked in the same old regulatory debate. This debate has focused largely on whether the United States should have more or less regulation rather than whether it should have a different kind of regulation.

Meanwhile, the problem stream evolved from a first generation of issues, such as industrial pollution and sewage, to more complex and less visible ones, such as indoor air pollution and diffuse sources of outdoor air pollution, global warming, nonpoint sources of water pollution, habitat loss, and loss of biodiversity. This latter set, often termed second-generation and even third-generation environmental issues, poses different kinds of challenges for policy makers and requires more varied kinds of solutions than were appropriate for earlier problems. The policy stream, especially beginning in the 1980s, adapted successfully to the need for change in many ways, but was constrained by the existing statutes and rules. Because of the high levels of conflict and frequent gridlock, especially within Congress, the politics stream could not respond to the need for statutory changes that would have enabled a shift from an old to a new environmental regulation.[38]

It will also be apparent that the environmental debate in the United States since the 1960s has been dominated by two story lines. The pro-regulatory story line has argued that the key to protecting the environment lies with increasingly stringent regulation. By having more rules, stricter standards, and more intense oversight, we will be better able to protect the environment. The anti-regulatory story line argues that stringent regulation stifles economic growth and undermines competitiveness. To maintain our economic prosperity, we need to reduce the stringency of environmental rules and generally relax government oversight, even if it involves some loss in environmental quality. This debate has focused almost entirely on how much or how little regulation we should have than what form it should take. What both of these story lines share is the assumption that there is an almost inevitable trade-off among environmental and economic goals. Any steps we take to protect or improve the environment will diminish economic growth. Likewise, economic growth nearly always involves damage to the environment.

We may date the beginnings of modern environmental regulation to the passage of the Clean Air Act in 1970, the formation of the EPA that same year, and enactment of the Federal Water Pollution Control Act in 1972.[39] Although federal pollution control programs had existed before then, they left most decisions up to the states and had a limited effect on industry behavior and pollution levels. They lacked the action-forcing mechanisms that would underlie the nation's legal strategies later. The year 1970 was a watershed year. Environmental regulation since then may be broken into three periods:

From 1970 to about 1983, the United States established the current system (the old regulation) with a burst of new legislation and rules that addressed many environmental problems. Despite several challenges, the system expanded, then faced major political opposition in the early 1980s.

The second period, from 1983 to about 1993, was one of reassessment, modest reform, and eventual stalemate. While the problem stream changed and actors in the policy stream tried to innovate, the politics steam was mired in conflict. Still, elements of a new regulation were explored, and promising innovations were incorporated into the regulatory system.

The third period, from 1993 to 2001, was the reinvention era. Actors in the policy stream tried, with mixed success, to address through administrative changes the widespread dissatisfaction expressed by the revisionist critics and others. Calls for a new regulation grew, but there was a limited consensus on just what that meant.[40]

Establishing Environmental Regulation: 1970–1983

In *The Morning After Earth Day*, Mary Graham argues that congressional action with respect to the environment between 1969 and 1973 was based on four ideas.[41] First was the perception that environmental problems were a crisis that required immediate action. Second was confidence that Congress could solve these problems through legislation. "Despite the growing skepticism of the time," she writes, "voters still believed that national laws could solve problems, if they were framed so as to avoid bureaucratic lobbying and maneuvering by industry."[42] The third idea was that state and local governments were not up to the task, either because they were unwilling to confront powerful economic interests, lacked authority beyond their borders, or did not have the institutional capacity to address environmental issues. Fourth was the idea that American business had the economic strength and technological prowess to control pollution, but would not be willing to control it without legal pressure from the federal government.

Each of these ideas contributed to the burst of legislative activity that created regulations in the 1970s. It began with the Clean Air Act and the Federal Water Pollution Control Act. These laws substantially shifted the locus of legal authority over pollution control from the state to the federal level. They set national goals that forced the development of new control technologies. Both challenged industry to meet federal requirements or face punitive sanctions. Together, these laws expressed optimism about technology and the capacities of government and law as instruments of change. They responded to the growing public demands for national action to deal with environmental problems, especially those related to pollution.

Especially important in the rise of modern environmental regulation was the shift from state to federal power that occurred in the early 1970s.[43] Pollution control advocates argued that national authority should take precedence over that of the states, for several reasons. The first and most obvious was that pollution does not respect state boundaries. Regional and often national policy responses were necessary. A second was the fear that states would lack the political will to regulate strong economic interests within their boundaries. The reasonable assumption of environmental advocates was that national authority could confront corporate power more effectively than states could. A third, related reason was that without minimum national standards, there would be a "race to the bottom" in which states would compete for economic development by adopting lax controls that could attract industry. For these reasons, environmental laws in the 1970s shifted authority for many issues to Washington, while leaving some responsibility and discretion to states, in a pattern that has been described as one of cooperative or conjoint federalism.

From the perspective of industry in the early 1970s, it was as if government had thrown down a gauntlet. Nearly thirty years of postwar economic growth had brought unprecedented prosperity, and it looked now as if it all would be risked on a dubious response to "soft" environmental concerns. The main targets of air and water regulation were large, pollution-intensive industries like electric utilities, iron and steel, petrochemicals, and automobiles. These industries resisted regulation in the political arena, in the courts, and through public appeals. The relationship between government and industry in these early days was largely one of conflict. Political events over the next few decades would only reinforce this tendency toward conflict. To establish the legitimacy of regulation, agencies needed to demonstrate their toughness and independence from industry, as well as be able to achieve concrete results through enforcement. This adversarial approach probably was politically necessary at the time, but it created a mold that has been hard to break.

This legislative decade of the environment continued after the air and water acts were passed. In 1974, Congress passed a Safe Drinking Water Act (SDWA), followed in 1976 by the Toxic Substances Control Act (TSCA) and the Resource Conservation and Recovery Act (RCRA). The TSCA granted EPA authority over the tens of thousands of chemicals in commerce and was viewed at the time as a means of filling in the gaps in the coverage of other laws. After the nation's attention to Love Canal and other waste sites in 1980, RCRA became the major vehicle for controlling the use and disposal of hazardous wastes. The decade drew to a close with passage of the Superfund law, which created a national fund for cleaning up abandoned waste sites and the legal mechanisms that enabled government to collect the costs of cleanup from waste generators. The air and water acts also were amended slightly and reauthorized later in the decade. In the space of just over ten years, Congress had enacted a comprehensive, if fragmented, statutory framework for pollution control.

Two sets of events in the late 1970s presented a major challenge for regulation. One was the troubled economy. By the end of the decade, inflation was escalating rapidly and economic growth was slowing down. In a zero-sum universe, critics of environmental regulation had little difficulty in casting blame for the poor economy on air and water pollution controls. At about the same time, limits on oil exports from the Middle East caused widespread shortages of gas and heating fuels across the country. Because pollution controls had limited the development of energy resources in many areas, and clean air rules sometimes increased the energy needed for transportation and other purposes, environmental regulation was assigned much of the blame.

Partly in response to these economic and energy challenges, the issue of regulatory reform first became prominent in the middle and late 1970s. The thrust of reform proposals was not to dismantle regulation (that would come a few years later), but to control its effects, especially those on economic growth and energy resources. One such reform was a greater use of economic analysis of regulations, including cost-benefit and cost-effectiveness analyses.[44] Although these reforms helped to make regulation more economically efficient, to the extent that they influenced decisions, they focused on the stringency of regulation more than on the form it should take. They were more about setting standards than about devising new models of regulatory governance.

Another reform, emissions trading, did focus on the form of regulation. Emission offsets were developed in the mid-1970s to reconcile Clean Air Act requirements with industrial development in southern California, and were incorporated into the 1977 revisions to the law. This was a forerunner of several trading programs for pollutants, which are based on the fact that marginal control costs among pollution sources vary, often considerably. The programs allow sources to trade, buy, or sell emission reduction credits so that sources with low costs may exceed the standard and earn credits, which they then may sell to those with higher costs. The environmental result is as good or better than it would have been and yet the overall costs are lower when they are calculated across all sources.

The accomplishments of 1970–1981 make it one of the more productive decades for any single area of domestic policy in recent U.S. history. Within this period the United States built the legal and institutional infrastructure for environmental regulation. It enacted a formidable array of laws, established a national regulatory agency, created a comprehensive system of regulation, and put major sectors of U.S. industry to the task of reducing and cleaning up pollution. To the extent that there was opposition to regulation, and there was, it usually took the form of limiting its unwanted by-products, not to dismantling the system itself.

It looked as if regulation had met the political test, but bigger challenges would come in the next few years. Although a national environmental regulation system would survive, it would be with political and legal consequences that hamper, to this day, the effort to build a new environmental regulation.

Reassessment (in the Policy Stream) and Stalemate (in the Politics Stream): 1983–1993

The early 1980s were a traumatic period for United States environmental policy. Little more than a decade after the Clean Air Act of 1970, regulation came under serious political attack. The Reagan administration came to Washington in 1981 with what it thought was a mandate to reduce the size and scope of government. Environmental regulation was a principal target. The views of the new administration were clear. Regulation interfered too much in private business and impaired growth and competitiveness. The goal of the critics during this period was less to reform environmental regulation than to dismantle it.

The effort failed. It was true that many people were unhappy with the more onerous aspects of environmental regulation. There were ample stories of higher-than-necessary costs, overbearing enforcers, nitpicking rules, and misplaced priorities, but people cared about environmental quality. Critics of regulation made a strategic error by not separating the goals of environmental regulation—clean air and water, safe drinking water and food—from the means that had been employed for achieving them. Their assault on regulation took the form of an attack on environmental values and programs rather than an effort to correct deficiencies in the system of regulation itself. Consider the effects on EPA, the national regulator. The first two years of the Reagan administration were the worst in EPA's history, in terms of accomplishments, reputation, staff morale, leadership, and most other measures. Although the Reagan administration's effort to rewrite the legislative framework failed, the effects of its assault on budgets, staffing, enforcement, and institutional credibility brought environmental regulation to the verge of crisis.

Nevertheless, crisis often is the handmaiden of change. Having reached a low point in public support, the administration decided in 1983 to abandon the more extreme elements of its antiregulatory crusade and place national policy in reliable hands. William Ruckelshaus was summoned back for a second tour as EPA administrator and given a free hand in filling top posts with people he knew could do the job.

Ruckelshaus returned with a deputy and group of assistant administrators that many consider the best in EPA's history. He set out to restore budgets and morale, rebuild public confidence, reestablish EPA's scientific competence, and, as it turned out, to begin to rethink environmental regulation.

Ruckelshaus did not set out simply to rebuild regulation on its old, tattered foundations. He realized after a dozen years of experience that cracks were beginning to appear in the system he had helped create. Certainly there was evidence that regulatory costs were high and mounting. Problems were emerging on the national agenda faster than policy makers could make sense of or set priorities among them. Patterns of conflict and mistrust were deeply embedded in the relationships of government, industry, and environmentalists, to the extent that cooperation in solving problems was almost nonexistent. Environmental progress seemed to depend on whatever brute political and legal force one side or the other could apply at any given time. Regulation was still focused on the narrow goal of controlling pollution rather than preventing it in the first place. More and more an array of critics pointed to the fragmentation of regulatory programs across environmental media as a source of inefficiency, lost opportunities, and unneeded complexity.[45]

The return of Ruckelshaus to EPA in 1983 sparked a decade of efforts to innovate within the policy stream under his leadership and that of his successors, Lee Thomas and William Reilly. Their approach was not just to innovate within the terms of the old regulation but also to plant the seeds of a new regulation, with innovations occurring mainly in four areas: (1) defining the environmental "problem" as more than just pollution control; (2) expanding the use of consensus-based processes, such as regulatory negotiation; (3) developing new policy tools to complement regulation; and (4) working to integrate across environmental media and policy sectors, such as agriculture and energy. Although each effort had mixed success, largely because of the recurring stalemate in the politics stream, they still make the 1980s a period of creativity and innovation that helped to provide groundwork for a new regulation.

Redefining the Environmental "Problem"   Definitions of the problem stream began to change. In the first era, the environmental problem had been seen mainly as one of controlling industrial pollution. Regulators focused their attention on large, visible sources. Moreover, they concentrated on controlling pollution as it came from manufacturing processes, where regulatory instruments, such as technology standards, could be best applied.[46] Regulation also had come to focus on protecting human health as a way of ensuring public support, rather than on ecological goals, such as protecting habitat and biodiversity.[47]

By the mid-1980s, this emphasis appeared to be too narrow. First, it neglected many sources of pollution that in combination are significant. For example, assessments at the time revealed that most water quality impairment was caused by nonpoint sources, such as agricultural and stormwater runoff, rather than industrial point sources. Second, the focus on controlling pollution at the end of a process led to many missed opportunities for preventing it further up the production line, through use of other raw materials, changes in manufacturing processes, reuse of materials, and other methods. Pollution prevention thus became a major policy theme of the 1980s, both in the private sector and in government. Policy makers also broadened the definition of environmental problems by looking beyond human health concerns, which had preoccupied them until now, to the well-being of the larger ecological systems on which human health depends. Ecological issues gained greater prominence on the policy agenda, as did such global problems as climate change, deforestation, and loss of biodiversity.

Expanded Use of Consensus-Based Processes   Conflict and mistrust were standard features of environmental policy making in the early days. The process of designing regulations and deciding issues consisted more of preparation for litigation by all sides than a search for solutions. In the Superfund program, for example, it was found in the early years that more funds were going to the legal and administrative task of assigning liability than to cleaning up waste.

The use of alternative dispute settlement (ADR) provided answers to some of these problems. Environmental mediation, a form of ADR, had been used in the 1970s to resolve local disputes on such issues as highway construction, facility siting, and habitat preservation. In the 1980s, EPA applied ADR techniques to rule making through a process of regulatory negotiation. Rather than develop a regulation through the conventional process, which typically ended in litigation, an agency convened a panel of interested parties to work together to reach a consensus on a proposed rule, which would be issued for public comment.[48] The EPA and other agencies also applied ADR techniques to broader issues through policy dialogues in the 1980s and 1990s.

New Policy Tools to Complement Regulation Until that point, the toolkit for environmental protection had consisted almost entirely of conventional regulation. Agencies would determine the best available technologies for different categories of industry, issue them as binding rules, monitor compliance, and take enforcement action when needed. Regulation was a blunt and often inefficient tool, but it was effective enough to show results in dealing with major industrial polluters. Even before the mid-1980s, however, regulators had shown a cautious interest in other tools, mainly market incentives like emissions trading and approaches based on the use of information. The apparent limitations of an entirely regulatory strategy, however, and the emergence of a second and third generation of environmental problems that were often not amenable to regulatory solutions (such as climate change, nonpoint water runoff, and indoor air pollution) stimulated even greater interest in tools that could complement or replace conventional regulation.[49]

One area of innovation was almost accidental. The 1984 catastrophe in Bhopal, India, involving a Union Carbide plant had raised chemical plant safety and a community's right to know as major issues. In 1986, in amending the Superfund law, Congress created the Toxics Release Inventory, which required several kinds of manufacturing plants to annually report to EPA their releases of any substances on a list of chemicals. The EPA would then publish information about each plant. The TRI and similar information disclosure requirements have had a more profound effect than most people could have anticipated. Combined with increasing corporate sensitivity and the availability of environmental data on the Internet, these requirements have pushed many companies to significantly reduce their environmental impacts.[50] In particular, activist groups have used TRI data to bring community pressure on manufacturing facilities.

Interest in economic incentives also grew in the 1980s, more so in air than in water programs. The EPA slowly expanded its use of emissions trading in controlling air pollution, but always within the context of the existing regulatory regime. Incentives complemented the existing regulation. In a major step forward, the emissions trading concept was incorporated in the 1990 Clean Air Act Amendments, in the form of a trading allowance for utilities that had to reduce their sulfur oxide emissions. Although at a slower pace, trading was applied to controlling water pollution as well, usually in the context of watershed protection programs.[51] This trend would continue into the 1990s and early 2000s, when trading was proposed internationally for dealing with carbon dioxide emissions and domestically for pollutants like mercury.

Integrating Across Environmental Media and Policy Sectors   The classification of pollution control programs by environmental medium had been both a blessing and a curse. By breaking large and complex problems into a series of smaller, more manageable ones, government could effectively apply technical expertise and legal tools to address a first generation of problems. By the 1980s, however, this method was causing problems, as the earlier discussion has suggested.[52]

From 1983 on, policy makers began to search for ways to integrate control across environmental media. One of the more ambitious efforts took place in mid-decade, in the Integrated Environmental Management Projects. The EPA launched projects to determine the feasibility and value of integrating analyses and strategies in three ways: by contaminant, by geographical area, and by industry. Later in the decade, it organized groups of issues into clusters. Some were based on the contaminant, such as lead. Others were based on the affected resource, such as groundwater, or the industry that was the cause of environmental concern, such as auto manufacturing. While the first exercise attempted to integrate risk assessments and policy options through complex analytical models, the second took a more pragmatic approach by assessing all the efforts under way and organizing them more effectively.

The various efforts made to change regulation between 1983 and 1993 had mixed success, largely because of the high levels of conflict in the politics stream. Indeed, while actors in the policy stream were struggling to modernize regulation with more flexible, integrated, and collaborative strategies, actors in the politics stream still were fighting over the contours of the old regulation. Even after Ruckelshaus returned to EPA in 1983, distrust of the administration by Democrats in Congress remained high. EPA rules still were subject to intensive review and delay by the Office of Management and Budget (OMB). Congress responded with highly specific and prescriptive laws that constrained the administration's and EPA's discretion, such as the 1984 Hazardous and Solid Waste Amendments and the Clean Air Act Amendments of 1990.

As indicated earlier, the Reagan administration came to office determined to roll back environmental regulation. The irony, given this goal, is that regulation in 1992 was more stringent and detailed than it had been in 1982. Democrats in Congress were committed to environmental programs and did not trust the administration. As Democratic Representative Henry Waxman put it: "The specificity in the 1990 Amendments reflects the concern that without detailed directives, industry intervention might frustrate efforts to put pollution control steps in place."[53] As a result, the law "is rife with mandates, deadlines, 'hammers,' and timetables, all geared to deprive bureaucrats and emitters of discretion and flexibility."[54] Partisan conflict had produced regulatory rigidity. Later efforts to change regulation would be frustrated by this statutory legacy of distrust.

The Reinvention Era: 1993–2001

The year 1993 was an auspicious time for environmental policy. After the environmental decade of the 1960s had come the antiregulatory assault of the early 1980s, followed by a creative period within the policy stream. By 1993, the pollution prevention movement was in full bloom. Agencies had become sophisticated in the use of such analytical tools as risk assessment and cost-benefit analysis. The value of information disclosure was appreciated more, as were the efficiencies and results that could be achieved with market instruments like emissions trading. Experience with environmental mediation and negotiation had shown that litigation was not the only way to end contentious disputes. It seemed that conditions were ripe for the politics stream to finally catch up with the policy and problem streams.

Other factors suggested that a change in the foundations of regulation was on the horizon. Internationally, the vague but compelling concept of sustainable development was gathering steam. The Earth Summit, held in Rio de Janeiro in June 1992, marked a new stage in the evolution of environmental issues. Protecting the environment was no longer seen as a narrow matter of instituting technical controls on pollution or of reconciling tradeoffs among economic and environmental goals. It was viewed as a fundamental aspect of social, human, and economic development.[55] Global issues like climate change, loss of biodiversity, and deforestation forced a recognition of interdependence among nations. The President's Council for Sustainable Development was created in 1994 to recommend strategies for change. People talked of new approaches for a new century and of alternative regulatory paths for a new era of regulation.

From industry, there were signs of a new attitude toward environmental protection. A philosophical underpinning of the old regulation—the notion that environmental and economic goals inevitably posed a zero sum—was increasingly seen as an artifact of less enlightened times. The pioneering efforts of companies like 3M to prove that pollution prevention pays had grown into a far more sophisticated set of ideas about the business value of strong environmental performance. Among leading firms, a "greening" of industry was under way, reflecting trends toward corporate stewardship and social responsibility. These changes are examined in detail in chapter 4. What matters here is that profound changes were occurring that could have set the stage for a new regulation.

Despite such influences, environmental regulation would change only at the margins between 1993 and 2001. As it turned out, applying the lessons of the past to the task of building a new regulation was not a priority of the Clinton administration. More significantly, conflict over the two old story lines—about whether we should have more or less regulation but not a different kind—erupted again in the politics stream. Indeed, the results of the 1994 congressional elections, when Republicans took control of the Senate and the House, led to the most concerted challenge to environmental regulation since the early 1980s.[56] Again, government's role and regulatory costs were major themes. And again, the prospects for a new regulation based on a new model of governance were lost in the political debates.

It is interesting that the solutions that were sought at the time would have done little to address the problems that motivated the conservative attacks in the mid-1990s. The main output of the antiregulators in 1995 was a House bill that would have required more elaborate quantitative analysis of risks and costs, formal peer review of agencies' analytical and science-based decisions, and more extensive judicial review of regulatory choices. Although this surely would have tied the regulatory system up in knots and slowed or stopped the flow of new regulations, it would have done little to address the many complaints about the existing system. Congressional reformers lacked the time, patience, and political support to undertake a comprehensive overhaul of the main environmental laws.

Still, the efforts of these potentially draconian proposals had two important effects on regulatory policy. First, they stimulated the Clinton administration to announce plans for an initiative, Streamlining Environmental Regulation, in March 1995. This defined the reinvention agenda for the rest of the 1990s. Second, the Republican assault largely killed chances for cooperative reform efforts within the political stream, including legislative change that would have addressed deficiencies in the old regulation. Notable proposals for second-generation environmental legislation that would have given agencies the authority to try innovative approaches were not enacted. There was little incentive for either side to seek a middle ground. And the administration, supported by environmentalists, decided not to risk the legislative gains of more than two decades by opening up any of the laws to revision. For the rest of the 1990s, any efforts to revise the old regulation and begin a transition to something new would have to occur administratively, without statutory change.

There is no better evidence of the gridlock in the politics stream than this: Legislatively, the only noteworthy changes in the 1990s were modest revisions in the pesticides and water quality laws. Both may be described as an incremental fine-tuning of the old regulation. In most respects, the political debates reprised the old pro- and antiregulatory struggle. Typically, these debates turned on how much regulation we should have and how strict it should be, rather than on whether regulation as it had been practiced in the United States was the best way to achieve the nation's environmental goals.

Still, despite the limited progress at the national political level, there were promising signs in the 1990s about the prospects for a new regulation in the near future. One was the widespread dissatisfaction with the existing system expressed by several influential people, many of them strong allies of environmental programs. These include what were described in the first chapter as the revisionist critics. The reports of such groups as the Enterprise for the Environment, the President's Council for Sustainable Development (PSCD), the Progressive Policy Institute, the National Academy of Public Administration, and the Aspen Institute reflected a broad consensus on the need for change.[57] Second, EPA's own initiatives, discussed in chapter 5, helped establish a basis for future change. Third, there were state innovations, often backed by legislation, as well as local initiatives that offered stepping-stones to a new regulation. These are examined in chapter 6.

What Next? Environmental Regulation in the Early 2000s
It is fair to say that the reinvention era ended with the 2000 elections. The period since President Bush assumed office in 2001 is difficult to classify. From the campaign onward, it was clear that the George W. Bush administration would not be progressive on environmental issues. Overall, it has pushed a pro-growth and development agenda, especially on the extraction and use of natural resources like the Arctic National Wildlife Refuge. On pollution control matters, it has consistently favored the interests of the fossil-fuel industry, an attitude that is most evident in its refusal to adopt more than voluntary measures to address the problem of climate change. It has also been criticized for its efforts to revise the New Source Review (NSR) program for controlling older sources of air pollution and for relaxing earlier proposals for reducing mercury air emissions from power plants and other industrial sources.[58] To no one's surprise, it has regularly drawn the ire of environmentalists and congressional defenders of environmental programs.

Yet it is inaccurate to describe the Bush administration as a reprise of the first Reagan term, at least regarding pollution control. In both the Reagan period and in the efforts by House Republicans to roll back environmental programs in the mid-1990s, Republicans had learned that to be perceived as weak on environmental issues could be an electoral liability. Probably for this reason, the Bush administration, at least in its first term, tread somewhat more softly on the pollution front than had its Reagan predecessor. The three EPA administrators who have served under Bush—Christine Todd Whitman, Michael Leavitt, and Stephen Johnson—have taken a generally moderate approach on most issues. Even the debate over something like New Source Review, where the administration took action that may increase air pollution, is not is simple as it appears. The NSR program has been described by critics as a cumbersome, expensive, and often ineffective way of upgrading standards for older sources of air pollution.[59] Indeed, the NSR debate demonstrates how difficult it is to separate these complex legal and administrative issues from the underlying issues of how to improve the environment. It is the very complexity of the system that makes discussions about changing the old regulation so difficult. That being said, this is the most politically conservative administration on environmental protection since the early Reagan years.

By 2001, the reinvention era was over, and nothing else had emerged to replace it. Reinvention as a concept surely had its limits, but it did provide a convenient conceptual and political umbrella for describing and justifying actions that were intended, in some small way, to move the United States toward a new approach to environmental protection. There still were initiatives aimed at changing the process for achieving environmental goals, but their significance was overshadowed by political struggles over the stringency of programs and the need for new ones to address issues like climate change. Even on climate, where innovative approaches based on the ideas of a new regulation might have been applied, the president's refusal to commit the United States to any kind of mandatory reductions in carbon dioxide emissions has blocked serious effort to find solutions. In general, the early 2000s may be seen as a time in which there were no clear directions for national environmental policy. There was a general sense, however, of opportunities being lost.

With the concept of reinvention dead as a guiding light, what became of the search for a new regulation in the early 2000s? To be sure, early in the Bush term, homeland security and the war in Iraq displaced the more routine domestic issues like environmental protection. When environmental issues did find a place on the agenda, however modest, partisan rancor and a legislative spirit of noncooperation got in the way of what necessarily should have been collaborative efforts to define a third way for environmental regulation. Still, there were signs that the spirit of reinvention was still alive. These signs are discussed in chapters 5 and 6; the political outlook for a new regulation is taken up in chapter 7.

Modern Environmental Regulation

The history of environmental regulation from 1970 to the present has been a productive one. What began as a movement in the 1960s had become an elaborate and highly developed set of laws, regulations, and programs by the 1990s. What had been a disconnected set of administrative units in 1970 had become one of the most powerful and technically sophisticated regulatory agencies in the world by the early 2000s. As discussed in chapter 3, pollution of many kinds has declined significantly or at least not gotten worse, despite substantial economic growth, economic development, and increased driving. Still, there was growing concern about second- and third-generation environmental problems, for which the old regulation is not especially well suited.

This has been a turbulent history. Advocates of the two story lines fought over almost every aspect of the system: the scope of regulation, the stringency of standards, the balance of federal versus state authority, the role of economic analysis, and the adequacy of the scientific base, to name a few. Each side used any available means to press its case, including the courts and the media. The shifting and unstable balance of political power in Washington contributed to the turbulence as well. Between 1970 and 2005, the same party controlled the White House and all of Congress for only ten years (four with Jimmy Carter, two with Bill Clinton, and four with George W. Bush). Ronald Reagan had a Republican Senate from 1981 to 1987, but faced a solidly Democratic House for his eight years in office.

It was a destructive pattern, one that William Ruckelshaus has likened to the swings of a pendulum: "The anti-environmental push of the mid-1990s was prompted by the pro-environmental excess of the late '80s, which was prompted by the anti-environmental excess of the early '80s, which was prompted by the pro-environmental excess of the '70s, and so on, for thirty years."[60] Because of these recurring swings in the political pendulum, Ruckelshaus has written, EPA was "not sufficiently empowered by Congress to set and pursue meaningful priorities, deluged in paper and lawsuits, and pulled on a dozen different vectors by an ill-assorted and antiquated set of statutes."[61] Furthermore, with each swing of the pendulum, different sides of the environmental debate worked hard to inject their own policy preferences in laws and regulations, thus narrowing the range of discretion available for later attempts to make the transition to a new regulation.

And yet, below this turbulence in the politics stream, there were efforts to adapt and innovate. A great deal of learning and improvisation was going on in the policy stream. Consider the efforts to redefine problems, use consensus-building techniques, apply new tools, and integrate strategies. Throughout this period there also was dynamism in the problem stream. The lessons of history are clear: We do not just "solve" environmental problems and move on. Reducing point-source water pollution made damage from nonpoint sources more apparent. No sooner did we learn how intractable the problem of ground-level ozone was than we discovered risks from the depletion of stratospheric ozone. Indoor air pollution, which had mostly been ignored, may pose greater risks to health than the outdoor kind. The social construction of problems has also changed— from pollution control to prevention, to eco-efficiency and cleaner production to sustainability; from a focus on health to worries about ecology; from national to global issues; from efficiency to social equity; and so on.

This chapter has suggested why regulation has taken the form it does in the United States and describes how we got to where we are today. Before we leave the old regulation, however, we need to evaluate it. To what extent has regulation solved problems? Is it still too expensive and cumbersome, given what it has delivered? Is it appropriate for the problems and circumstances of a postmodern era in public policy? If environmental regulation has been so successful, as many have claimed, and much of the evidence appears to suggest, then why not leave it as it is? Why change it at all?

3

Why Change? Evaluating Environmental Regulation

Centralized, detailed, and programmed regulation can be a powerful social instrument, but it is not a subtle one.[1]

The history of environmental regulation in this country has reinforced the very tendencies that influenced its initial design. The tug-of-war between parties and among branches of government caused each side to seek whatever short-term political advantages they could gain at any time. Our incremental tendencies led policy makers to react to problems as they appeared on the policy agenda, leading to fragmented strategies. High levels of political conflict meant that each side struggled to get its views codified into law, then resisted changes to avoid losing what they had achieved. Prescriptive, detailed laws invited judicial interventions that reinforced the legalistic and adversarial tendencies that had been hard-wired into the system. Through it all, distrust among parties remained high, making a transition toward a new regulation all but impossible, both politically and legally.

The regulations that Congress launched in 1970 have sailed through troubled seas, but the regulatory approach has not changed fundamentally for over thirty years. If anything, the initial predispositions have been reinforced by partisan conflict and adversarial relationships. We now have more rules, more complicated laws, and more intricate systems for permitting and reporting than ever before. Despite the many incremental innovations discussed in the later chapters in this volume, it is fair to say that the old regulation not only has survived, it has prospered. While other countries have evolved toward new models of regulation, the United States has continued to elaborate, often in fine detail, on the old rules-and-deterrence model.

One explanation for the absence of change is that we are still caught up in the debate over the two story lines. Recall that one story line links environmental protection inextricably to continued or expanded regulation, while the other calls for dismantling or rolling back regulation as we know it. Despite the good ideas and proposals for change that have been brewing in the policy stream, the politics stream has been unable to get outside of the proverbial box of these two story lines. Most recently during the George W. Bush administration, the terms of the environmental policy debate have revolved around whether there will be more or less regulation and enforcement rather than the need for changes in regulatory governance.

The political process has shown time and again that the antiregulatory story line is unacceptable. Voters are not ready to toss out the framework of regulatory controls that have delivered results. Despite the many complaints about environmental regulation, it has enjoyed steady public support.[2] It is essential to remember that for over thirty years, every effort to reduce the scope and stringency of environmental regulation through legislative action failed. To the extent that regulation was cut back significantly at all, in 1981–1983, it was due to administrative, not legislative action, and these actions were later reversed by the proregulatory, proenvironmental, Democratic Congresses of the 1980s.

So why not buy the second story line? If environmental regulation as we know it has delivered results and the public has rejected efforts to dismantle it, why not stick with what we have?

This chapter evaluates current environmental regulation and responds to the question of why it should or should not be changed. It begins by looking at what regulation has accomplished, in itself an impressive picture. Many kinds of pollution have decreased substantially. Others have not increased, despite nearly four decades of economic growth and increased driving. Taking advantage of its political stability, administrative and legal strengths, and economic success, the United States has built an impressive capability for managing the more serious forms of pollution. On the other hand, as is argued here, the old regulation has unwanted side effects and is unsuited to the task of protecting the environment in a rapidly changing world. These criticisms and the case for change are discussed later in the chapter.

What Has Environmental Regulation Accomplished?

First, the good news: Regulation has delivered results. Testimony to this effect runs throughout the literature. Terry Davies and Jan Mazurek conclude that the amount of pollution released to the environment has declined since the 1970s. This has occurred despite the fact that, between 1970 and 1995, "the total United States gross domestic product increased 99 per cent; population climbed 28 per cent; and vehicle miles traveled jumped 116 per cent."[3] Richard Andrews sees regulation as being extraordinarily successful in reducing pollution, at least from major industries and municipal sources.[4] Michael Kraft and Norman Vig conclude that the record of the past thirty years demonstrates convincingly that the United States government is able to produce significant environmental gains through public policies. "Unquestionably," they add, "the environment would be worse today if the policies enacted during the 1970s and 1980s had not been in place."[5] Gregg Easterbrook has gone so far as to describe United States environmental protection policy as the leading success story of postwar liberalism.[6]

This is impressive testimony, to be sure. As the following discussion details, environmental regulation has delivered results, and it has saved this country from serious and costly damage. Nevertheless, keep two qualifications in mind. First, as Davies and Mazurek point out, many of the accomplishments consist of not allowing problems to get worse in the face of economic growth. Second, and more important, as Andrews points out, most of these results were achieved for industrial and municipal point sources, a first generation of problems that were the main targets of regulation in the 1970s. There are many second- and third-generation problems—nonpoint, diffuse, emerging, and persistent ones—for which the old regulation has been less successful. Increasingly, these are the problems that require attention. Indeed, Vig and Kraft later observe that in the future, further advances will be more difficult, costly, and controversial.[7] The main reason for this, they add, is that "the easy problems have already been addressed, and at this point marginal gains . . . will cost more per unit of improvement than in the past."[8]

Before making the case for a new regulation, this chapter briefly evaluates what the existing approach to regulation has accomplished, from two perspectives. One is measurable results. What effect has regulation had on the problems it was created to solve? The second is capacity building. What have we accomplished in terms of enhancing our ability to solve problems? The assessment on both counts is positive but mixed.

What Have Been the Measurable Results of the Old Regulation?
Any attempt to assess the measurable results of regulation must deal with limited and uneven information. The best information exists for air emissions and air quality, where we can identify national trends in major pollutants. Although there is information on water quality, it varies by region and has not been collected consistently over time. There is information on some chemicals, such as polychlorinated biphenyls (PCBs) and DDT, but much less about most others. We know least about waste generation and disposal. This section gives a brief summary of what is known, based on Terry Davies's and Jan Mazurek's 1995 evaluation of United States pollution control, the United States Environmental Protection Agency's 2003 *Draft Report on the Environment*, and other recent assessments.[9] The goal is not to provide a comprehensive assessment of environmental conditions but to evaluate what regulation to this point may have generally achieved since the early 1970s.

What is clear is that emissions of many common air pollutants have declined significantly. The most complete information is for the six "criteria" pollutants covered by the National Ambient Air Quality Standards (NAAQS). Emissions of several of these peaked between 1965 and 1975, when they were two to three times higher than they are estimated to have been in 1900. The greatest success has been lead emissions, which fell by 98 percent between 1970 and 1995. In the same period, emissions of sulfur oxides fell by 41 percent; fine particulate matter (PM-10) by 79 percent, volatile organic compounds by 25 percent; and carbon monoxide by 28 percent. Of these six pollutants, only nitrogen oxide emissions rose, by 6 percent. This record is all the more remarkable when one considers that United States gross domestic product and driving (as measured by vehicle miles traveled) both roughly doubled during this period.[10]

Similarly, in a more recent analysis, EPA concluded that ambient concentrations of criteria air pollutants have fallen significantly in most parts of the country. Between 1982 and 2001, for example, average atmospheric ozone levels fell by some 11 percent. Still, in 2001, more than 110 million people lived in counties with ozone concentrations higher than the eight-hour standard for that pollutant, and 73 million people lived in counties where levels of very fine particles (less than 2.5 micrometers) exceeded national standards. For toxic air pollutants, where monitoring data are much less available than for the criteria pollutants, there are mixed trends. Despite large reductions in pollutants like benzene in the 1990s, EPA has concluded that emissions of air toxics may still pose health and ecological risks in certain areas of the United States.[11]

The record for water discharges is not as easily described because the information is less consistent than it is for the criteria air pollutants. Concentrations of water pollutants linked to industrial and sewage treatment plants (the point sources) have declined substantially. For example, concentrations of fecal coliform bacilli (commonly discharged from sewage treatment plants) and phosphorus have fallen sharply, the latter because of the phase-out of phosphorus in detergents. Levels of dissolved oxygen, a positive measure of environmental quality, increased sharply in the 1970s and more slowly in the 1980s. Nitrate levels, a negative measure of water quality, increased sharply in the 1970s as use of nitrogen fertilizer grew, but fell again in the 1980s. Overall, because of controls on industrial and municipal sources, pollution concentrations in rivers and streams have decreased over time according to Davies and Mazurek.[12]

Most water quality problems today are the result of diffuse, nonpoint sources of pollution, such as agricultural and stormwater runoff: "Rain carries the leavings of daily life—fertilizer and pesticides from fields, golf courses, and lawns; oil from driveways and streets; sewage from leaky septic tanks; and the land itself—into rivers, lakes, and bays."[13] These diffuse sources are more difficult to regulate than point sources and have major effects on the environment. For example, phosphorus and nitrogen loadings from nonpoint sources account for up to 44 percent of total water pollution in Chesapeake Bay.[14] Each summer, farm and city runoff into the Mississippi River accounts for a 7,000-square-mile "dead zone" off coastal Louisiana, where shrimp and fish cannot survive.[15] Low oxygen levels are a recurring, seasonal problem in areas that include Chesapeake Bay, Long Island Sound, and Tampa Bay.

The data on nonpoint source pollution are difficult to interpret. For example, EPA reported that 14 percent of the river miles, 28 percent of the lake acreage, and 100 per cent of the Great Lakes and their connecting waters were under fish consumption advisories in 2002. These per centages had increased steadily since 1993. However, the increases, EPA reported, "are most likely the result of more consistent monitoring and reporting and decreases in concentration criteria, and are not necessarily an indication that conditions are getting worse."[16] Sometimes what appears to be bad news is relatively good news. Although wetlands acreage declined nationally at an annual rate of nearly 60,000 acres between 1986 and 1997, that was an 80 percent reduction in the rate of loss from the previous decade.[17] Overall, the evidence suggests that remaining water quality problems are the result of diffuse, nonpoint sources and patterns of growth and development that are not amenable to traditional, technology-based regulation.

The effectiveness of regulating solid and hazardous wastes is especially hard to evaluate because the data are so poor. Federal regulation focuses largely on hazardous wastes—those that may pose a threat to human health. Because these wastes are tightly regulated, methods for their handling, storage, and disposal have greatly improved since the 1970s. For example, the practice of disposing of hazardous waste in landfills, especially liquid wastes, has been greatly reduced. However, this is because more waste is being treated on site and in incinerators rather than not being generated in the first place. This is a deficiency that the pollution prevention movement in the 1980s was designed to address, but it has been difficult to correct under a regulatory approach. In addition, many kinds of industrial wastes, such as those from mining, have not been regulated as "hazardous." The EPA estimates that the 20,000 businesses generating more than 2,200 pounds of legally hazardous waste in 1999 produced some 40 million tons of such waste. It was unable to compare this with previous years because of changes in data collection over the years.[18] As for the more routine municipal waste, per capita generation increased from about 2.7 pounds per day in 1960 to 4.5 pounds in 2000 (although the rate has remained relatively constant since 1990).[19]

Another set of impacts associated with industry are releases of toxics into the environment. The best source of information is the Toxics Release Inventory, although that did not begin until 1987, has been modified several times (making precise comparisons difficult), and excludes several sources of releases, such as mobile sources and the mining industry. "The good news from the TRI data is that a dramatic reduction has taken place in direct releases to the environment."[20] Many of these reductions have been attributed to the effects of TRI disclosure on firms' behavior. At the same time, total production of many chemicals increased as the economy grew. Still, there were decreases in such chemicals as lead and mercury, both of which were tightly regulated by EPA under multiple legal authorities and routes of exposure. Monitoring data also show reductions in concentrations of some chemicals. Exposure to PCBs, for example, has declined significantly. Of thirty chemicals tracked by EPA as high priorities for reduction in recent years (lead, mercury, cadmium, and twenty-seven organic chemicals), releases of seventeen have been declining since 1993. Overall, amounts of these chemicals in the environment fell by 44 percent between 1991 and 1998.[21] In later years, however, many categories of TRI releases fell at a much slower rate or increased.[22]

In evaluating the old regulation, it is important to consider what it has not addressed as well as what it has accomplished. When it regulates manufacturing, the United States achieves results that exceed or at least compare favorably with other nations, but there are gaps in the regulatory framework. A glaring one is carbon dioxide (CO_2) emissions, the main contributor to global warming. These have been growing steadily, although transportation and other activities separate from industrial production are a large part of the increase. Similarly, energy, materials, and water use are not directly affected by existing regulation. Overall, the United States economy is relatively more energy intensive than other industrial nations, relatively low in waste recycling rates, and relatively high in waste generation rates per dollar of GDP. National environmental regulation affects these areas of performance only indirectly, if at all.[23]

Other than limited information, the major difficulty in assessing the measurable results of regulation is linking causes and effects. Many people have argued, for example, that air pollution is down less because of regulatory controls than changes in the structure of the economy, patterns of fuel use, and weather. Like other advanced economies, that of the United States is increasingly based on services rather than manufacturing, which lessens the amounts of industry-based emissions that regulation may cover. Davies and Mazurek try to separate the effects of regulation from other factors in an analysis of air quality over twenty years in three industrial, urban areas. They conclude that mandated air pollution control investments have often had a significant effect in reducing air pollution levels. At the same time, however, they determine that the effects of air quality regulation generally have been overshadowed by the effects of economic changes, weather, and other factors.[24]

The reality is that we cannot separate the effects of the old regulation from the other factors that influence environmental quality. Still, the evidence and common sense suggest that regulation has had some substantial effects in reducing pollution and other damage. Many harmful pollutants are now gone or remain at far lower levels than they would have been without regulation. More than two decades of new technologies have been installed. Cars today are one-fortieth as polluting as those made in 1970. Hazardous wastes are managed and treated in ways that will prevent future Love Canals and avoid costly cleanups. Microbes in drinking water are lower; far more sewage is treated—the list goes on. It seems clear that if government had not intervened in the 1970s and forced industry to account for its actions, environmental conditions in the United States surely would have been far worse than they are today. At the same time, the evidence suggests that for many environmental problems, much remains to be done.

Based on what we know now, it is reasonable to conclude that regulation has resulted in:

· reductions in common air pollutants, or little increase despite significant economic and population growth

· virtual elimination of several harmful pollutants that were banned or tightly regulated, such as lead, mercury, PCBs, and phosphorus

· reduced emissions and concentrations of several common water pollutants, largely owing to technology controls on industrial and municipal point sources

Regulation has been less effective in other areas, some of which it was not designed to affect. These include:

· pollution from diffuse, nonpoint sources, especially those that damage water quality

· volumes of wastes generated and energy or materials used, much of which are a result of consumption and transportation patterns that are beyond the scope of this discussion

· emissions of carbon dioxide and other greenhouse gases

· volumes of toxic chemicals that have been accumulating in the environment

What Progress Has Been Made in Problem-Solving Capacities?

Results are one measure of progress. Another is the capacity for solving environmental problems. In studies of how different nations responded to pollution, Martin Janicke and colleagues at the Free University of Berlin stress the need for capacity building. This describes the process of creating within policy systems the ability to identify and respond successfully to environmental problems.[25] Institutions, laws, political culture, technical skills—all of these and others may affect problem solving capacity. The approach in these studies is to identify cases of successful problem-solving, then work backward to determine what factors most likely are associated with that success.

The United States enjoys many of the conditions this research associates with successful problem solving. Political stability is an obvious one. Others include an open political system, with avenues for political opposition and dissent, such as a free flow of information and competitive elections; the existence of advocacy groups that bring problems to light and place pressure on government and industry; a well-developed administrative and legal infrastructure; a strong base of scientific and technical knowledge; and enough wealth to be able to afford environmental controls and cleanup. In addition, the United States policy capacity includes a relatively strong and professional civil service, at all levels of government, as well as highly developed legal institutions and a respect for law.

In nations that have not responded well to environmental problems, often by not allowing them even to emerge on the policy agenda, many of these conditions are absent. Until recently, examples were the Former Soviet Union and parts of Eastern Europe. Their history demonstrates the effects of unchecked industrial development and resource exploitation on environmental quality. Similarly, many developing nations lack the stability, financial resources, administrative-legal infrastructure, and other conditions necessary for success in dealing with environmental problems, as studies by the World Bank and others have concluded.[26]

In contrast, the United States, the nations of western and northern Europe, and Japan fare well in overall capacities. In addition to its general political, administrative, and legal capacities, the United States has developed many more specific environmental capacities since the 1960s. They include:

1. A comprehensive, if not integrated, legal and regulatory framework. At both the national and state levels, there is substantial legal authority for dealing with pollution and related problems. Air and water quality laws in the United States are often used as models in other parts of the world. After several decades of evolution (remember that there were limited national pollution laws before 1970), the United States has built an impressive legal framework that is implemented through comprehensive regulations. Although deficiencies in state programs justified the creation of strong national regulation in the 1970s, the American states today are for the most part strongly committed to having effective environmental programs.[27] Their statutory frameworks are as comprehensive and often more innovative than EPA's.

2. Well-developed administrative capacities within government and the private sector. To administer this legal framework, in both the public and the private sectors, there now exists an impressive set of organizations, networks, and specialists. The EPA is respected internationally for its technical, scientific, enforcement, and administrative skills. Thought of as likely weak links in our environmental protection system in the early 1970s, most state agencies now are considered to be highly capable and powerful. These government capacities are enhanced by the resources dedicated to environmental compliance in the private sector, at least among larger firms. The legal and public relations stakes are so high that most firms have built strong compliance and management functions at the corporate and facility level. For most firms, legal compliance is a non-negotiable goal that comes above all others. Networks of professional organizations (such as the Air and Waste Management Association and the National Pollution Prevention Roundtable) exist to build professional competencies and relationships in all aspects of environmental compliance and management.

3. Scientific knowledge and resources. A special strength of the United States is the level of scientific knowledge and research that is available. Although we tend to focus in our regulatory debates on what we do not know, the reality is that we still know a great deal. A high level of knowledge and strong capacity for scientific research have enabled the United States to maintain its leadership in international scientific communities. Whether the issue is stratospheric ozone depletion, dioxin, lead, radon, or climate change, the United States has been a leader. Indeed, Richard Andrews has observed that the United States has developed probably the most extensive scientific and technical capacity of any country to support environmental policy making.[28]

4. Public commitment to environmental values. As important as institutional and scientific capacities is the level of public support for environmental programs and values in the United States. Survey data consistently show strong support for environmental programs, despite periods of skepticism about government itself.[29] Both of the obvious efforts to roll back national programs—in the early 1980s and mid-1990s—failed. Both also caused political damage to their Republican Party sponsors. Curiously, despite the political struggle among elites about regulation, the public has been willing to countenance even more stringent regulation if it is necessary to preserve air or water quality. The sensitivity of many firms to information from the Toxics Release Inventory and other unfavorable disclosures further testifies to the power of public opinion, especially when highlighted in the press and mobilized by activist groups.[30]

However, this public support may be vulnerable in times of stress. Opinion surveys in 2004 documented slippage in public support for the environment, including a noticeable decline in the percentage of Americans who would give precedence to the environment over economic growth. This decline coincided with the September 11, 2001 terror attacks, and it probably was reinforced by public concern about rising gasoline prices and the economy. In addition, the historically low salience of environmental issues compared with other issues and the Bush administration's success in framing protection of the environment as involving tradeoffs with energy and economic concerns helped to reduce public concern about the administration's policies.[31] These recent trends show that public support should not be taken for granted and emphasize that environmental goals should be achieved in ways that do not unnecessarily compromise other policy goals.

In both measurable results and environmental capacities, one can point to accomplishments from the United States approach to environmental problems, specifically in controlling pollution. Especially regarding industrial point sources, auto emissions, and certain high-profile pollutants, there are successes. Of course, there is one question this review of the evidence does not address: At what cost were these results achieved? Many people argue, with good evidence, that some regulatory programs, hazardous waste principally among them, have delivered little ecological and health protection at a high cost. Others have argued that specific policies, such as certain drinking water or hazardous air pollutant standards, have cost more than their benefits justify.[32] On the other hand, the health benefits of reducing air pollution appear to be substantial, exceeding the costs in some cases by a large ratio for such common air emissions as fine particles and lead.[33]

The cost-benefit issue has been one of the most debated and analyzed topics in United States domestic policy. Advocates of cost-benefit analysis argue that government should not pursue any policy in which monetized benefits do not exceed costs. Although many, if not most, people accept this argument in principle, in practice there are methodological and other issues associated with this kind of analysis. These include how to attach dollar values to benefits that are not traded in markets (such as ecological or aesthetic benefits) and to premature deaths that are avoided. Among cost-benefit analysts, the consensus is that regulation of air quality has delivered net benefits, although marginal costs increased as stricter controls were adopted; that regulation of water quality has often not delivered net benefits, although some benefits may not be sufficiently appreciated; and that regulation of hazardous wastes has delivered fewer benefits than the costs justify. In designing new regulatory standards and strategies, however, the critical question is the marginal costs of further gains. Achieving these results cost-effectively, especially for the smaller and more diffuse sources that account for a larger share of pollution, will pose a major challenge for designers of a new regulation.

To Change or Not to Change? A Critique of the Old Regulation

This section considers the complaints about the old regulation and the case that many people, including strong supporters, have been making for changing it. However plausible it may have been as an initial response to environmental problems, and it clearly has shown success, the existing approach carries within it characteristics that will limit its effectiveness over time. Because of the dynamism in problems, institutions, and economies in recent decades, the limitations in the old regulation are becoming increasingly apparent. Even among proponents, it was widely held by the 1990s that U.S. pollution control institutions, once seen as a model for the world, were beginning to be a cumbersome, inefficient anachronism.[34]

These limitations of the old regulation fall roughly into five categories. It impedes innovation; it is legalistic, inflexible, and fragmented; it is expensive; it is increasingly irrelevant and thus ineffective for many issues; and it faces an implementation deficit. These complaints, however, do not always fall neatly into categories. For example, one reason regulation may inhibit innovation is that legalism and distrust discourage the constructive dialogue that may support innovation. Similarly, high distrust increases transaction costs, such as reporting and permitting, which add to the expense and inflexibility of regulation. Regulation is expensive in part because definitions of problems and strategies to address them are fragmented. Still, these categories offer a framework for discussing the limitations of the old regulation. They provide a basis for considering which of its aspects should be preserved and which should be modified in the years to come.

It Impedes Innovation
A common complaint about the old regulation is that it fails to promote or even impedes innovation. On its face, this is a surprising claim. Consider the number of technology innovations that were adopted and diffused under the old regulation: catalytic converters for vehicles, scrubbers for power utilities, advanced sewage treatment techniques, organisms that render hazardous waste harmless. How can a system that has brought such innovations be criticized for impeding innovation?

To be sure, the old regulation has generally been successful in promoting innovation at one level. It has forced industry to adopt technologies that are commercially available or nearly so. Indeed, this is precisely what a technology-forcing strategy is designed to do. In the air and water laws, for example, Congress directed EPA to determine what technologies or practices are "best available" or "best achievable" and require their adoption. Government determines what technologies or practices meet this legal standard and then requires their use by regulated firms. The threat of legal sanctions and the negative publicity that comes with them induce firms to adopt the specified technologies.

However, the old regulation has been less successful in creating conditions under which long-term, continuous innovation occurs. To appreciate this issue, consider the distinctions made in the Dutch National Environmental Policy Plan (NEPP) among short (less than five years), medium (five to ten years), and long-term (more than ten years) innovations. By identifying and forcing the adoption of technologies that are available or nearly so, government may bring regulated sources up to a level of performance that is effective in the short term. However, as the Dutch recognized in their NEPP, achieving a sustainable economy over time requires a capacity for continuous innovation over the longer term. A technology-forcing strategy may not always be the best way of achieving this.

Indeed, in their essay arguing the business case for high environmental standards, Michael Porter and Claas van der Linde argue that short-term pressure for results based on known and economically achievable end-of-pipe technologies may sacrifice opportunities for longer-term, continuous innovation. They illustrate their point by comparing the regulation of pulp and paper mills in the United States and Scandinavia.[35] The United States required rapid adoption of end-of-pipe technologies based on secondary treatment of effluents. The more flexible Scandinavian approach allowed mills to evaluate and adopt changes in production processes that led to more significant improvements in technology over time. They applied stringent regulatory pressure, but allowed mills time and flexibility to discover solutions they could integrate into their operations. These observations are reinforced by an Organization for Economic Co-operation and Development (OECD) survey of environmental managers in seven countries, which concluded that "environmental innovations are more often closely identified with cleaner production measures than with end-of-pipe technologies, which reduce environmental impacts by using add-on measures without changing the production process."[36] The point for this discussion is that technology-forcing, end-of-pipe regulation may not always be the best approach for promoting longer-term innovation.

A persuasive critique of the effects of the old regulation on technology innovation is a 1998 study by the Environmental Law Institute (ELI). In evaluating the barriers to innovation in six industries (baking, dry cleaning, electric utilities, iron and steel, pulp and paper, and wastewater treatment), ELI found that "barriers specific to environmental technologies stem from the way environmental regulations are designed and enforced, and how these in turn affect business decision-making."[37] It further concluded that "technology-based emission limits and discharge standards, which are embedded in most of our pollution laws, play a key role in discouraging innovation."[38]

The existing approach to regulation, and specifically technology-based rules, may discourage innovation in several ways. One is the emphasis on end-of-pipe controls. A facility may be able to achieve better environmental results through changes in materials, product designs, and up-stream process changes, but these changes may not meet the specific technology requirements needed to demonstrate compliance. In addition, ELI concluded, regulations often favor end-of-pipe technologies that consume significant resources and generate high wastes.[39] For example, scrubbers reduce sulfur oxide air emissions but consume lots of lime and generate solid waste for disposal. Hazardous waste rules often require the treatment and disposal of residuals that could be recycled but cannot be done so legally.

Administrative requirements often pose barriers to innovation. To adopt a new technology, a facility typically must apply for a new permit or modification of an existing one. Permitting processes are often lengthy and uncertain, and approval sometimes must be gained from more than one level of government. These requirements greatly increase the cost and time to innovate.[40] From an agency perspective, technology standards are developed and updated through lengthy and complex rule making, which means that they often lag behind advances in the field. Adding to this lag is the lack of agency resources for updating technology standards on schedules called for in the statutes, usually every four or five years.

Other aspects of the old regulation may inhibit innovation. What may be called the compliance imperative within firms makes them reluctant to deviate from government-prescribed technologies, even when an alternative delivers better results more efficiently. Innovation may involve risks that firms worried about reputation and legal status are unwilling to take. Finally, there is no incentive to perform beyond what is needed to maintain compliance. As a result, the ELI report concludes, most firms "fail to develop a culture of continuous environmental improvement necessary to sustain research, development, and investment in innovation."[41]

The ELI report focuses on the technology-forcing aspects of the old regulation and how the definition and enforcement of standards is a barrier to innovation. Others look to even more fundamental issues—to relationships and patterns of governance—in making their case about innovation. An example is David Wallace, who argues in a comparison of innovation in six nations (the United States, the Netherlands, Germany, Denmark, France, and Japan) that patterns of governance in a policy regime determine the capacity for innovation more than any specific policy instruments that may be used. He argues that two aspects of governance matter: government autonomy from industry influence and the quality of dialogue among actors. Regarding the first, government must be able to maintain some degree of independence from industry influence if it is to sustain pressure for improved performance. At the same time, there must be a reasonable degree of trust, a potential for collaboration, sharing of information, and respect for mutual competence among government and industry. A combination of high independence and poor dialogue increases compliance costs and lowers the capacity for long-term innovation; high independence combined with effective dialogue leads to the use of flexible regulatory mechanisms and schedules that accommodate innovation.[42]

Wallace rates the United States as high on independence from industry but low on the quality of dialogue, at least compared with three (Denmark, the Netherlands, and Japan) of the other nations he examines. Government has enough political power to pressure industry to improve its performance, especially through technology forcing. The cost, however, is uncertainty for regulated firms, which in turn creates barriers to long-term innovation: "Uncertainty arising from environmental policy adds to the existing technology and organizational risks of technology development and adaptation."[43] Regulation in the United States is characterized by high conflict, adversarial relationships, and low trust. Requirements often are unpredictable because they are subject to changes in political coalitions or statutory interpretations that are difficult to anticipate. Both sides are reluctant to share information, so as not to concede to the other side any advantage in litigation or future standard setting.

The result is a regulatory system with the characteristics described in ELI's analysis; industry is unwilling to take risks, focuses narrowly and safely on compliance, and has little incentive to do more. Government locks in technologies, forces short-term compliance, and loses the benefits of the extensive industry knowledge that could be applied to achieve long-term, continuous innovation.

Wallace's analysis lacks a firm empirical foundation. It is based on his interpretations of several case studies. However, his arguments about the importance of predictability and dialogue in inducing a commitment to long-term innovation are based on a careful review of the literature on organizational change. His evaluation of the United States is consistent with the wider writing on environmental policy and conclusions reached in other studies. The contrasts with nations like Denmark and the Netherlands suggest differences in the capacity for innovation that are worth evaluating. Despite the many cultural and institutional differences between the United States and these other nations, they offer lessons to consider for the new regulation.

It is Inflexible, Legalistic, and Fragmented

The old regulation is dichotomous. A regulated entity is either in compliance or it is not. If it is in compliance, it usually has been of little interest to government. If it is not in compliance, it is a subject of great interest to government, which has mechanisms at its disposal to punish and correct the noncompliance. As indicated earlier, the division of environmental laws, programs, and agencies along medium-specific lines tends to fragment regulatory strategies, leading to missed opportunities and higher-than-necessary compliance costs.

From a company perspective, noncompliance is to be avoided if at all possible. Not only may a violation entail financial penalties, it may involve harm to one's reputation and to relations with customers, communities, and public officials. As a result, "It is not surprising that companies spend considerable sums on lawyers and lobbyists, but comparatively little on creating new and better means of controlling pollution at their plants (a task for which they are uniquely suited)."[44]

This compliance imperative has several consequences. First priority within a company, and each of its facilities, must be given to maintaining an airtight compliance status. This is no simple task. Even a medium-sized chemical processing facility must regularly comply with hundreds of federal, state, and local regulatory provisions. When the pharmaceutical firm Schering-Plough and the New Jersey Department of Environmental Protection piloted facility-wide permitting in the late 1990s, they were able to combine several hundreds of individual permits into one consolidated permit.[45] A large, complex facility, such as a chemical manufacturer or petroleum refinery, may have to comply with possibly thousands of specific regulatory checkpoints a month. Even government enforcement officials readily concede that full compliance all of the time is a near-impossibility for most large and complex facilities.

Our society places high value on legal compliance, as well it should. The problem with the old regulation is that so many specific provisions have been codified into law that much of the effort devoted to maintaining compliance is delivering little environmental value to society. Many violations have little to do with any actual environmental harm. They involve deviations from permitting, reporting, or notification provisions that even well-managed firms commit from time to time. For example, a joint study done by EPA and the chemical industry in the late 1990s found that about 40 percent of noncompliance events were in reporting and record keeping.[46] It is a kind of vicious circle in which extensive compliance reporting that is aimed at poor performers creates yet more opportunities for noncompliance for good performers. Too often, minor compliance issues take attention away from larger environmental issues that are regulated less closely but may matter far more to society. A premise of the proposed new regulation is that government should focus more on meeting a set of core environmental indicators and less on administrative violations.

The causes of this proliferation of rules may be found in Bardach and Kagan's "logic of regulatory expansion," an almost inevitable outgrowth of a strategy based on bureaucratic control.[47] Regulators are paid to be risk averse. They see their task as preventing problems that *might* occur. They gain little credit for granting firms flexibility or allowing them to operate more efficiently. However, they know they will be criticized mightily if problems do occur. So they feel compelled to adopt a strategy of control by uniform, detailed, and stringent rules. Should anything go wrong, agencies want to be able to demonstrate they are keeping industry on a tight leash, even if that interferes with the behavior that leads to innovation and continuous improvement. Firms try to maintain some control over their own actions by finding loopholes in the regulatory scheme. Agencies, in turn, seek to close those loopholes with even more rules. The cycle continues in a progression toward more costly, detailed, and intrusive forms of regulation.[48]

Another consequence of this either/or emphasis on compliance is the inability to distinguish good from bad performers. Regulators know that environmental compliance by firms varies widely. For purposes of discussion, assume that 80 percent of regulated firms generally are good compliers or better (good apples) on core standards, with the rest exhibiting sporadic or outright noncompliance (bad apples). Most environmental regulation is designed for the bad apples. It assumes that firms will try to evade the rules, that every legal loophole must be closed, and that every firm must regularly document compliance. A high level of intrusiveness and oversight may be necessary for the bad apples, but it is self-defeating for the good ones. It increases transaction costs for all parties. It creates resentment and resistance, undermines cooperation that may lead to better results, and diverts resources and creativity into often pointless legal conflicts.[49] And yet the regulatory system is designed around the bad apples.

A further consequence of the compliance focus is that opportunities for reducing pollution are missed. The old regulation requires agencies to determine how and where to impose controls on many diverse and complex manufacturing processes in industry. The managers and designers of these production processes must react to government's commands. So the people who know the most about the business are not the ones making the rules; they are responding to rules imposed on them from outside. If the mind-set within firms is to maintain compliance more than to improve environmental performance, and if compliance is defined by those outside the firm who know less about the firm's processes, inevitably there will be lost opportunities.

An illustration of missed opportunities may be found in New Jersey's experiment with facility-wide permitting. The program involved making complete inventories of releases throughout a facility. State regulators and company managers found that existing permits missed about half of the total emissions of a typical facility. In addition to lost opportunities for reducing pollution, this may also lead to higher costs. Similarly, a joint project of EPA and Amoco Corporation in the early 1990s found that air emissions from leaks at an Amoco refinery were tightly regulated at high costs, while petroleum transfer operations from ships into the refinery were not regulated at all, even though they offered a far more cost-effective way to control emissions. If Amoco had been allowed to determine how best to reduce emissions overall, rather than have to comply with detailed controls on specific emissions as prescribed in the rules, it could have achieved a better result, and at less cost.[50]

It Is Expensive
A recurring complaint about the old regulation is that it costs too much. This complaint may be separated into two more specific ones. The first is that regulation has cost more than it has delivered in benefits. This is mostly an issue of how environmental goals are determined and priorities set. The second complaint is that actions taken to achieve those goals are more costly than they should be and thus are inefficient. Because the focus here is on how the United States achieves goals rather than how they are set, the issue at hand is the second. Once we select an environmental goal, how efficiently do we achieve it?

Some people have argued that cost efficiency is not a valid goal for environmental agencies, whose task they feel is to squeeze as much environmental improvement out of industry as possible. Many agency staff think they should not worry about how efficient Ford, Intel, a small metal finisher, or a midrange chemical processor is. However, they should be worried, for at least three reasons.

First, Congress and the president, the two institutions that most clearly reflect the will of the American people, have made it clear that economic and cost issues must be considered in regulatory decisions. Nearly every statute has provisions for balancing economic with environmental factors, either by matching benefits to costs or pursuing the least-cost means of achieving a goal. Every president since 1970 has issued an executive order requiring economic analysis for environmental regulations.

Second, economic success helps to maintain political support for environmental protection. Opinion surveys show that such public support tends to weaken during periods of economic stress. To the extent that regulation is seen to impose high costs with few benefits, to increase unemployment and prices, or to limit growth and competitiveness, support for environmental values is likely to soften. By designing regulations that allow society as well as firms to achieve environmental goals more efficiently, policy makers may help to maintain public support and demonstrate that economic goals need not be given up.

Third, and most important, there is growing evidence that environmental and economic success may go hand in hand. I once asked the environmental, health, and safety vice president of a major pharmaceutical company why so many firms within that sector were seen to be environmental leaders. His immediate response was that, as a highly profitable and financially successful business sector, these firms had the resources to invest in innovations and exercise leadership. Indeed, a growing body of research, discussed in chapter 4, strongly suggests a positive relationship between top environmental performance and financial success.[51] Although this is often cited as evidence that environmental excellence promotes financial success, the causality may very well work the other way. Firms doing well financially may also be able to perform better environmentally. So many firms now have committed to going beyond compliance in their environmental performance that it is obvious they see a financial advantage in doing so. Well-designed regulatory policies that allow firms to be more efficient may help them be better, more innovative environmental performers, as well as reconcile the apparent tradeoffs between environmental quality and economic growth that reduce public support.

This association between economic and environmental performance has been demonstrated on a macro level as well. Studies of American states demonstrate that the more affluent among them tend to have stronger environmental policies.[52] Again, the direction of causality is unclear. For now, however, two points are worth bearing in mind. First, people tend to be more willing to protect the environment when they have achieved a level of material comfort. Second, economic success generates resources for developing the institutional capacities and technologies that reduce pollution, as well as the political will to protect habitat and other amenities. Furthermore, at a macro level, there is potential for designing policies that promote win-win relationships among environmental and economic goals, through a strategic approach known as ecological modernization.[53]

What is it about the old regulation that makes it more expensive than it should be? The core reason is that regulation based on technology controls and uniform treatment of diverse sources fails to account for the often large differences in marginal control costs among those sources. In a review of the research on air pollution control costs, Paul Portney concludes that a very large body of research has clearly demonstrated that existing limits on pollutant emissions—and perhaps current air quality goals—could be met at a fraction of what is now being spent.[54] In a range of studies reviewed by Portney, the technology-based approach was found to be two to fourteen times more costly (on average, three to four times more costly) in reducing air emissions than a least-cost approach that allowed emissions trading or another market-based approach. Another reason regulation is more expensive than it needs to be is high transaction costs and uncertainty. In part, this is the result of lengthy permitting processes and highly specific permits that allow firms little flexibility in controlling their releases in more cost-effective ways. Evaluations of EPA's initial rounds of flexible air permits have documented not only the business value they offer to firms but also the emission reductions that may be achieved.

In fact, the United States has made progress in modifying the old regulation to allow more flexibility in how marginal control costs are distributed.[55] As discussed in chapter 2, emissions trading programs have been an important set of innovations since the 1970s and will be an essential element in any program for reducing greenhouse gas emissions, as well as for dealing with other environmental problems. Allowing even more flexibility for lower-cost approaches will enable us to meet environmental goals more efficiently. For these reasons, market incentives are stressed in chapters 6 and 7 as elements in the new regulation.

It Is Irrelevant to Many Problems and Thus Ineffective

The old regulation was designed to respond to a 1970s view of environmental problems, which were seen to consist of obvious pollution from large industrial sources. For these sources, selective intervention by government, based on a strategy of bureaucratic control, was a reasonable and generally effective response. Environmental problems have changed, however, both objectively and in how we perceive them. We have moved from a concern with just controlling pollution to also preventing it, reducing risk, promoting eco-efficiency, advancing stewardship, and achieving a sustainable economy and society over the long term. The environmental "problem" has continually evolved and been redefined. This means that in addition to worrying about pollution, we now want to use energy, materials, and water efficiently; design environmentally friendly products; think about the impacts of products over their life cycle; preserve habitat and species; protect the global commons; and worry generally about the effects of today's actions on future generations.

With concerns that now are far broader than simply controlling pollution, it is clear that the old approach to regulation has become increasingly irrelevant to environmental protection. First, it does not address many aspects of performance in the industrial sector that significantly affect environmental quality, such as use of energy, materials, and water. For example, the energy intensity of industrial production has implications for environmental quality that extend well beyond traditional concerns with air pollution. Yet there is little pressure or incentive in the current regulations to improve energy efficiency. The effects of product use and disposal is another example. For products like motor vehicles or household appliances, some 80 percent of their environmental impacts lie in their use rather than in their manufacturing, yet product use and disposal are barely addressed under the old regulation.

Another way to look at the growing irrelevance of the old regulation is through the economic activities that affect environmental quality. A business tool called the value chain helps in breaking down these activities. Used to analyze a company's value-creating activities, the six links in the chain also offer a framework for evaluating the environmental impacts of a firm's actions.[56]

The six activities are (1) research and development and investment, covering the design of new products or services; (2) raw materials sourcing, including decisions about inputs into production, such as materials, energy, and water; (3) manufacturing and service delivery, in which inputs are transformed into the final product or service; (4) marketing; (5) customer service; and (6) end-of-life disposal. Although each activity determines the environmental impacts of the firm, regulation typically influences only a few. Indeed, regulation is focused almost entirely on the third activity, mainly manufacturing processes. It may influence the second activity by banning or controlling the use of certain toxic materials, such as asbestos or lead, but has little influence on decisions about other material, energy, and water inputs. It may influence design activities, but only indirectly. It may affect marketing only peripherally, through labeling or product warning provisions, and it has no practical effect on research and design and customer service activities.

The point is not that government should intervene in all these activities, and certainly not with conventional regulation. For much of the product chain, policies outside of regulation make more sense, such as eco-taxes, preferential purchasing, or consumer labeling. The point is that the old regulation focuses intensively on one and secondarily on a few other activities in the value chain, while ignoring most of the others. Better results could be achieved at less cost, in ways with more potential for win-win solutions, if government could create mechanisms and incentives that led to more environmentally beneficial outcomes at other stages of the value chain. A new regulation could contribute to these broader environmental goals by complementing other policy strategies, such as tax or purchasing policies.

It Faces an Implementation Deficit

The old regulation makes so many demands on government that it cannot be fully implemented. There is an implementation deficit, which John Dryzek terms "a substantial gap between what legislation and high-level executive decisions declare will be achieved and what is actually achieved at the street level in terms of attainment of environmental standards."[57] At the start of the modern era of environmental regulation, in the 1970s, it may have appeared to most people that this implementation deficit was a temporary condition and eventually would be overcome. The scope of what was perceived to be the environmental problem was limited to large industrial sources and point sources of pollution from them. The importance of small, diffuse, and nonpoint sources was not fully appreciated, nor were the possible effects of improper waste disposal and exposure to toxic chemicals. Longer-term issues, such as global climate change, loss of biodiversity, and persistent pollutants, were not yet on the policy agenda.

Regulators simply cannot do everything that the law and their own rules require them to do. Consider the number of sources covered by the old regulation. In 1999, EPA's enforcement office published what it described as "a rough picture of the universe of facilities that need to comply with environmental regulations and the statutes under which they typically fall."[58] They included some 40,000 stationary air sources, 90,000 facilities with clean water permits, more than 400,000 hazardous waste facilities, and 173,000 drinking water systems. This does not even include some categories of regulated facilities. For example, EPA rules under Section 112(r) of the 1990 Clean Air Act Amendments require risk management plans from some 15,000 facilities nationally. Nor does this include chemical reviews under the Toxic Substances Control Act or pesticide registrations, among other regulatory functions.

Another way to illustrate the demands of the existing regulations is with permitting requirements. There are two dozen federal environmental permitting programs. The main water quality permits program, the National Pollutant Discharge Elimination System (NPDES), covers half a million sources. Although most are regulated under general permits that include many facilities, some 90,000 have individual permits, of which about 10 percent are considered major. The permits expire after five years. As of October 2000, for major sources, 44 per cent of federal and 25 per cent of state permits had expired. For minor sources, 78 per cent of federal and 31 per cent of state permits had expired.[59] It is a constant struggle for EPA and states to keep up with these permitting obligations, especially in an age of declining agency resources. Permitting for existing sources of air pollution is authorized under Title V of the CAAA of 1990. The EPA estimates that this will cover about 22,000 major facilities. By July 2001, less than two-thirds of the permits had been issued by state agencies; usually the easiest permits were done first. Title V permits expire after five years. "In many states," Terry Davies notes, "the initial title V permits will begin expiring after all sources have received their first permit."[60]

Another illustration of the implementation deficit is the difficulty in evaluating and reissuing emission and discharge standards under statutory schedules. For example, new source performance standards under the Clean Air Act should be updated every four years to keep pace with technology, while water effluent guidelines are to be revised every five years. These schedules are almost never met. The point of this discussion is not to criticize regulators for sloth or inefficiency, which would be unfair. It is that there is so much to do, under such complex procedures, for so many sources and substances, that fully implementing the old regulation is simply not possible with what society is willing to invest.

Determined advocates of the proregulatory story line may argue that we can close this deficit by adding implementation capacity. Accepting for a moment the value of the old regulation on its own terms, there are two responses to this argument. First, American society will not support any significant expansion of the regulatory state. There is not enough money, given the many financial pressures on and expectations of government. In addition, there is now considerable skepticism about expanding government's conventional regulatory authority, as the legislative gridlock of the past decade documents.

A second response is that even if one assumes it would be politically possible to expand governmental capacities to close the implementation deficit (say, by doubling or even tripling the resources now available), such an expansion would have serious consequences by reinforcing the weaknesses in the old regulation that have been discussed. More regulators—rule writers, permitting staff, inspectors, and so on—would almost inevitably increase the inflexibility, cost inefficiency, and legalism that exist now. We would see efforts to exercise even more control, close more loopholes, catch people with paperwork violations, throw more barriers in the path of innovation, and elaborate the old regulation in even finer detail. Such a strategy would increase the costs of an old, outdated policy strategy.

This issue of the implementation deficit in the old regulation brings its weaknesses together in sharp relief. Whatever purpose it served in the past, the old regulation increasingly is a system that inhibits innovation, discourages continuous improvement, breeds legalism and distrust, and costs more than is necessary. It misses opportunities for environmental improvement. There is a gap between what regulation requires to be fully implemented and what is available or even possible. Even if we could close the implementation deficit, we should not, because that would only magnify the limitations of the old regulation.

The Risks of Changing and of Business as Usual

In the third of its assessments of environmental policy in the 1990s, the National Academy of Public Administration concluded that the United States "must continue to transform its environmental management, not because innovation is good *per se*, but because the present system will *not* solve the most pressing of the nation's outstanding environmental problems."[61] The NAPA report added that "the statutes and the system they support are not keeping up with changing technology, changing public attitudes, or changing global relationships."[62]

For nearly forty years, the American public has consistently rejected the arguments of the antiregulatory story line. People do not want to dismantle the core system of laws, rules, and institutions that have protected them from serious environmental damage. One need only look at the nations of the former Soviet Union or at air pollution in major cities of developing nations to understand the environmental consequences of unchecked industrial development. It is clear by now that the proregulatory story line is considered suspect as well. The reason that voluntary programs and the other innovation activities discussed in chapter 5 have been growing is that there is little political support for simply expanding upon or tightening the old approach. Since the Clean Air Act Amendments of 1990, there has not been a consensus in favor of introducing more stringent regulation overall, despite the strong public support for environmental quality. The argument here is that rather than debating whether or not there should be more or less regulation, we should be working to build a different kind of regulation that responds to the criticisms of the revisionists.

The evaluation in this chapter suggests many directions for such a new regulation. At the level of relationships, it seems clear that reducing distrust and increasing constructive dialogue should be primary goals. Flexibility, diverse policy tools, lower transaction costs, and more predictability could reduce costs and promote innovation. A shift in emphasis from compliance to measurable performance should also be part of the design. A new regulation should take into account the limited resources and capacities of government, while aiming to use industry's knowledge and motivations more effectively. Underlying it all should be sustained pressure from government and the public for high levels of environmental performance. Indeed, a core lesson of the past forty years is that pressure from government is an essential element in the formula for environmental protection. The question is how that pressure should be applied.

Fortunately, trends and initiatives in business and government have been converging toward a new regulation. These are discussed in the next two chapters. Chapter 4 examines trends in industry, where many firms are making commitments and achieving results that exceed their legal obligations. To the extent that we can understand why, the chapter argues, we may be able to design a better regulation. Chapter 5 considers government's efforts to change regulation in response to the criticisms that have been described here. Together, these chapters set the stage for outlining the conceptual basis for and elements of a new environmental regulation in chapters 6 and 7.

4

From Zero-Sum to Win-Win? Industry Goes Beyond Compliance

Various indirect indicators of environmental strategy suggest that a sea change in corporate attitudes toward the environment may indeed be taking place.[1]

The old environmental regulation is based on the notion that the interests of society and industry regarding protection of the environment are mutually antagonistic. Under this presumed zero sum, the thinking is that business will consider environmental values only when it is forced to by government. The assumption is that any action by a firm to reduce emissions, control wastes, use resources efficiently, or protect habitat is due to the coercive powers of the state as expressed through regulation. This was the view that influenced regulatory designs in the late 1960s and 1970s, and it still shapes the style as well as the substance of interactions between regulated firms and government.

To even a casual observer today, the world has changed. Indeed, much of what is happening in the business world now would have been unthinkable only twenty years ago. Consider these examples:

· Hundreds of U.S. companies now voluntarily issue annual environmental reports, many with quantitative performance targets and a self-assessment of their progress in meeting them.

· Some 13,000 organizations, most of them from the private sector, participate in voluntary programs with EPA in which they agree to do more environmentally than the law requires.

· Trade associations and other industry groups have adopted codes of environmental conduct or other agreements that encourage or in some cases even require their members to exceed government standards.

· Some five thousand U.S. facilities have invested time and money to seek formal certification under ISO 14001, an international standard for environmental management systems (EMS); far more have adopted a formal EMS.

· Despite the U.S. government's unwillingness to require mandatory reductions in greenhouse gas emissions, many U.S. companies have made voluntary public commitments to reduce them on their own.

These examples are part of a broader trend described in the literature on business and the environment as the greening of industry. Although there are reasons to question the scope and durability of this trend, as many people have, it still is an important behavioral shift with profound policy implications. It is true, for example, that most of these changes are occurring within a subset of large and visible firms, including many multinational corporations. It is also true that these changes began in a period of relative economic prosperity; a tighter economy has tested the commitment of many firms to progressive environmental policies.[2] It is also fair to say that much of the initial motivation for the greening trend was a desire in many industry sectors, especially the chemical industry, to improve their public image as well as to forestall more stringent regulation, and more substantive improvements only came later. To be sure, many industry initiatives do have as a goal preventing more stringent regulations.[3] Indeed, that has been a long-standing criticism of the chemical industry's Responsible Care program discussed later in the chapter.

Still, the greening of industry should be taken seriously. The steps that many firms have taken—BP-Amoco, Johnson & Johnson, IBM, Dupont, General Electric, and Pfizer are some that come to mind—are so public and so much a part of their corporate strategies that they are almost certain to continue. More important, the forces driving this trend are likely to grow even stronger. For many reasons, regulation is only one of several forces shaping environmental practices by firms. Regulation still matters a great deal, to be sure. However, public image, customer and investor pressures, internal operating efficiencies, community and employee expectations, and corporate values are also driving firms to achieve and maintain higher standards of environmental performance.[4]

This chapter describes this greening of industry, considers its causes, and discusses what it means for public policy, specifically for a new regulation. The issue of what greening means for policy deserves serious attention. On the one side, many people argue that a long-term transformation of industry is under way, so that government intervention is increasingly irrelevant. In this view, multinational corporations are so powerful, and any one government's authority so limited, that only business may lead us to a sustainable environment. On the other side is the view that greening lacks substance and durability. Until there is irrefutable evidence that it is widespread and irreversible, many have argued, government should not make any changes in its approach to regulation.

Both views are rejected here. Public policies, especially regulation, have profoundly affected the actions of business over the past four decades. Government wielded the regulatory stick that forced industry to pay attention to environmental damage. Through regulation and other policies (e.g., taxes, subsidies, and information), government will continue to influence industry behavior. Only the state has the legitimacy to set collective goals and balance the demands of competing interests in society. We cannot rely on Dupont, General Motors, or Volvo to make critical social choices. Government also plays a necessary role in keeping irresponsible firms in line, by not allowing them to gain competitive advantage from their poor performance. Indeed, ask someone from nearly any large, successful firm if government should significantly pull back its regulatory oversight of their industry and they will say "no." They see credible and fair enforcement as underpinning not only society's efforts to protect the environment but their own as well.

Nor should government sit on the sidelines and wait to see how this greening trend turns out. To continue with business as usual by simply relying on the old regulation ignores the potential for change that greening represents. It consigns us to an outmoded strategy in a rapidly changing, postmodern world. The dynamism of contemporary economies, new expectations about governance, and changes in environmental problems are driving change in business as well as stimulating the shift toward a new regulation. Many in the business community are responding. Government needs to respond as well.

The key public policy question is not whether the greening trend will continue. It will, in some manner, if only because the forces behind it are so compelling. How broad and lasting the greening trend is depends in large part on the actions of government itself. The key question, then, is this: How do we design and build a regulatory system that will promote a continuing, broad, and enduring greening of industry that builds on the demonstrated achievements of the leading firms?

What Is the Greening of Industry? The Overall Logic and Trend

There has always been a tendency in environmental policy discussions to think of "industry" or "business" in monolithic terms. Regulators and environmental activists in particular often talk of business firms and the people who run them as if they are similar in goals, constraints, opportunities, and values. Yet there is tremendous diversity among the firms that are subject to regulation. They include United Technologies, Intel, and Ford. They also include, in far greater numbers, auto repair shops, metal finishers, and batch chemical processors. Some are publicly traded, others are privately held. Some firms have easy access to capital, while others have little or none. Some make products; others deliver services. Some firms are constantly innovating in highly competitive environments, while others change products or processes very little from year to year.

There is also a wide variation in the environmental intentions and capabilities of firms. The goal for many firms, especially smaller ones, is simply to stay below the regulator's radar screen. They want to avoid detection, often in order to evade compliance. In the middle and larger size ranges, most regulated firms are probably in compliance with the law most of the time. Their intention may be to remain fully compliant, but financial and information barriers—especially given the sheer number and complexity of federal, state, and local regulations—make full compliance all the time a difficult and often elusive goal. Many firms these days not only comply consistently (if not perfectly, given realities), but do far better. They use less energy or water, lower their emissions, or redesign products, not because government tells them to, but for other reasons. Moreover, they do these things in publicly verifiable ways. These firms are the locus of the greening of industry. Although they surely represent a distinct minority of the business community—most firms at best struggle to stay in compliance—they may offer useful lessons on how to design regulation to take advantage of the forces that are influencing their behavior.

Among this subset of progressive firms—those who not only consistently meet but verifiably exceed legal requirements—the old pattern of resistance to regulation and hostility to public pressures for responsible environmental behavior is distinctively out of fashion. To be sure, even these firms still complain about specific rules.[5] Their complaints, however, typically relate to a lack of flexibility or time for planning how to comply with regulations, or the high transaction costs that accompany them, or a lack of clarity, rather than the fact of the regulations themselves. A frequent focus of industry criticism, for example, is the multiple permitting requirements across different programs and levels of government. They involve cumbersome, costly procedures and uncertainty, often without clear environmental benefits. Despite such complaints, however, most medium and large firms accept compliance as necessary. They take elaborate steps to comply as fully and consistently as possible, often by overcomplying to create a margin of safety.

For present purposes, greening involves a constant and verifiable effort to do better than compliance. More specifically, it means that a firm tries to account for the many effects it has on the environment, whether it is required to by government or not. These include more than the effects that are usually regulated, such as air and water releases. They also include the use of resources, such as energy, water, or materials. Many firms also consider the effects of product use and disposal and the actions of their suppliers. The concept of greening also implies a different approach to dealing with employees and people outside the firm, such as communities and environmental groups. Several elements of greening are discussed here.

The greening of industry is reflected in what has been a rapidly growing literature. Most early work consisted of case studies, with an emphasis on documenting the economic and financial benefits of pollution prevention and other actions that led to bottom-line payoffs.[6] Later work considered greening from a more strategic perspective, as part of a long-term transformation.[7] It went beyond describing cases to analyzing the forces that shaped greening and explaining the conditions under which it occurs. Other studies have looked at more specific aspects of greening, such as industry codes and the consequences of firms' adopting environmental management systems, environmental accounting, life-cycle analysis, and other tools.[8]

Greening typically has been presented as an evolutionary process. In an early essay on greening, for example, Kurt Fischer and Johan Schot described it as occurring in three phases.[9] The first began with the emergence of environmental regulation in the early 1970s. The initial response of business was to resist regulation and comply only when it was legally necessary, through a strategy of "resistant adaptation." The environment was hardly viewed as a business and strategic opportunity. Instead, it was seen as a source of costs that had to be borne as a result of external legal and political pressures. The focus was on compliance, which was handled by specialized environmental staffs assigned to specific manufacturing sites.

This began to change in the middle 1980s, at least among a subset of firms. The period of roughly 1985–1992 was one of "embracing environmental issues without innovating."[10] Regulation was a large part of the reason for change. By increasing the costs of environmental mismanagement, government forced business to think more tactically, if not strategically, about the consequences of producing toxic wastes or using certain raw materials. Increasingly, firms responded to pressures from sources other than regulation as well, including customers, communities, employees, investors, and activists.

During this period, many firms began to expand their environmental staffing, integrate their compliance functions, and issue environmental policy statements. Companies like 3M showed that "pollution prevention" saved money. The chemical industry created the first major industry code of conduct, known as Responsible Care. With the 33/50 program, EPA launched its first voluntary challenge initiative in 1991. (The numbers refer to discharge percentages.) It called on firms to reduce their releases of harmful chemicals voluntarily, in return for EPA recognition, and as an alternative to stricter regulation. This was a precursor of several voluntary, beyond-compliance programs at EPA, several of which are discussed in chapter 5. In this period, firms focused in particular on ways to reduce costs, on changing their relationships with regulators and communities, and on reducing potential liabilities. For most, the environment was not yet seen as a strategic opportunity.

These efforts presaged yet a third stage of greening in the 1990s. Leading firms began to view environmental excellence as a strategic resource. They adopted proactive environmental strategies, not just to avoid such negative consequences as penalties, bad publicity, or financial liability, but to gain market share, optimize resources, increase operational efficiency, create a positive public image, and enhance their long-term business success. Firms began to compete on the basis of the environmental quality of their operations, their open relationships with communities and others, and the environmental attributes of their products. These firms talked less of environmental management and pollution prevention and more in terms of sustainability and environmental stewardship. They aimed, not only for bottom-line value from their environmental policies by reducing costs, but also for top-line value in terms of enhanced market share.

A sampling of the literature helps in understanding the thinking behind this greening trend. An oft-cited exposition of the case for greening is a 1995 article by Michael Porter and Claas van der Linde.[11] They argue that environmentally progressive firms will be more competitive than those that think narrowly about compliance. They reject the view that good environmental performance detracts from a firm's financial success. That only holds, they assert, if one adopts a static view of the economy–environment relationship, in which everything except regulation is held constant.[12] However, business firms operate in a dynamic and competitive world, not a static one. They are constantly pressed to innovate if they are to succeed. Rather than diminish a firm's chances for success, Porter and van der Linde argue that "Properly designed environmental standards can trigger innovations that lower the total cost of a product or improve its value."[13] The result is enhanced resource productivity that makes firms more competitive. When a company responds to pressures for improving its performance, whether from regulation or another source, it uses materials more efficiently, eliminates unneeded activity, and increases product value.

The core of the Porter and van der Linde argument is that pressure to perform better environmentally—whether driven externally by stringent standards or internally by leadership or cultural factors—produces behavior that may lead to better financial performance. This is often cited as an argument in favor of stringent regulation because it asserts that strict standards create pressures that make firms use resources more productively. Critical to the argument is their distinction between good and bad regulation. Good regulation sets high standards and holds firms accountable for meeting them, but gives them room to discover how best to get the desired result. In contrast, bad regulation is prescriptive and poorly designed; it often deters innovative solutions or renders them impossible.[14] Examples are rules that stress cleanup over prevention, that mandate specific technologies, that set unrealistic compliance deadlines, and that subject firms to delay and uncertainty. The problem is not the strictness of regulation, they argue, but "the way in which standards are written and the sheer inefficiency with which regulations are administered."[15]

Another early statement of the theoretical case for greening comes in a 1997 essay by Stuart Hart. He argues for a strategic approach to environmental issues in a firm and the need for a "sustainability vision."[16] The early case for greening, he argues, typically was based on the potential for achieving bottom-line cost savings, largely by preventing pollution. There is more to be gained from a proactive environmental strategy than cost cutting, however. Firms may use such a strategy as a source of revenue growth as well, by pursuing opportunities for product stewardship and clean technologies. He proposes a framework that will help firms assess their "sustainability portfolio" and position them for business advantage. This opens the door for top-line as well as bottom-line returns on environmental performance. "In the final analysis," he concludes, "it makes good business sense to pursue strategies for a sustainable world."[17]

An excellent analysis of greening from the perspective of the firm is Forest Reinhardt's *Down to Earth: Applying Business Principles to Environmental Management.* Its premise is that companies are in business to make money for their owners, and that they can satisfy other stakeholders only insofar as it serves this basic purpose.[18] Business behavior is viewed as a series of pragmatic choices that aim to reconcile environmental performance with shareholder value. Similarly, Reinhardt sees environmental management as an activity comparable to others in the firm, so that fundamental business principles of strategy, finance, marketing, and organizational design can contribute to solving firms' environmental problems.[19] Building on this business perspective, he asserts that if the goal is to devise responsible, realistic, solutions to environmental problems, "it is neither necessary nor desirable to stray far from basic management principles."[20]

Reinhardt defines five ways that firms may increase shareholder value through their environmental performance: by differentiating products environmentally from those of competitors, thereby gaining an edge in the marketplace; by managing competitors through collective action or influencing regulation to gain first-mover advantage; by lowering costs within the firm by reducing treatment costs, using fewer raw materials, or stimulating other efficiency improvements; by redefining the markets in which they compete by changing how they create and deliver value to customers; and by reducing risk and uncertainty, which allows them to lower their economic and political liabilities.

These and other writers on greening offer lessons for designing a new regulation. Porter and van der Linde assert the potential for win-win solutions in how firms reconcile environmental with financial success. They also underscore the role of regulation in achieving results, while stressing the limits of the kinds of inflexible, uncertain, and intrusive approaches that have characterized the old regulation. Hart proposes that business move beyond greening to sustainability and act more strategically based on that concept. He argues that the firms with a "sustainability vision" will position themselves for business success. Finally, Reinhardt sets out a strategic business view of environmental behavior from the perspective of the firm. His framework is used later in this chapter to explain why firms go beyond compliance and what this tells us about how to design a new regulation.

Not everyone agrees with what is known as the Porter hypothesis on the business value of beyond-compliance environmental performance. In a critique of the case that ample opportunities for win-win solutions exist among environmental and economic goals, Noah Walley and Bradley Whitehead assert that we should be realistic and recognize that regulation requires firms to incur many costs they will not be able to recover. Although win-win environmental investments exist, "they are very rare and will likely be overshadowed by the total cost of a company's environmental program."[21] Similarly, other writers have argued that the innovation and efficiency-enhancing effects of regulation are easily overstated. Public policy should be based on an analysis of costs and benefits and be designed to allow firms to achieve environmental goals cost-effectively; it should not be based on a vague notion that stringent regulation promotes resource efficiency among firms.[22] These are valid arguments, and they help to put the Porter hypothesis in perspective.

Several points can be made here regarding the potential for win-wins and its relevance for a new regulation. Remember that Porter and van der Linde state that only properly designed regulations will push firms to be more efficient and innovative. Poorly designed standards impose higher than necessary costs on firms and impair their ability to find innovative and resource-efficient solutions, as was argued in chapter 3. Certainly regulation has pushed firms to be more resource efficient. The entire pollution prevention movement might not have been possible, for example, without the action-forcing effects of government standards.[23] More important, we have to accept that regulation does impose costs on firms that they cannot recoup. That is a central lesson of the analysis in *Shades of Green*, discussed later in this chapter. To think otherwise is unrealistic. Still, successful firms will find ways to create value through their environmental policies, if not all of the time, then at least some of the time.[24] Furthermore, a well-designed and managed regulatory system will create more win-win opportunities for firms. The role of government then is to create the conditions that will enable well-run firms to be more efficient and innovative while still achieving society's environmental goals.

Still, theoretical arguments aside, the empirical question remains: Does it pay to be green? The relationship between environmental performance and financial success obviously does matter both for government policy makers and business managers. Much of the theoretical literature argues that there is or at least could be a positive relationship, if a firm operates strategically. Research on the response of financial markets to environmental events has found that firms lost market value when they were the subject of bad news.[25] Several studies found that stock prices declined, if only briefly, following the release of TRI data that put firms in a bad light.[26] Certainly the growing volume of case studies asserting the financial benefits of strong environmental performance add weight to the scale, as do the documented efforts by many companies to go beyond legal compliance. The last point is compelling. If many successful companies are going well beyond compliance, they must have good business reasons for doing so. Still, it is worth looking at the evidence. What do we know empirically about the link between financial and environmental success?

One of the more systematic investigations of this link was a 2001 study by Andrew King and Michael Lenox.[27] Using toxic emissions as their indicator of environmental performance, they analyzed a sample of 652 firms for the years 1987–1996. They controlled for several factors that could influence the results, such as firm and sector characteristics, the relative stringency of regulation, and the number of environmental permits held by a firm. They did indeed find evidence of a real association between lower pollution and better financial performance.[28] This association held when they controlled for characteristics of the firm, industry sector, regulatory environment, and other factors. What they could not determine was the direction of the causality—whether good environmental management contributes to financial success or just being profitable allows a firm to be better environmentally. It may pay to be green, they conclude, but it is unclear from the evidence why or when.

Others have reached similar conclusions. After reviewing the research, an EPA advisory group concluded "Overall, the empirical evidence appears to lay to rest the argument that the investments required to achieve sound environmental performance are a net drag on financial performance; rather, it suggests that a positive relationship between the two kinds of performance is likely."[29] A thorough review of the literature by an OECD team in 2001 found that "the results of such studies appear to reveal that there is a significant and positive relationship between environmental performance and commercial and financial results."[30] Again, the direction of causality could not be clearly established. Similarly, a more recent OECD review and survey of private sector environmental managers in seven nations concluded that "companies that find innovative solutions to reduce their environmental impacts are benefitting substantially by increasing resource productivity and cost savings, as well as marketing their environmental actions as being selling points for their products."[31]

Another way to assess the link between environmental and financial performance is to look at what at least part of the investment community is doing. For Innovest Strategic Advisors, a firm that rates socially responsible investments, environmental policies and management are a key indicator of a company's likely financial success and value to investors. In making its ratings, Innovest evaluates companies on several factors—including their risk management systems, disclosure and verification policies, process and eco-efficiency, health and safety policies, and board oversight of environmental issues. It also analyzes corporate documents, security filings, and EPA data sources, such as the TRI and air and water compliance sources. In a 2002 report on the utility sector, Innovest concluded that as "has been the case in nearly every other sector . . . environmental leaders . . . consistently out perform in the stock market by 300 to 3000 basis points (30 percentage points) per year."[32] This occurs largely, the report adds, because "environmental performance turns out to be an excellent proxy for management quality, the primary determinant of stock market returns."[33] To be fair, this emphasis on environmental performance is not shared overall by the investment community, except to the extent they look for negatives like major environmental liabilities or systemic compliance issues. Still, it is clear that socially responsible analysts like those from Innovest view environmental performance as an indicator of financial success and stake their recommendations to investors on that view.

In sum, there is impressive evidence that the more profitable firms tend to do better environmentally as well. The reasons behind this association are unclear. It could be that the more profitable firms simply have more resources to invest in environmental protection. Or, as is likely, well-managed firms demonstrate success on multiple dimensions. Still, it is possible that firms may use environmental excellence as a strategic means of improving their profitability. As Lenox and King conclude, the important question may not be whether or not it pays to be green, but under what circumstances and with what strategies it pays. The connections between environmental and financial success could be more a matter of astute firms taking advantage of a business opportunity than a sign of any inevitable relationship. It may be that well-managed firms will find ways to make it pay to be green.

What Are Firms Doing?

This section further illustrates the greening trend with three kinds of changes that have occurred: the expansion of corporate goal setting and reporting; the spread of environmental management systems; and the evolution of Responsible Care, the chemical industry's collective environmental management system. These trends both illustrate greening in more detail and suggest some important lessons for the new regulation.

Environmental Goal Setting and Reporting

The first illustration is the expansion of corporate goal setting and reporting. There was a time when firms would not voluntarily share information about their environmental performance and activities. Although many still take this view, others are committed to sharing information with the public on a wide range of environmental indicators. Some of the information now available is required under federal and state law, but most of it at a corporate level is provided voluntarily. This is especially the case in the United States, where there are minimal environmental reporting requirements at the corporate level.

Since the late mid-1990s, there has been steady growth in the number and quality of corporate environmental reports. A 1999 KPMG survey found that 35 percent of Fortune Global 250 firms issued a separate corporate environmental report.[34] By 2005, that number had increased to 52 percent.[35] Also since 1999, far more firms have been issuing sustainability as opposed to just environmental reports, although environmental issues were still covered more substantively than economic and social ones. The highest percentage of corporate environmental reports came from the electronics and computer, utility, automotive, oil and gas, chemicals, and pulp and paper sectors—all manufacturing industries that are heavily regulated. Countries with the highest rates of corporate reporting were Japan, the United Kingdom, Canada, and France. In 2005, just under a third of U.S. companies in the Global 250 issued corporate responsibility reports that covered environmental and other sustainability issues, compared with 80 percent in Japan and 71 percent in the United Kingdom.

Moreover, the quality of many such reports has improved. Many early ones were public relations exercises designed to showcase a firm's achievements and little more. They did not reveal much of substance about compliance or performance. Over time, however, there has been increased reporting on such factors as compliance, emissions, energy and materials use, worker safety, and waste generation, as well as on such management indicators as third-party audits, training, supply chain management, and life-cycle analysis. A growing number of companies set corporate goals and report regularly on their progress.

The pharmaceutical company Bristol-Myers Squibb (BMS) is a leading illustration of this trend toward setting goals and reporting on them.[36] It reports annually on several indicators, including materials, energy, and water use; air and water releases; waste generated; products and services; and supplier practices. For most of these, BMS bench marks its performance against others in its industry. It has set public goals for 2010 that include 10 percent reductions (from a 2001 baseline) in energy use, greenhouse gases, and water use, as well as large reductions in offsite air and water releases and product packaging. For its efforts, BMS has been recognized as one of the top U.S. firms in environmental reporting. Other firms that set public goals include Dow Chemical, Johnson & Johnson, and 3M. One recent survey found, however, that only about a third of a sample of 150 environmentally aware firms set public targets in their reports. Most of the indicators that this sample of firms reported on described their performance in terms of environmental impacts but did not set public targets or use measures of eco-efficiency, which would allow more accountability and comparability among firms and over time.[37]

A major development in this area is the Global Reporting Initiative (GRI), which was developed as a response to the growing number and variety of corporate environmental reports.[38] Its purpose is to develop formats and standards comparable to those used for financial indicators that firms may use voluntarily in their own reporting. The GRI is the product of a coalition of socially responsible investors, accounting organizations, advocacy groups, and firms and is sponsored by the Coalition for Environmentally Responsible Economies and the United Nations Environment Programme. It covers social as well as economic and environmental indicators, so it may be seen as a form of sustainability reporting.

The GRI includes a core set of sustainability reporting guidelines as well as sector supplements tailored to specific industries, technical protocols, and "issue guidance" on special topics. The GRI is enjoying at least some level of acceptance among multinational firms; the 2005 KPMG survey cited earlier found that of the Global 250 firms preparing corporate reports, 40 percent based their content at least to some degree on GRI guidelines.[39] In August 2005, some 70 U.S. organizations and 600 globally were listed as using the GRI.

Still, despite such efforts, "a persistent lack of consensus on what and how to report raises concern about the content and quality" of corporate reports.[40] There is far more information than in the past, but it is still difficult to compare performance across firms or facilities and evaluate progress over time. As more manufacturing shifts overseas, levels and kinds of production change, and firms contract out their production processes, making comparisons and evaluating performance becomes even more challenging. What may be most valuable in coming years is not that firms just describe their performance but that they provide indicators of eco-efficiency, set and report on goals, and enable comparisons of their products and effects on such long-term issues as climate and biodiversity. In addition, there is more attention to better environmental reporting at a facility level. CERES and the Tellus Institute are sponsoring a facility reporting project that has developed initial guidelines and is testing them with a variety of organizations.[41] The EPA's Performance Track program also has stressed the need for consistent and comparable reporting from its members.

Environmental Management Systems

Another trend in the past decade is the growing use of environmental management systems by private and public organizations. An EMS may be described as "a formal set of policies and procedures that define how an organization will manage its potential impacts on the natural environment and on the health and welfare of the people who depend on it."[42] Of course, firms have always had an EMS of a sort, if only to manage their legal compliance. The trend more recently has been to adopt far more systematic and comprehensive management tools. Organizations with an EMS typically adopt a written environmental policy; identify aspects of their activities, products, and services that affect the environment; set objectives and targets for improved performance; assign responsibility for implementing the EMS, such as training; and evaluate and refine the EMS in an effort to improve it and the results it helps them achieve.

Several EMS models exist, including versions adopted in Great Britain (BS 7750) and the European Union (under the Eco-Management and Auditing Scheme, or EMAS). By far the most influential model, however, is one developed by the International Standards Organization (ISO), known as ISO 14001. Developed at the initiative of business firms after the Rio Earth Summit, and issued in 1996, 14001 serves as a reference point for EMS generally. Facilities may certify their EMS with third-party registrars. As of December 2004, nearly 4,800 organizations (public and nonprofit, as well as private business) had been certified in the United States. This represents only the tip of the iceberg, however; many organizations adopt an EMS but do not seek formal third-party certification. An OECD-sponsored survey of U.S. firms conducted in 2003–2004 found that about half of those that had adopted an EMS had been third-party certified.[43] This suggests that perhaps twice as many organizations in the United States may have adopted an EMS of some form, say some 10,000, but this is only a rough estimate.

Most people view the spread of the EMS as positive. It is hard to disagree with the claim that "systematic efforts yield better results than nonsystematic or haphazard efforts."[44] Yet calls for recognizing the EMS in public policy are often met with skepticism. Because it is a management tool, it neither prescribes nor guarantees a particular result. If government is to use the EMS to complement or replace regulation, we need to know more about its effect on environmental performance. Although there are no clear answers, research and experience suggest several conclusions. First, people in organizations that use an EMS mostly think it has been an effective tool for improved environmental performance, better compliance, cost savings through internal process efficiencies, a better image with customers, and greater employee participation. In sum, many surveys of EMS adopters have shown that they find real and valuable benefits from doing so.[45]

A more useful guide for public policy is less what managers think an EMS is doing for them than what it appears to be delivering in compliance and performance. A study by the Environment Agency of England and Wales drew attention a few years ago when it concluded that the compliance records of EMS-adopting facilities were no better than those of nonadopters.[46] The study did, however, find evidence that having an EMS helps a firm identify other opportunities for improved performance. Two more recent studies in the United States found that an EMS does appear to be linked with better compliance and overall improved environmental performance. One study of the clean air compliance records of 3,700 facilities found that ISO-certified ones had better compliance records. The researchers carefully controlled for other factors that could affect a firm's compliance.[47] Looking beyond compliance measures, another study found that "the extent of EMS adoption has a significant negative impact on the intensity of toxic emissions particularly among firms with past release intensity that exceeded that of the median firm."[48] In other words, a more complete EMS was associated with better eco-efficiency, at least as measured by toxic releases.

Another comprehensive study by the University of North Carolina and the Environmental Law Institute concluded that "the introduction of an EMS can be expected to be at least somewhat beneficial to the environmental performance of most facilities, as well as to their operating and management efficiencies, and in some cases to their compliance patterns."[49] At the same time, they cautioned, having an EMS (certified or not) is not necessarily a clear signal regarding a facility's actual environmental performance, compliance, or rate of improvement.[50] Within these general conclusions were other, more specific findings. Environmental management systems varied considerably in their content and completeness. The contents of the EMS (e.g., the scope of activities covered or the objectives and targets selected for improvement) are more reliable indicators of positive effects than the mere existence of an EMS or even ISO registration. Other studies have found that the quality and scope of the EMS, its integration with other business activities, and the management commitment behind it are more important than the simple fact of whether an organization has one.[51]

In sum, the connection between having an EMS and environmental performance is far more complicated than one might think. Research studies try to isolate the EMS as the independent variable, with measures of environmental performance (including compliance) as the dependent variable. What if the relationship works the other way? Adopting and implementing an EMS may be an important sign of management commitment to improved compliance and performance. Some of the research suggests that management commitment may be a source of much of the observed differences in performance. In their study of the pulp and paper industry, the authors of *Shades of Green* conclude that the environmental management style of a mill's leadership is a crucial intervening variable that shapes the influences of external regulatory, economic, and social pressures on a facility.[52]

A study of the Finnish pulp and paper industry reinforces this point. It concludes that "the greatest positive impacts [of an EMS] arise when the system identifies areas of improvement that hitherto have not been recognized."[53] The EMS may promote an effective learning process in an organization that leads to incremental improvement, but not necessarily to major innovations that require substantial investment. For these, pressure from government may be necessary. An EMS, the study concluded, should supplement regulatory instruments but cannot replace them.[54] Similarly, *Shades of Green* and other studies conclude that core regulatory requirements for new technologies drive the basic upgrades among firms, but using management tools like the EMS may help to sustain a process of continuous improvement in performance.[55] In sum, an EMS may promote the "reflexivity" that is discussed in chapters 6 and 7 as an element in a new regulation. On its own, however, it is not a substitute for the regulatory pressure that government is in a position to apply.

If we are looking for conclusive evidence about how an EMS affects performance, it is fair to say that the jury is still out. Although more research may shed light on this question, it probably cannot be answered definitively. It is difficult to control for all the factors that affect performance. Moreover, factors other than having or not having an EMS matter—such as management commitment, employee involvement, and resources—and influence behavior in ways that are hard to measure. The evidence suggests that the EMS could play a role in a new regulation as a vehicle for promoting continuous improvement, especially when it is reinforced by regulatory pressures and complemented by other forces both within and external to the organization.

Collective Action by Industry Groups—Responsible Care

A third area worth considering in an analysis of greening is efforts by trade associations and other industry groups to take collective action for achieving environmental goals that are beyond compliance. For most of the past thirty years, trade associations were among the most vocal critics of regulation. They fought nearly every expansion of the government's regulatory authority. It was a rearguard action, to be sure, but was seen as necessary to protect members' economic interests. For many associations and issues, conflicts with regulators are still the rule. Others have worked to change this relationship, and some have created codes of environmental conduct to improve the performance of their members.

The leading example is Responsible Care, described as "the most sophisticated and far-reaching regime of self-regulation to be found in the world."[56] Begun as a voluntary initiative by the Canadian chemical industry in the 1970s, Responsible Care spread globally after the 1984 Bhopal tragedy. In the United States, the Chemical Manufacturers Association (now the American Chemistry Council, or ACC) adopted its own program in 1988 in response to negative public views of the industry.

For much of its life, Responsible Care consisted of ten guiding principles, six codes of practice, and over one hundred management practices grouped under each of the codes. Much of this material covered aspects of environmental performance that were not addressed by existing law. This was especially so in the community awareness, distribution, and product stewardship codes, which made firms look beyond their fence lines to the environmental impacts of products, as well as to the actions of suppliers, transporters, and customers. Participation was a condition of membership in the ACC. Members were expected to follow the principles, implement the codes in stages until they were fully in place, and continuously improve under the management practices. The codes did not set quantitative performance standards; they defined qualitative expectations that member firms had to document that they had met.[57]

As important as the principles, codes, and practices was the network of resources, relationships, and pressures that backed them up. Responsible Care reflected an awareness that problems in one firm may taint the entire industry. "What this means, in practical terms, is that each company in the chemical industry must act as its brother's keeper."[58] The program was reinforced by a network of committees, work groups, manuals, and other resources. Responsible Care was distinctive in the comprehensiveness of its codes and practices, as well as the networks and resources for implementing them.[59] Other similar codes, such as the American Textile Manufacturing Institute's "Encouraging Environmental Excellence," are far less developed. Their influence on the behavior of firms is probably minimal at best. Most associations lack the resources available to large chemical firms for implementing Responsible Care.

In 2002, the ACC decided to make several changes in Responsible Care. These were the product of a strategic review by ACC members, who concluded that "a program originally designed to demonstrate leadership beyond compliance could no longer claim that it was pushing the performance envelope."[60] Responsible Care had become more the norm of performance in the industry than a program driven by the leaders. Reinforcing this perception were research studies suggesting that at least some firms were using the program to brand themselves as high performers when they were not. One study, for example, found that Responsible Care companies reduced their toxic emissions (as measured by the TRI) at a slower relative rate than nonmembers.[61] In addition, the ACC found that the program was pushing firms to go beyond regulatory compliance less aggressively than it had in the past. In its early years, 13 percent of Responsible Care's content was covered by regulations; by 2000, 75 percent of its content was codified in regulations. The program could no longer be seen as encouraging beyond-compliance behavior.

As a result of this review, in 2003 the ACC announced that it would strengthen Responsible Care by making four changes. First, the old system of codes would be replaced with a "modernized" management system (known as the Responsible Care Management System or RCMS) that incorporated prevailing standards, such as ISO 14001. Second, all ACC members would undergo an independent, third-party certification process at a corporate level and at a sample of their sites. Third, members would be required to track and report their performance under a set of indicators, including toxic releases, energy efficiency, and greenhouse gases. A fourth set of changes instituted additional plant security provisions.

The final chapter of this book considers how these and other greening trends may be incorporated into a new regulation. Consider some brief examples: Government could use facility and corporate-level reporting as a substitute for much of the routine compliance reporting that companies currently provide. This could define a basis for facility-level environmental agreements similar to the Dutch covenants. Similarly, agencies could use industry codes like Responsible Care as the basis for negotiated agreements that commit firms to achieving measurable and verifiable results more quickly than could be achieved under a standard regulatory process. Environmental management systems also could be used to complement regulation in several ways. Currently, EPA may require in settlement agreements that firms with compliance issues adopt a management system. An EMS is one of the four criteria for acceptance into EPA's Performance Track program (discussed in the next chapter). In addition, EPA and state agencies are taking preliminary steps to try and integrate EMS provisions into their regulatory programs. These illustrate how in some ways the transition to a new regulation already has begun but could be accelerated with more careful thought and structured innovation.

Why Are They Doing It?

These examples of beyond-compliance behavior challenge the zero-sum assumptions behind the old regulation. If one accepts the premise that firms will act responsibly only when they are forced to do so by regulators, then why is it that some firms are acting to benefit the environment without direct government pressure?

Untangling the direct effects of regulation from other pressures that shape industry behavior is a tricky business. The answers will vary across firms, over time, even within the same firm. A virtue of the behavioral theory underlying the old regulation was its simplicity. "These are the rules," government says, "and if you do not follow them you will be punished." There was no need to worry about the dynamic business environment in which firms operated, the values and motives of their leadership, or changes in environmental problems and the institutional landscape. The price of this simplicity was that the behavioral theory of the old regulation became less valid, given the changes that have been occurring.

For insight into what motivates industry to go beyond compliance, consider two kinds of explanations from the literature. One is from *Shades of Green*. The second is *Down to Earth*. The first adopts a public policy perspective. The second takes a business strategy approach. Together, they help to explain beyond-compliance behavior of firms and suggest general directions for designing a new regulation.

Once among the most polluting of all sectors, pulp and paper mills have greatly improved their environmental performance over the past three decades. In a study of several mills in the United States, Canada, Australia, and New Zealand, the authors of *Shades of Green* seek to explain why some mills go well beyond compliance while others aim just to meet their legal obligations. The explanations lie in a combination of internal and external factors. The most important external factor is regulation: "Government regulation has been primarily responsible for the large improvements that are associated with the installation of costly pollution prevention technologies."[62] This is consistent with surveys of corporate managers, which find that regulation is the single most important driver of improved environmental performance.[63] In the pulp and paper case, the costs of investing in the technologies needed to reduce pollution significantly were so high that only government pressure, applied across all mills, could induce the needed investments. Regulation may even lead firms to go beyond compliance when they anticipate the need to comply with more stringent rules later and when they overcomply by building a margin of safety into environmental investments.

At the same time, the authors found that a simple compliance model is inadequate for explaining greening. Their research on fourteen mills in four countries suggests that greening involves "an economic calculus that is significantly broader, and more sensitive to political and cultural values, than the narrowly economistic 'amoral calculator' model suggests."[64] Regulation drives core technology upgrades, to be sure, but other improvements are the result of "a commitment to effective employee training, preventive maintenance, systematic environmental management, and 'operating excellence.'"[65]

In addition to regulatory pressures, the mills faced social and economic pressures that affected their environmental performance. They responded strategically to social pressures by increasing their "reputation capital," which translates into the trust of regulators, greater community acceptance, more tolerance by NGOs, and access to government officials. Economic pressures generally served to constrain their environmental improvements, at least when it came to making major technology changes. Within that context, however, economic pressures motivated mills to search for operating efficiencies and other opportunities for win-win solutions. External factors influenced their behavior, but these were mediated by factors internal to the firm as well. Principal among these were the attitudes, skills, and capacities of managers; the effective use of management systems; available resources; and an organizational capacity for learning.

A second view on greening is Reinhardt's analysis of how environmental practices may increase the chances of financial success in a firm. While *Shades of Green* studied facility behavior, Reinhardt analyzed the case for greening at the corporate level. As discussed earlier, he argues that the environment may be used as part of a firm's overall business strategy in five ways: by differentiating products, managing competitors, reducing operating costs, redefining markets, and reducing risk and uncertainty.

Many firms have found that differentiating their products on the basis of environmental attributes may yield business benefits. By reducing costs to customers, delivering better value, or emphasizing the social benefits of a product, a firm may increase its market share. Patagonia, the Body Shop, and Ben and Jerry's use preferable products to increase their appeal to consumers. Industrial marketers may seek economic advantage from environmentally preferable products as well. Reinhardt presents a case study of a low-salt textile dye in the mid-1990s that lowered wastewater treatment costs at the same time that it improved product performance.[66] When a firm can offer a product that increases environmental benefits or lowers environmental costs for its customers, it may use that to gain an advantage in the marketplace.

Another strategy is managing competitors by using environmental practices that competitors are forced to match. Firms that have a greater capacity for adopting such practices may gain a first-mover advantage over those that are in a less favorable position. One way to manage competitors is through collective action programs like Responsible Care.

Typically, leading firms in an industry sector will adopt relatively more stringent environmental policies or practices that other firms are forced to match if they are to remain in a position to compete with the leaders. Another way to manage competitors is through the regulatory system. In the 1980s, Dupont used its formidable resources and market dominance to get ahead of competitors by developing substitutes for chlorofluorocarbons (CFCs), then promoting regulation that restricted CFCs in favor of less environmentally damaging alternatives.[67] Dupont thus gained a first-mover advantage.

A third way to reconcile environmental and financial goals is by reducing internal costs. This is the most obvious explanation for greening. It captures what Aseem Prakash calls Type 1 behavior, when firms take actions, not because they are legally required, but because they offer a return on investment that is more favorable than other options.[68] Early pollution prevention programs, such as 3M's Pollution Prevention Pays and Dow's WRAP (Waste Reduction Always Pays), documented the savings that could be gained by preventing pollution rather than controlling it at the point of release. The essence of a cost-reduction strategy is that "by scrutinizing their operations and investments in light of environmental considerations, firms can realize costs savings that will more than offset the additional cost of providing higher levels of environmental goods."[69] These savings may come in several forms: reducing waste treatment and disposal costs, using less raw material, avoiding future liabilities, reducing legal penalties and expenses, lowering insurance premiums, and stimulating continuous learning and innovation that may lead to longer-term reductions in costs.

The opportunities for reducing costs are well documented in the literature on greening, pollution prevention, and EMS. What is less clear is the extent to which most firms are looking for and taking advantage of them. Generally, firms operating in a competitive business environment need to reduce costs whenever they can. At the same time, critics complain that firms are not looking aggressively enough for ways to reduce costs through environmental improvement or are not pursuing ones they know are available. Are firms not responding to opportunities to reduce costs? Are the proverbial $20 bills lying around that even profit-seeking firms fail to pick up? If so, the assumption of potential win-wins from environmental innovation may be exaggerated. Such questions have led researchers to ask whether firms are pursuing opportunities to reduce costs, and why or why not.

In one revealing study, James Boyd examined three cases of pollution prevention decisions at global chemical producers based in the United States. His objective was to determine how well firms evaluate the financial benefits of preventing pollution. The research was provoked by concerns that firms were failing to take advantage of opportunities that offered financial and environmental benefits. Boyd saw three reasons firms might not pursue prevention opportunities. Each has different implications for government. First, firms may find opportunities to save money by preventing pollution, but decide not to pursue them. In this case, "only the blunt instrument of command-and-control regulation can be counted on to get the job done."[70] Second, there may be internal barriers to evaluating prevention options, such as a lack of information, few managerial incentives, or poor accounting tools. In this case, government should lower barriers by providing technical assistance, new incentives, or better tools. Third, there may not be as many chances to profit from prevention as the conventional wisdom suggests. Environmental investments may not stack up well against other uses of capital that are available to the firm.

Boyd finds that the third reason describes his cases. All three of the prevention options he studied showed a positive return according to methods typically used by the firms. Still, two did not survive the firms' capital budgeting analysis and were not funded because they did not compare favorably with other investment options. Although there were uncertainties, "the cases suggest that firms are quite capable of identifying the actions that are in their greatest financial self-interest."[71] The firms decided against the investments, not because they lacked information, incentives, or tools, but because they could not justify them financially. The lesson is that environmental investments must compete with other financial options.

These cases involved global chemical firms. Smaller ones may lack the tools or incentives to identify even highly cost-effective pollution prevention opportunities. Indeed, EMS research suggests that small firms especially may benefit from government and other technical assistance to help them identify such opportunities. Some firms may miss even highly favorable investment opportunities because of limited information, organizational inertia, a lack of incentives, or for other reasons.[72] This analysis reinforces a conclusion reached in *Shades of Green* and other studies regarding the need for government regulatory pressure to drive basic investments in new technologies and practices. Within this context, firms may then search for investments that reduce their operating costs. The challenge for regulatory design is to apply this pressure in ways that are flexible, have low transaction costs, and operate on predictable timetables. It is a matter, as Porter and van der Linde would say, of changing behavior through good rather than bad regulation.

A fourth explanation for greening is that firms are redefining markets. When they redefine markets, firms "find ways to reconfigure the whole system by which they create value and deliver it to customers."[73] They transform relationships with customers by rethinking their products and services. An example is leasing rather than selling products to customers. Ray Anderson, chief executive officer of Interface Carpets, decided years ago that the practice of selling carpeting to customers that was later removed and disposed of in landfills made little sense. His company developed an innovative practice of leasing carpeting until it was due to be replaced, then removing it and recycling the raw material to make a new product rather than simply throwing it away. Xerox has for many years seen itself as a provider of business services rather than a marketer of products. It pioneered the practice of remanufacturing—of leasing copiers and other equipment, then taking it back and using the parts again.

An even more compelling explanation for performing beyond compliance is to manage risk and uncertainty. Like most people, business managers dislike uncertainty. All kinds of uncertainty may interfere with business success—from trends in the global economy, to election results, to the prices of raw materials in international markets, to the weather. To succeed, business managers need to manage uncertainty by reducing it whenever possible. Much of the behavior associated with the greening of industry may be explained as efforts by firms to manage risk and uncertainty.

Consider the steps firms take to exceed existing legal standards (i.e., overcompliance) or to voluntarily meet standards in advance of their possible adoption by government. Firms often overcomply as an insurance policy against future legal interpretations by regulators or to provide a buffer for any internal missteps that may lead to even small and temporary lapses in compliance. For example, there have been instances in which firms treat a waste as legally hazardous even though the waste appears not to be covered under the relevant definition, just in case an agency interprets it differently later. Firms also comply in advance of a possible future requirement as a hedge against regulatory uncertainty. When a facility upgrades a process, it may decide to go beyond existing technology standards in anticipation of more stringent standards later. Examples are Aseem Prakash's case studies of E.I. Lilly's and Baxter's decisions to go well beyond the EPA requirements when they replaced underground storage tanks in the late 1980s and 1990s.[74]

Anticipated regulation presents a credible threat of government intervention later on. Industry may be motivated to act before the government does because firms may prefer to address an issue on their own terms rather than on the terms set by potentially inflexible government rules. People in industry often say they would meet stricter performance targets if they had more control over how they comply and had predictable timetables for meeting them. Indeed, a letter from EPA Administrator William Reilly inviting participation in the 33/50 program for toxics reduction implied that it was an alternative to "the detailed direction which is likely to be demanded if voluntary efforts are not fruitful."[75] The clear message was that if industry did not participate, stricter EPA regulations were a possibility. As stressed later in the discussion of voluntary programs, a credible threat of more regulation later on may stimulate firms to take aggressive action now.

These examples illustrate the ways in which current and anticipated regulation may induce beyond-compliance behavior. In practice, however, firms seek to manage uncertainty through good environmental performance in ways that are not related directly to compliance. Three examples follow.

Improving Relationships with Regulators   Officially, of course, under the old regulation everyone is treated the same. Unofficially, people recognize that some facilities and firms are better managed and more responsible than others. Many leaders in greening explain their behavior as a way to gain credibility with government regulators, which they see as having long-term business value. Greater trust and credibility with regulators, or what may be termed regulatory capital, pays off in many ways. One way is obtaining exceptions to rules. The inflexibility of regulation means there are times when firms are forced to do things that do not make economic or environmental sense. Regulatory law and procedure recognize this in allowing regulators to exercise discretion by granting exceptions to general rules.

An example is a procedure in which a facility petitions EPA to de-list a waste stream from coverage under hazardous waste rules. De-listing petitions may be granted when there is no risk of environmental harm. They are a way of building some flexibility into an otherwise inflexible system. Ideally, agencies would grant them when the facility could make the necessary case. In practice, however, they are yet another demand on scarce agency resources, take time to process, and may not be justified, given the other workload demands that agencies face. Good relationships with a regulator may translate into expedited action on a de-listing petition, agency attention in resolving administrative issues, or informal resolution of a minor enforcement action that saves the firm time and resources. Members of EPA's Performance Track (discussed in chapter 5) have cited this opportunity to create regulatory capital as the main benefit of being in the program. It means they are not just another face in the crowd.

Another benefit of trust and credibility is being included in the advisory groups and policy debates that influence legislation and regulation. In his analysis of E.I. Lilly's motives for greening, Prakash cites an internal company document stating that "gains have been made in our efforts for a proactive involvement in legislative and regulatory issues at the federal and state level."[76] Especially as opportunities for dialogue between government and industry improved in recent decades, being included in advisory groups allowed many firms to have their views heard and gave them more credibility with government.

A third example of how better relationships with regulators deliver value to firms is in making them eligible for expedited and other forms of preferable permitting. The business costs of delay and uncertainty in permitting processes are well documented.[77] Changes in production processes often require that a facility obtain a new or modified permit from regulators. For businesses that change processes frequently, such as specialty chemicals, the delay and uncertainty associated with permitting slows their ability to respond to customers. Several government voluntary programs grant permitting caps, regulatory waivers, and expedited response times to participants. In 2004, for example, EPA announced it would give priority to Performance Track members in expanding the use of flexible air permits and encouraged states to do the same. Many firms have realized tangible business value from having these flexible air permits. An EPA study of the early implementation of flexible air permits documented not only reduced emissions but also business benefits to firms that were granted such permits, among them Baxter, 3M, Saturn, and Daimler-Chrysler.[78]

Reducing Uncertainty in the Supply Chain   Most business firms depend on others to supply raw materials or intermediates they use to make their own products. In addition to looking at price and quality, they look for suppliers who will be reliable and responsible. Having a reliable supply chain is especially critical in these days of just-in-time delivery, in which firms maintain low inventories to reduce costs. Experience shows that a lack of environmental or social responsibility in the supply chain may have repercussions. Consider the problems that firms like Nike and Home Depot faced when activists became critical of their suppliers' labor practices (Nike) and forest management practices (Home Depot).

Increasingly, manufacturers are demanding evidence of environmental responsibility from their suppliers. Xerox, IBM, Johnson & Johnson, and Hewlett-Packard evaluate their suppliers or require audits by third parties. Both General Motors and Ford now require ISO 14001 certification for first-tier suppliers. Although there are many reasons for this oversight of suppliers, Reinhardt observes that business interruption risk, risk of liability, reputation risk, and regulatory risk are the most prominent.[79]

Improving Industry Performance through Collective Action   Programs like Responsible Care and the Sustainable Forestry Initiative may be seen as strategies for managing competitors. They serve yet another, even more important role in improving industry performance and public perceptions of its performance. After Bhopal, one executive stated that the chemical industry would have to earn a "license to operate" in communities. A poor public image for the industry translates into more regulation, community opposition to facilities, and financial liability for everyone. Programs like Responsible Care help firms reduce risk and manage uncertainty.

Reinhardt's analysis offers a useful framework for explaining beyond-compliance behavior. For example, the growth of corporate environmental reports may be seen as a way to differentiate products and performance on environmental grounds as well as a way to manage competitors. The spread of environmental management systems has been fueled by evidence that an EMS may help identify opportunities for internal cost reductions, by the efforts of large customers (such as General Motors) to manage uncertainty in the supply chain, and by the desire to reduce regulatory risk and uncertainty. By leasing rather than selling products (as with Xerox and Interface) and providing services rather than goods, firms seek to gain competitive advantage. The lesson of Reinhardt's analysis is that creative and innovative firms find ways to reconcile environmental performance with financial success. A major goal of a new regulation should be to maximize the opportunities for these kinds of solutions. A new regulation should be aimed at creating "maximum opportunity for innovation by letting industries discover how to solve their problems."[80]

The history of Responsible Care illustrates how dynamic the greening process has been. Its origins may be explained as an interest by large firms within the chemical sector to improve the industry's collective image and manage their competitors. As Responsible Care evolved, it began to serve other purposes. The pollution prevention codes helped firms lower costs. The product stewardship codes helped reduce risks in the supply and distribution chains. It is not just the codes and practices, but the entire system of networks and resources behind them, that enable firms to take advantage of potential win-win opportunities. Of course, to fully take advantage of the potential business value of industry codes, they must been seen by regulators and the public as transparent, effective, and credible. This need explains the enhancements that were made in Responsible Care over the past few years, to stress third-party verification and measurement.

Lessons of Greening for a New Regulation

It is no exaggeration to say that a sea change in the environmental attitudes and practices of leading firms has occurred over the past forty years. At a minimum, these changes cast doubt on the simple rules-and-deterrence model of the old regulation and the assumption of the inevitable zero sum that underlies it. To be sure, businesses exist to make money, and their survival depends on it. However, as the studies in this chapter document, the business logic that motivates environmental behavior is much more complex than the traditional thinking would lead us to believe. Although we do not fully understand the nature of the relationship between environmental and economic performance, that there is a positive relationship is well documented, both in the empirical literature and in the behavior of leading firms.

One lesson of greening is that firms make environmental improvements in response to more than just short-term legal coercion. They anticipate new requirements and frequently overcomply with existing ones. They seek operating efficiencies, set expectations for suppliers and customers, redesign products, commit to and report on public goals that go beyond regulation, build complex management systems, and adopt collective codes of conduct that demand more than government requires. They seek collaborative relationships with regulators, provide information to communities, regulate actions of their suppliers, and take steps to reduce future liabilities even when the short-term payoffs are unclear.

Another lesson from this chapter is that there is tremendous diversity among and within firms regarding their commitments to and capacities for strong environmental performance. This chapter examined the leaders, not because they are typical, but because they are not. We should study them, however, because by understanding their behavior we may gain insights for a new regulation. This chapter also suggests how varied the motives for greening are. Firms do better than comply for many different reasons that are shaped by their internal organizational dynamics; their relationships with suppliers, customers, and regulators; the nature of their products; the resources that are available; and many other factors.

Yet another set of lessons lies in our growing knowledge of what works and why. With a management tool like the EMS, for example, experience so far suggests that it is best used to complement regulation, not to replace it. When there is a lack of management commitment and too little attention to results, the EMS may have limited value. Although there is evidence that a strong and well-integrated EMS may be an engine for process innovation and continuous improvement, government pressure is still necessary to sustain the technology and behavioral upgrades on which long-term progress depends. By encouraging the use of an EMS, along with other tools and practices, government may equip firms to engage in a process of continuous improvement that not only meets society's environmental goals but that also may have business value. At the same time, it would be a mistake for government to prescribe the use of an EMS. This would take us away from an emphasis on environmental results—a core premise of the new regulation—and reinforce the emphasis on process and prescription that has characterized the old regulation.

Likewise, experience with corporate reporting and Responsible Care shows that transparency and accountability are important but not easily obtained. Until recently, many reports were seen to be public relations exercises. Because of trends like the Global Reporting Initiative, intense scrutiny from NGOs and others, and efforts of firms like Bristol-Myers-Squibb to set standards, corporate reporting is now more legitimate. The history of Responsible Care shows that credibility is the ultimate test of industry codes, a point the ACC is stressing in efforts to improve measurement and accountability. Whether the new version of Responsible Care will meet the larger tests of legitimacy and accountability remains to be seen. The argument here is that efforts like Responsible Care deserve serious attention from regulators and careful evaluation by researchers to determine what role they might play in the transition toward a new environmental regulation.

Another lesson is the importance of knowing what motivates behavior. Gunningham and co-authors put it well when they write: "progress in improving the environmental performance of industry generally, or in redesigning environmental regulation, is more likely when policy makers have a detailed understanding of how and why firms go about addressing environmental risks."[81] If the biggest conceptual error of the old regulation was assuming an inevitable zero sum, its biggest behavioral error was pretending that the firm was a black box rather than a composite of individuals working under shared rules, structures, and procedures, and as part of an organization. A premise of the new regulation is that policy makers will try to understand the factors that motivate, constrain, and improve environmental behavior among firms. They do this with research, dialogue, information sharing, and systematic learning through experience.

In thinking about what greening means for public policy, Porter and van der Linde's distinctions between good and bad regulation are critical. Government standards that define core obligations are a necessary element in the new regulation. Still, it should be clear that there are different kinds of regulation. What they term *good* regulation focuses on outcomes, not processes. It sets stringent goals, yet may still be developed collaboratively with industry. It allows firms to innovate, not just add to existing end-of-pipe techniques; and it grants the flexibility needed for creative solutions that maximize win-win opportunities.

Of course, the fear among defenders of the old regulation about flexibility and collaboration is the potential for regulatory capture. To be sure, financial scandals raise doubts about the confidence we may have in corporate responsibility. However, conditions in the early 2000s differ greatly from those of the 1970s, enough to make capture of agency regulators increasingly unlikely. There is far more information, accountability, and scrutiny now than there was even twenty years ago. By building transparency and accountability for results into the new regulation, it is possible to further reduce the risk of capture. A premise of the new regulation is that flexibility and collaboration do not inevitably lead to a dependence of government on industry or a weakening of environmental standards. It is a matter of institutional design.

The experience with greening suggests two more specific lessons for designing a new regulation. One is that government should officially recognize different levels of performance. Chapter 7 argues that performance tracks should be a key element in the new regulation. Second, a variety of policy tools may be used to induce the kinds of behavior that will achieve policy goals. In addition to conventional regulation, government may incorporate information disclosure, market incentives, and management systems into its program designs. There is ample evidence that carrots influence behavior as much as sticks do. These other policy tools are as much a part of the new regulation as regulatory standards themselves.

Having looked at the industry side of what has happened in recent decades, the discussion now turns to what was happening in government. The calls of the revisionist critics, reinforced by the political challenge to regulation in the 1990s, stimulated efforts by government to adapt. These efforts enjoyed mixed success for the most part, but they may offer useful stepping-stones toward a new regulation.

5

Stepping-Stones or Just Rocks in the Stream? The Reinvention Era

Stepping stones lead to evolutionary, not revolutionary, change.[1]

At a public session on regulatory innovation, one panelist was a lawyer from a national environmental group who was critical of proposals for a more flexible, performance-based approach. He dismissed the many reinvention proposals of the 1990s as merely the Clinton administration's political reaction to the 1995 Republican assault on regulation. Here was a clever rhetorical strategy: Present reinvention as a case of defensive politics, rather than as a more reasoned and principled attempt at change, and cast doubt on the legitimacy of the whole enterprise.

In fact, many people accept this formulation of what may be termed the reinvention era of the 1990s. Certainly, there is some truth to it. It is no accident that proposals for streamlining environmental regulation were unveiled in March 1995, at the height of Republican attacks on environmental programs. At the level of partisan politics, events were pushing the Clinton White House and EPA to respond to complaints that regulation had become too inefficient, cumbersome, and intrusive. Still, as argued here and chapter 6, deeper forces were at work. Consider that:

· A range of advisory bodies, including established supporters of environmental programs, were calling attention to the weaknesses in the current system and calling for change.

· The federal government itself, responding to trends in the private sector, initiated efforts to improve processes, structures, and relationships as part of a much broader program to "reinvent" government.

· State governments were searching for ways to introduce flexibility, tailor regulations to diverse circumstances, and recognize different levels of performance.

· The greening of industry trend, discussed in chapter 4, moved many firms from reluctant compliance to being leaders and innovators.

· Other nations, most notably the Netherlands, were modifying traditional regulatory practices and relationships after realizing that the old system would not deliver the necessary environmental results.

· Governments around the world were experimenting with voluntary initiatives with industry as complements to or replacements for conventional regulation.

This chapter discusses how the federal government in the United States responded to calls for change in the 1990s. Although it appeared to be little more than a superficial reaction to political events, reinvention also expressed deeper, longer-term forces that were in play. As argued in chapter 3, dissatisfaction with regulation had grown in the 1980s and 1990s. Whatever had been accomplished, and certainly much had, it was clear to many people that the world had changed and regulation had to change with it.

This and the next chapter are exercises in what Richard Rose calls lesson drawing in public policy. Typically, Rose argues, people in government and many outside of it prefer the status quo. At times, however, a sense of dissatisfaction disrupts routines and leads people to question business as usual. Dissatisfaction stimulates a search for solutions, for "actions that will reduce the gap between what is expected from a program and what government is doing."[2] This dissatisfaction was increasingly evident in the 1980s and 1990s. Chapter 3 examined the concerns about adversarial relations, missed opportunities, inefficiency, rigidity, unresponsiveness, and a simple lack of resources. Many states, including leaders in environmental protection, tried to adapt to a changed operating environment. Leading firms took greater responsibility for their environmental behavior, but still faced criticism from EPA and state regulators for regulatory violations that often appeared to be trivial in the context of their overall accomplishments.

Later in this chapter is a discussion of what William Ruckelshaus called an extraordinary convergence of ideas on the need for change, toward what the authors of *Thinking Ecologically* termed "not only the middle ground but the higher ground."[3] Like Ruckelshaus, many of these revisionist critics had helped to create the system they now wanted to rebuild. They saw regulation as it had evolved in the United States as increasingly flawed. Before looking at the United States, however, it is important to examine the trend toward voluntary environmental programs that involved government and industry more generally because they are an important indicator of the search for a new regulation, not only in the United States but in other countries.

Voluntary Programs and Environmental Policy

A theme of this chapter is that events in the United States were by no means atypical. In Europe and Japan as well, governments had been experimenting with a variety of initiatives for complementing or replacing conventional regulation. Especially for issues like climate change, nonpoint-source pollution of water, and persistent pollutants, governments took advantage of the flexibility, potential for collaboration, and results orientation of voluntary approaches. Indeed, reinvention in the United States may be seen as relying on voluntary industry efforts as a potential stepping-stone to broader change.

Several features distinguish voluntary programs from conventional regulation.[4] The former usually are "extralegal" in that they are undertaken without specific legislative authority. As a result, participation by industry and others is voluntary. This idea of voluntariness should be viewed cautiously, however. Many initiatives, including the more successful ones, carry a direct or implied threat of more stringent regulation if policy goals are not met. Voluntary programs may be more goal oriented than regulation and leave the details of meeting the goals to participants. They ask for effort or results that go beyond compliance and typically carry no legal sanctions for nonperformance, although there is the likelihood of adverse publicity if a firm fails to meet a commitment it has made publicly.

An OECD study of these initiatives in 1999 divided them into four types: unilateral actions by industry, private agreements between industry and nongovernmental organizations, government challenge programs that invite industry participation, and negotiated agreements between industry and government.[5] Chapter 4 discussed unilateral actions by firms through programs like Responsible Care.[6] The second type includes initiatives like the Environmental Defense's partnerships with McDonald's and Federal Express, in which they worked with companies to achieve specific goals. The focus here is on the third and fourth types. In the third, government challenges industry to achieve environmental results that are not legally required. In the fourth, government is party to a negotiated agreement in which it grants benefits in exchange for an industry commitment to achieving results that go beyond compliance.

Even within these third and fourth types, there are variations. One is government's leverage in getting participation, commitments, and performance from industry. This leverage may come from either sticks or carrots. As an example of sticks, a Dutch energy benchmarking program allowed firms to demonstrate that they were in the top 10 percent globally in their energy efficiency as an alternative to facing stricter regulation and emission fees. Participation in EPA's 33/50 program was probably increased by the hint that more regulation would be necessary if releases of listed chemicals did not decline. Indeed, a consistent theme in assessments of voluntary programs is that the threat of future regulation makes them more effective. One review of the research concludes that the effectiveness of a voluntary program increases when there is a credible regulatory threat.[7]

Carrots also may offer leverage to government and make voluntary programs more effective. The theory behind EPA's Project XL and Performance Track programs (discussed later in this chapter) was that flexibility and other benefits will induce firms to achieve more than they would under regulation alone. The more value firms attach to these benefits, the more leverage government has in changing their behavior. If EPA has more legal discretion in granting flexibility under such programs as Project XL, for example, it might be able to negotiate more significant improvements from firms. Other carrots that encourage industry participation in government-sponsored initiatives are recognition, the prospect of a different working relationship with regulators; access to technical assistance and resources; and lower regulatory transaction costs, such as less routine compliance reporting or streamlined or expedited permitting.

Voluntary programs also vary in the extent to which they allow free riding among participants. Free riders enjoy the benefits without having to meet the obligations of these programs. Free riding is worrisome enough for government when it only recognizes firms for their participation. Free riding becomes even more serious when government offers regulatory inducements, such as the low inspection priority provided under EPA's Performance Track, exemptions from reporting requirements, or streamlined permitting. It reduces confidence in the reliability and quality of participants and thus affects the program's public credibility. In many if not most voluntary programs, particularly of the "challenge" variety discussed later, firms may enjoy recognition and other benefits of participation without having to meet obligations, such as progress reports or other monitoring and documentation of results. Of 137 voluntary agreements studied by the European Commission in 1997, for example, 118 did not require firms to report the results of their performance monitoring, and 47 had no monitoring requirements at all.[8]

The reasons governments use voluntary initiatives vary as well. In Japan, they provide a bottom-up solution to the limited authority of the national government over pollution problems. Negotiated between local governments and firms, the agreements usually are a precursor to national law. Some 34,000 such agreements were in place in Japan by 1999.[9] In the United States and Europe, voluntary initiatives are used more commonly to augment existing legislation. They encourage better-than-compliance behavior and allow policy makers to adapt more quickly to new issues than a conventional regulatory approach would. For their proponents, voluntary initiatives offer "a chance to address environmental problems in a flexible manner at low cost, based on consensus-building between the different stakeholders."[10] In the United States, voluntary programs are generally used more to complement than to replace conventional regulation.

The key policy question, of course, is whether voluntary initiatives work. Measured only by environmental results, the record is decidedly mixed. An OECD review in 2002 found that the initial, publicly stated targets of most such initiatives are met. The report argues, however, that in many cases it is unlikely that the results achieved were much different from what would have been achieved under business as usual. Similarly, a thorough review of voluntary programs published more recently found that few voluntary approaches in the United States have resulted in anything greater than a moderate reduction in emissions.[11] In the OECD study, certain characteristics were associated with more effective programs: provisions against free riding; credible and reliable monitoring; transparent and clearly defined goals; networks for sharing information; and most important, the presence of a credible threat of regulation or other government action, such as an emissions tax, that puts firms on an equal footing and compels them to change their technology and behavior.[12] The argument in this chapter is that voluntary programs on their own are not likely to show much in the way of environmental results. When combined with either the right sticks or carrots, however—or a combination of both—and designed properly, they offer a valuable and effective addition to conventional regulation and should be a core element in the new regulation.

Still, voluntary programs should not be evaluated solely on the basis of measurable environmental effects, particularly when they are seen as part of a transition from an old to a new regulation. They offer many advantages as "stepping-stones" to a new system because they provide experience for transforming relationships and building trust, allow us to explore new kinds and combinations of policy instruments, offer practical lessons on measuring performance, enable policy makers to respond to new issues flexibly and collaboratively, spread information and tools across organizations and settings, and allow government to experiment with new roles. Indeed, it is fair to say that voluntary approaches may have the greatest potential in areas where it is especially difficult to measure behavior.[13] In the long run, these results may prove to be more important in making the transition to a new regulation. Still, measuring both the "hard" (environmental) and the "soft" (effects on relationships, learning, trust, and so on) results is vitally important in deciding the future role of voluntary programs in a new environmental regulation.

The last part of this chapter returns to the issue of evaluating voluntary programs. The topic now is how voluntary programs in the United States offer lessons and stepping-stones for a new regulation. The following section begins with the "extraordinary convergence of ideas" Ruckelshaus cited in making the case for change.

"This Extraordinary Convergence of Ideas"

William Ruckelshaus holds the distinction of serving as the both first and fifth administrator of the U.S. Environmental Protection Agency. Probably no other public official outside of Congress has had more influence on environmental policy in the past four decades. As the first administrator in 1970–73, he established EPA's credibility and mobilized the legal resources of the federal government for the job of controlling pollution. He returned in 1983–85 to restore the agency's effectiveness and public image after two years of the Reagan administration's efforts to reduce both. He is highly respected on both sides of the political aisle.

So it was no small matter in 1996 when, thirteen years after his second term at EPA, he announced his intention to organize an effort to assess national environmental policy and recommend improvements. Called the Enterprise for the Environment, it brought together some forty people from government, business, environmental groups, universities, and other interests. They committed to work in good faith to try and agree on changes in environmental policy that would overcome the limitations examined in chapter 3, including distrust and conflict, inefficiency, a focus on means over ends, and the barriers to innovation.[14]

The E4E participants met several times over a period of eighteen months. They proposed a broad vision for a new system that included such ideas as the need to set and pursue clear goals, offer flexibility with accountability, promote collaborative and integrated problem solving, encourage stewardship and continuous improvement, and involve stakeholders in decisions. They also recommended tools and strategies, such as more use of market incentives, for incorporating these ideas into public policy. In the end, however, the group was unable to reach a consensus on specific proposals for implementing their vision. Environmentalists would not endorse even the broad E4E proposals. Representatives from the Natural Resources Defense Council and Friends of the Earth withdrew from the process. They disagreed on the need for overall change and were reluctant to endorse the idea of relying more on long-term goals, which they thought would require more definitive burdens of proof from regulators and hinder government's ability to respond to pressing issues.[15]

The E4E was in many ways a culmination of efforts to reach a consensus on a new system for environmental protection in the 1990s. It had several predecessors. Formed in 1994, with the usual constellation of stakeholders, the President's Council for Sustainable Development took the design and operation of regulation as one of its topics. Among the PCSD's conclusions was that the adversarial nature of the existing system and heavy reliance on technology-based standards posed barriers to progress. It called for more flexibility, backed by accountability for results; more use of partnerships and collaboration; and greater reliance on tools like extended product responsibility and market incentives. The PCSD called for a two-level approach: make the old system more efficient and effective and "create a new alternative environmental management system that achieves more protection at lower cost."[16]

In the first of three reports issued between 1995 and 2000, the National Academy of Public Administration evaluated the old regulation and proposed changes. It reiterated what had become the standard elements of the revisionist critique: rigidity, lack of cooperation, bureaucratic fragmentation, and so on. Among its conclusions, the NAPA panel urged EPA and Congress to develop policies that would encourage firms to go beyond compliance and reward them for doing so. It also stressed the need for better measurement of performance and more flexible policies that would encourage and enable firms to innovate.[17]

Another group with similar ideas was the Aspen Institute, which proposed an alternative path for regulation. Its core principles included clear goals, flexibility, innovation, integration, and stakeholder participation, among others. Firms would qualify for this alternative path by demonstrating a strong record of compliance, performance, and leadership. It would be designed to supplement but not replace the current system and offer another option for firms willing to commit to superior performance, involve stakeholders, and work collaboratively with regulators. This proposal was incorporated to some degree into EPA's Project XL, which is discussed later. Aspen also proposed a two-level "performance track" concept, which was applied in EPA's National Environmental Performance Track, also discussed later.[18]

Similar themes were echoed in the broader literature. The authors of *Thinking Ecologically: The Next Generation of Environmental Policy*, argued for "a next generation of environmental policies that are not confrontational but cooperative, less fragmented and more comprehensive, not inflexible but rather capable of being tailored to fit varying circumstances."[19] In *Smart Regulation*, Neil Gunningham and Peter Grabosky observe "there is some evidence that a new paradigm for the analysis of regulation may be evolving: one capable of transcending the regulation-deregulation dichotomy and of providing a much broader perspective of what regulation can involve."[20] Generally, the academic literature since the mid-1990s echoed these calls for a new approach to environmental regulation and the general form it should take.[21]

Ruckelshaus was right; here was an extraordinary convergence of ideas on the need for and general outline of a new regulation. The challenge lay in translating these ideas into actions. The fate of the E4E itself is emblematic of what occurred in the politics and policy streams in the 1990s. Even with the leadership of a respected figure like Ruckelshaus, the E4E group as a whole could not agree on more than broad principles. This is not to say that EPA and the states did not try to respond to the ideas coming from the E4E and other revisionist critics. In fact, attempts were made in the 1990s to apply these ideas for innovation, with varied success. The rest of this chapter analyzes selected EPA efforts as case studies of reinvention in practice and as possible stepping-stones to a new regulation.

Regulatory Reinvention at EPA

Founded in 1970 under an executive order, the United States Environmental Protection Agency is one of the foremost regulatory agencies in the world. It exercises authority under more than a half dozen major statutes and dozens of lesser ones. Its technical, scientific, and legal resources are formidable. Many nations took EPA and its enabling laws as a point of departure for their own environmental policies.[22]

Like the system it administers, EPA draws both praise and criticism. Despite the complaints of some critics that it relies on weak, even "junk" science, EPA generally is seen to be highly competent technically. In a turbulent political environment, responsible for implementing complex and often contradictory laws, it usually is credited for building an effective system of environmental controls and administering it capably. Most of the complaints about EPA may be linked to the scientific uncertainty that surrounds its work, the many conflicts among goals, a fragmented legal framework, and the complex system of political oversight under which it has had to operate.[23]

These forces combined to shape EPA's agenda in the 1990s. To be sure, this was not the first time the agency had been pressed to change its approach to regulating industry. The idea of regulatory reform is as old as EPA itself. Many such reforms were discussed in the brief history of environmental regulation in chapter 2. Among the more important ones were the use of such market mechanisms as emissions trading, cost-benefit and other forms of economic analysis, the use of consensus-based processes like regulatory negotiation, and efforts to integrate across program and sector lines.

Still, what was called reinvention in the 1990s differed from earlier reforms. It was directed not just at applying new tools (cost-benefit analysis) or procedures (regulatory negotiation) but also at changing patterns of relationships among government, business, and others. It also reflected broader trends that were apparent in other industrial democracies, as argued in this and the following chapters. In short, the reinvention era was very much about governance, and not just about fine-tuning analytical tools or improving information flows. A careful look at the statements of the E4E, the NAPA panels, the PCSD, or the academic literature reveals this shared concern with governance among the revisionist critics.

EPA's reinvention efforts in the 1990s enjoyed mixed success. To be fair, it undertook these initiatives with the political and legal equivalent of having one hand tied behind its back. Despite the dissatisfaction with regulation as it existed then, there certainly was no consensus in the politics stream as to what should replace it. Nor had any statutes authorized these initiatives. Decades of political conflict and distrust had created barriers to change. A clearer political commitment and more skillful leadership might have delivered more impressive results, but the barriers nonetheless were formidable.

The first major reinvention initiative of the Clinton years, begun in 1994, illustrates the pitfalls of innovating under less-than-favorable circumstances and without a clear sense of purpose. Called the Common

Sense Initiative (CSI), it assembled representatives of many points of view to recommend policy changes in six industry sectors: iron and steel, petroleum refining, computers and electronics, metal finishing, printing, and auto manufacturing. The EPA's goal was to work with six stakeholder groups (one per sector) to devise "cheaper, cleaner, smarter" policies. Reflecting a core idea of revisionist critics, EPA stated that the CSI was "based on the principle that we best protect the environment by setting tough environmental goals while encouraging flexibility and innovation in how the goals are met."[24]

The CSI was aimed at responding to complaints about regulation. As in Project XL, launched the next year, there was a concern that uniform national rules often did not make sense when they were applied to diverse circumstances. With its focus on industry sectors, the CSI was designed to overcome the mentality that categorized problems and their solutions by environmental medium. The use of stakeholder panels reflected a perceived need to involve diverse interests in a collaborative process.[25] Conceptually, the CSI incorporated many elements of the revisionist critique under one big tent.

It probably was too big a tent and not well constructed, as it turned out. The goals were so vague, the means so diffuse, and the procedural rules of the game so open-ended that the enterprise was doomed almost from the start. It would be an understatement to say that the CSI accomplished little, at least in terms of lasting policy change. The petroleum refining group in particular foundered on the deep distrust that existed among industry and environmentalists. Some modest proposals came out of the auto, computer-electronics, iron-steel, and printing groups, although they fell well short of the expectations set out in the CSI charter. The metal-finishing group achieved more, largely because it had been working under a well-defined plan, using ground rules that preceded the CSI.[26] Still, some participants saw value at least in the attempt. It certainly presented opportunities for interaction. In 1996 and 1997 alone, Jan Mazurek reports, the various panels and subcommittees making up the CSI met 319 times. "CSI's primary benefit," she observes, "was of the 'soft' variety."[27] Indeed, it is fair to say the CSI offered useful lessons for the reinvention initiatives that followed, but actual policy and environmental results were limited in their effects.[28]

The CSI and the cases that follow were not the only significant efforts at EPA to reinvent regulation. For example, in April 1998, EPA issued a final rule that combined water and air standards for pulp and paper mills. It defined effluent guidelines for water discharges, limits for wastewater discharges, and standards for hazardous air pollutants. In addition to combining rules across different media, however, this "cluster" rule also offered "incentives to reward and encourage mills that implement pollution prevention beyond regulatory requirements."[29] Mills committing to advanced technologies that would push the edge of the envelope and set a course for the "mill of the future" could qualify for reduced monitoring, reduced inspections and penalties, and greater permit certainty, as well as public recognition. In the end, few mills took advantage of the advanced technologies program. The incentives that were offered apparently were not enough to justify the firms making possibly risky investments in new technologies and paper products made with a chlorine-free process.

Another promising innovation undertaken in the late 1990s and early 2000s is flexible air permits. As noted earlier, firms often complain about the time and uncertainty involved in permitting, especially when they want to get approval for new processes that respond to customer demands on a tight schedule. Flexible permits address this concern by allowing plants to operate within plant-wide caps that are more stringent than individual permit limits but that allow more flexibility and do not require specific permit approvals for process changes. The EPA implemented several such permits on a pilot basis and found they encouraged emission reductions and pollution prevention beyond the existing permit limits; they also helped companies operate more efficiently by reducing the time and uncertainty in changing production processes. By 2005, EPA was developing a rule to authorize flexible air permits more broadly and apply the lessons learned from the pilot projects.[30] Although these were not multimedia permits like the New Jersey pilots that are discussed in chapter 6, they took an administratively challenging process and accommodated the needs of permitting agencies and industry while delivering a better environmental result. They illustrate the kind of incremental innovation that will promote the transition to a new regulation discussed in chapter 7.

To explore the lessons of reinvention further, the next section presents three case studies of other innovation programs: voluntary challenge programs, alternative regulatory agreements (Project XL), and the Performance Track. They shared two features common to voluntary initiatives generally. First, they were carried out without specific statutory authority. Legally, EPA was freelancing. This was a weakness because it limited what EPA could do. It also was a strength because it enabled government to respond to issues and try new ideas without having to meet detailed legal prescriptions. The second shared feature is a consequence of the first. Participation was voluntary. Firms took part because they saw benefits in doing so. Just why they participated has been the subject of research that is discussed later. What matters is that firms stepped forward and entered into new relationships with agencies. This simple fact may be more important in the long run than any actual results that were achieved.

The OECD report cited earlier defined two types of government-sponsored initiatives: negotiated agreements between industry and government and those in which government invites participation from industry. Of the cases discussed here, Project XL clearly illustrates the first. Voluntary challenge programs and the Performance Track fit the second type. This chapter briefly describes the iniatives, the motives for participating in them, and the lessons that may be drawn. We begin with voluntary challenge programs. They came first and built a foundation for what would follow.

Voluntary Challenge Programs

Several federal initiatives in the 1990s tested the notion that firms improve environmentally only when they are forced to do so by regulations.[31] In challenge programs, government selects an issue, usually one for which it lacks legal authority to do much of anything, and challenges industry and others to voluntarily achieve measurable results. Participants usually report on their progress and receive recognition and possibly other symbolic benefits from government for their accomplishments. In the United States during the 1990s, many voluntary challenge programs were designed to achieve climate change and pollution prevention goals, especially measures incorporated under the Clinton administration's Climate Action Program.

Not all voluntary programs fit this description of a challenge program. By late 2005, of more than sixty voluntary programs listed on EPA's "Partners" web site, fewer than ten involved efforts to get industry and others to commit to achieving and reporting on measurable goals.[32] The other programs are technical assistance or partnership activities that offer information and promote cooperation but do not necessarily challenge participants to achieve measurable goals. Examples of programs that do not ask for action toward specific goals are the Landfill Methane Outreach Program, Design for the Environment, and the Water Use Efficiency Program. These may produce environmental and business benefits and change relationships between government and industry, but they do not ask participants to publicly define and report on quantitative goals, so they are not the topic of this discussion.

The mold for challenge programs based on voluntary commitments was cast with the 33/50 program launched by Administrator William Reilly in 1991. Early rounds of reporting under the Toxics Release Inventory had revealed that many kinds of toxic releases were not covered by existing regulations. Rather than seek legal authority to control them, Reilly challenged industry to reduce them voluntarily. The EPA invited firms to commit publicly to reducing releases of seventeen priority TRI chemicals by 33 percent in 1992 and 50 percent in 1995. In exchange, EPA would recognize the companies for their participation and achievements. To encourage participation, Reilly and EPA implied that a failure to voluntarily make reductions could lead to new regulations.

According to EPA's accounting, 33/50 succeeded. In the end, reported reductions exceeded the original 33 and 50 percent goals, leading to emission cuts of 491 million and 744 pounds, respectively. Nevertheless, there has been criticism of this accounting. Studies by the General Accountability Office and INFORM concluded that EPA had overstated the program's success by counting reductions achieved before 1991, when it began, and by including reductions from firms that were not part of the program. Another criticism was that the reductions were achieved mostly through pollution control and recycling, not by reducing pollution at the source, which was the preferred method.[33]

Still, the 33/50 program—not just its results but the very idea of 33/50—struck a chord. Until then, industry had acted to protect the environment when it was forced to do so by government rules. In a zero-sum universe, amoral calculators do not act to protect the environment unless they are legally compelled to do so. The 33/50 program suggested that the potential for win-win solutions was not just a theoretical construct. If firms will voluntarily reduce releases of harmful chemicals to gain recognition from EPA as well as to avoid more stringent and unpredictable regulation what else would they do if they were challenged by government?

This initial response to 33/50 triggered a steady flow of programs based on voluntary commitments in the 1990s, stimulated and funded in large part by the Clinton administration's Climate Action Plan. Begun in 1994, WasteWise challenged firms to commit to reducing the volumes of solid waste they generated. ClimateWise (later replaced by Climate Leaders) induced firms to reduce releases of greenhouse gases. In what became the largest voluntary program of all, Energy Star challenged computer makers, and later manufacturers of other products, to achieve more energy-efficient designs. Later, the federal government announced it would give preference to Energy Star products in purchasing decisions, an action that offered clear business value to participants.

By the early 2000s, voluntary challenge programs were active in several areas. In Climate Leaders, launched in February 2002, whether or not firms commit to measurable goals is optional. Of some seventy partners listed in August 2005, thirty-nine had made such commitments. For example, S.C. Johnson committed to a 23 percent reduction in greenhouse gases per pound of product by 2005, using a 2000 baseline; Pfizer committed to a 35 percent reduction per dollar of revenue by 2007, with a 2000 baseline; and Eastman Kodak committed to a 10 percent reduction between 2002 and 2008.[34] Others that may be classified as challenge programs included the Green Power Partnership, National Partnership for Environmental Priorities, and WasteWise, which by mid-2005 had grown to more than 1,400 partners. The Performance Track resembles these challenge programs but it differs in so many respects that it is discussed separately.

A recurring issue for EPA is how challenge programs fit together and how they link with the regulatory programs that overwhelmingly define its work. An EPA study in 1999 found that less than 1 percent of agency resources went to voluntary programs; the bulk of that was for the well-funded Energy Star. Most were started at the initiative of specific offices or as a broader effort to address issues for which an administration did not have or seek statutory authority. Although many industry leaders have participated in these programs, many firms also complain that the range and variety of such programs and the lack of business benefits beyond that of recognition limit their value.[35] In recent years, EPA has initiated efforts to achieve more coherence and coordination among its voluntary programs. Still, although there is some coordination, there are few or no strategic links among them or an overall plan for how they should fit with regulation.

Why the interest in challenge programs? From the agency side, they responded to the gap between what many people thought needed to be done and what the prevailing political climate allowed them to do. As the old regulation came under growing criticism, support for merely expanding it and making it more stringent declined, especially after passage of the revised Clean Air Act in 1990. In John Kingdon's terms, the problem stream was changing, but the politics stream was at a stalemate. The policy stream adapted by getting results through voluntary action that did not require the consent of the politics stream.

In addition, for their advocates, these programs were a way of changing the old adversarial relationships among government, industry, and environmentalists. Here at last were things that everyone could agree on: that greenhouse gases should be reduced, that less solid waste should be generated, and that products should be designed to use less energy. Debates about legal rights and regulatory controls could be replaced with discussions about preventing pollution, working with stakeholders, using resources more efficiently, and raising the performance bar. After decades of often intense regulatory conflict, challenge programs were a breath of fresh air for people in government and industry. Although the results are difficult to measure, the programs surely have had positive effects on government–business relations, at least among the more progressive firms that participate in them.

Why did industry cooperate? Why would some 13,000 firms agree to work cooperatively with EPA, in most cases committing to report publicly on their ability to meet goals that went beyond any legal obligations? This question has drawn a great deal of interest from researchers.[36] Their answers reflect the changes that occurred in the strategic context for environmental management in the 1980s and 1990s, as assumptions about an inevitable zero sum were replaced by a belief in potential win-wins. This belief that environmental and economic successes are not always at odds made voluntary challenge programs possible.

The available evidence suggests four main reasons why firms participate in challenge programs. All are consistent with arguments used in chapter 4 to explain the greening of industry. One is recognition from government and by extension, from others, such as investors, employees, insurers, and communities. Firms compete on many dimensions, including public image and reputation. Customers, suppliers, employees, communities, investors—all may be favorably impressed by EPA recognition of a firm's environmental achievements. In the terms of Reinhardt's analysis, firms take part because it helps to differentiate them and their products and perhaps to gain a first-mover advantage over their competitors.

Another reason for participating is the opportunity to develop positive relationships with regulators. To qualify for these programs, a firm or facility must pass a federal and state compliance screen. This means it has an acceptable compliance record and may be recognized as a good actor in a legal sense as well as being committed to achieving certain goals. Furthermore, should compliance issues arise, a firm may be better able to resolve them cooperatively, with fewer legal sanctions and harm to its reputation. Administrative changes, such as permitting modifications, may come easier and faster. A firm may also have better access to government when it wants to influence policy. In Reinhardt's terms, taking part in challenge programs helps firms manage risk and uncertainty by developing more predictable, collaborative relationships with regulators. It also may help them deal with competition by giving them access to information about possible regulatory changes or providing them with opportunities to participate in innovative projects—such as flexible permitting—that could give them an advantage over their competitors.

A third reason companies participate is to gain access to information and resources. This may be especially appealing to small and medium-sized firms. The EPA does provide limited forms of technical assistance for firms that want to commit to reducing waste, improving energy efficiency, using less water, or preventing pollution in other ways. A firm may become part of a community for developing and sharing best practices. This may help cut internal operating costs and reduce regulatory uncertainty. Small firms also may benefit from opportunities to interact with the larger, more innovative ones and have access to their resources and expertise as a result of their involvement in voluntary challenge programs.

Yet a fourth reason that has not been appreciated sufficiently in the literature is that participation in voluntary programs gives leverage to internal change agents in firms. Often the agent is a plant or corporate environmental manager; at other times it may be someone in the corporate business unit. People within a firm that want to strengthen its commitment to pollution prevention, environmental management systems, product stewardship, or other aspects of its environmental policies may use government voluntary programs to obtain a public commitment and hold the firm or facility accountable for its performance. Once a commitment is made publicly and a company begins to receive attention as part of a program, internal change agents may find that their leverage for getting the necessary investments and decisions made to achieve those commitments is far greater than it might have been. These internal dynamics should receive more attention in the research on voluntary programs. All four of these reasons apply to the two other voluntary programs that are discussed in the next section. What the next two offer that challenge programs do not, however, is some kind of connection to how one is treated under the regulatory system.

What is missing in challenge programs is that link with regulation. Taking part in WasteWise, Climate Leaders, or other such programs does not lead to more flexible permitting, less reporting, or other preferential treatment. At the same time, however, the costs of participating are minimal. Firms may commit to goals in writing, but they do not assume formal legal obligations. They may report their results, often without verification. Often, reporting is not even required. Challenge programs offer modest benefits but at the same time impose few burdens. If they are to provide stepping-stones to a new regulation, they need at some point to connect with the regulatory programs that overwhelmingly define government's relationship with industry. Two other programs coming out of the reinvention era—Project XL and the Performance

Track—were designed explicitly to link voluntary efforts by industry with regulation. Although they were built upon government's experience with challenge programs, they differ in this crucial respect.

Project Excellence and Leadership (XL)

A core premise of reinvention generally is that the people closest to the action (on the proverbial shop floor) know more about how to solve problems than those farther away. A corollary is that the people making the chemicals, semiconductors, autos, or steel know more about how to reduce pollution and make safer products than regulators. Yet regulation in the United States is based on the premise that government knows best, not only in defining what goals to meet but deciding how to meet them.

Often failed policy innovations turn out to be successful because they are so instructive. This was the case with a project EPA undertook with the Amoco Corporation at a refinery in Yorktown, Virginia, in the early 1990s. The project originated with a conversation between an EPA policy official and an Amoco manager in 1989. The topic was how regulation and information drive behavior at an industrial facility. Typically, facility environmental managers are focused on maintaining compliance—responding to a range of specific rules, by category of release, from many levels of government—rather than on reducing environmental impacts in a comprehensive or cost-effective way. If facility managers knew more about overall releases and had flexibility in deciding how and where to reduce them, could they deliver better results than they do under current regulations?

With this question, the project was born. The EPA and Amoco agreed to conduct an inventory of environmental releases at the Yorktown plant. Their goal was to determine the best overall strategy for the facility. They found that the existing rules did not offer the most cost-effective approach for controlling pollution. For example, to meet existing rules, Amoco had to reduce air emissions of hydrocarbons that are due to fugitive releases (i.e., leaks) at a cost of $2,400 per ton. However, the project team found that Amoco could reduce hydrocarbon even more by controlling emissions from its dock transfer operations, where the oil is unloaded from ships, at one-fifth the cost per ton.[37] These emissions were unregulated. Here was a chance to get a better result, and for less money.

This also was an example of Bardach and Kagan's concept of regulatory unreasonableness, in which uniform rules do not make sense when they are applied to specific circumstances. In the end, EPA decided it lacked the authority to trade off one set of controls (on fugitive emissions) for another (those from the transfer operations), regardless of the better results that could have been realized at less cost. Still, the Amoco project illustrated what was widely known in business circles: Many opportunities for cost-effective pollution reduction are not pursued because of highly prescriptive rules. In *The Death of Common Sense*, his critique of what he argued were the stultifying effects of overly prescriptive regulations, Philip Howard later cited the rule in the Amoco case as "almost perfect in its failure: It maximized the cost to Amoco while minimizing the benefit to the public."[38]

Project XL drew its inspiration from the Amoco experience. The lesson drawn by later policy makers was that government should specify results but should allow industry more discretion in determining how to achieve them. If opportunities for cost-effective environmental improvement were being lost at this one facility, then what opportunities were being lost every day, around the country, because of overly specific rules that allowed no flexibility for "common sense" solutions?

Announced as part of the program for Reinventing Environmental Regulation in March 1995, Project XL offered a simple quid pro quo: Regulated firms would have "the flexibility to develop alternative strategies that will replace or modify specific regulatory requirements on the condition that they produce greater environmental benefits."[39] Government and industry would work together to improve the environment *and* the economy. It was the classic win-win situation. Government would pressure industry for results, but empower managers on the shop floor to decide how best to achieve them. Stakeholder panels would represent community interests and provide a citizen perspective for changes that, admittedly, would test the limits of EPA's legal authority.

The mechanics of XL went like this: Once EPA approved an initial proposal, the applicant worked with federal, state, and local authorities and citizen groups on a final project agreement. The agreement defined the steps the company would take to improve its performance, the flexibility (in the form of exceptions to existing rules) regulators would provide, the ways to measure performance, and the expected environmental benefits that would be achieved. Once the agencies approved and local stakeholders agreed, the final project agreement became legally enforceable, allowing a company to implement its program. Still, these agreements may be the subject of litigation if they are challenged under the citizen suit provisions of environmental statutes. This concern about litigation had a chilling effect on what the government thought it could commit to in the agreements and made companies more cautious as well.[40]

The public announcements for XL set a goal of fifty applications within the first year. At first, there was a flurry of interest. Over a dozen companies applied in the initial round. Most were large firms like Intel, 3M, Union Carbide, and Merck. Soon after the launch, however, the flow slowed to a trickle, as several policy issues arose and other applicants waited to see how they were handled.

Three issues in particular dogged the XL process over the next few years. One was the level of environmental benefits a project should have to deliver. The original notice asked for benefits greater than what would be achieved under existing rules. This implied a modest goal of incremental benefits. Under pressure from environmentalists, EPA soon turned this into a goal of "superior" performance, which many interpreted as superior in an absolute sense rather than just measurably better than existing performance. Like such absolutes as truth or justice, the concept of superior environmental performance is, in a practical sense, undefinable. It could be and often was debated endlessly. In the Intel negotiations, for example, although the local stakeholder panel had endorsed the agreement, the Natural Resources Defense Council (not a member of the panel) kept pressing for more. An Intel issues manager expressed her frustration with the NRDC and EPA by commenting at one point that "We're being measured against some theoretical nirvana. No matter what we do. It's not enough."[41] Similar frustrations surely were expressed in the 3M and other negotiations as well.

A second issue went right to the heart of reinvention as it was practiced in the 1990s—the design and legitimacy of stakeholder processes. The best illustration is the Intel project, which EPA eventually did approve. Intel worked closely with its local stakeholder group, holding hundreds of hours of meetings as it negotiated the final project agreement. The local group raised issues, but it supported the agreement that came out of the negotiations. As the process unfolded, however, national advocacy groups like the Natural Resources Defense Council, and even some regional groups from other parts of the country, pressed for a role in the Intel discussions. They argued that if, as EPA said consistently, Project XL was a way to test ideas locally that could be applied nationally, stakeholders from elsewhere should have a say in the result.

This is an interesting theory of political representation. If we adopt the premise, as most reinventors did, that those affected by a decision should be part of the process for making it, and if the purpose of a program is to generate ideas for national policy change, then perhaps EPA should have expanded representation beyond the local stakeholder groups. However, this quickly reaches a point of absurdity. For example, a facility manager in Minnesota told me that at one point an EPA staffer proposed to him that all state environmental agencies should have been among his project stakeholders because the project could generate lessons that would be applied nationally. Although it was obviously impractical, this comment suggests where an uncritical approach to stakeholder involvement may lead.

The third issue was the lack of a statutory basis for XL. Voluntary challenge programs are appealing because they enable people to think about the environment without being too constrained by legal prescriptions. In contrast, Project XL was designed specifically to modify requirements. The particularity of most environmental laws, the complexity of the regulations already on the books, and disagreements within EPA over how much flexibility to allow imposed major constraints on what the project agreements could authorize. Like other reinvention efforts, XL suffered "from the general problem that no legal authority exists for EPA to relax certain requirements in exchange for greater environmental benefits."[42] The very prescriptiveness of the existing laws and regulations that XL was designed to overcome became an important limiting factor in the project agreements.

The first few years of XL were difficult. Within EPA, there were disagreements over the goals, criteria, and even the legal validity of the program. Still, even after the hard lessons of these first years, XL began to show progress. The last year of the Clinton administration brought a renewed commitment to making XL work and completing the many negotiations under way. The EPA showed an excellent capacity for learning by attempting to clarify several issues that had come up and providing guidance to participants.[43] In a September 2000 report on XL, EPA was finally able to list fifty projects meeting the target set in March 1995. These included projects with International Paper, IBM, Anderson Corporation, NASA White Sands, and PPG Industries, among others. The transaction costs of negotiating the project agreements could be substantial. In the seventeen months of negotiation needed to get the Intel agreement in place, for example, the firm and the government together spent nearly $600,000.[44] There was a learning curve, however; by 2001 the average cost of negotiating an XL agreement had fallen to about $100,000.[45]

The EPA's *Comprehensive Report* on Project XL, based on the experience through 2000, documents many of the results. It provides a detailed assessment of each project and the lessons learned. Whether the long-term effects of these projects will come even close to the expectations XL created is uncertain. The EPA lists some seventy innovations coming out of the more than fifty projects. At times these led to visible policy change. An example is the air permitting innovation known as plant-wide applicability limits that was tested in the Intel, Merck, Weyerhaeuser, and Anderson projects. This experience later proved to be useful in developing EPA's new system for flexible air permits in the early 2000s. Other researchers have found evidence that participants in XL were able to deliver better environmental results than they otherwise would have shown.[46] Consistent with the original intent of the program, the EPA *Comprehensive Report* concluded that the "true value" of XL lies in "revealing improvements that can be applied either voluntarily or through regulatory change to achieve better results on a much broader scale."[47]

Whatever its long-term effects, Project XL is worth studying for several reasons. Unlike challenge programs, it aimed to engage the regulatory system. It was designed to link measurable improvements to enhanced flexibility that would yield economic benefits to firms, as well as give them an opportunity to do better environmentally. It also acknowledged that the old regulation, with its rigidity, high transaction costs, and philosophy of bureaucratic control, could hinder performance improvements as well as being costly for firms. Here, in EPA's own program, was a validation of much of the revisionist critique. Project XL also provided experience with negotiated agreements, which have been used far more extensively in Europe and Japan than in the United States. If, as my final chapter suggests, negotiated agreements between government and industry offer a promising tool for a new regulation, then the XL experience offers some important lessons.

The National Environmental Performance Track

A characteristic of the old regulation is that at least officially, everybody is treated pretty much the same. The goal is total compliance. Those who fall short face the prospect of financial penalties and public shaming. Those who do better are not of much interest to regulators until the next inspection occurs. Interactions among agencies and industry emphasize the negative, with many sticks and few carrots.

There are several problems with this approach. First, it means that regulators may not be using their resources wisely. They may be spending as much time and effort overseeing the very good actors as they are overseeing the very poor ones. Second, it means all facilities are subjected to the same transaction costs—in reporting, monitoring, record keeping, and permitting—regardless of how well they perform. Because the system has to be designed to ensure the compliance of the lowest common denominator (that is, the likely noncompliers), these transaction costs are substantial. Third, this "everybody is the same" approach offers the better facilities little incentive to do more than comply. Their overwhelming concern is with avoiding sticks, not earning carrots, especially when there are few carrots to be earned.

When much of industry was resisting environmental controls, and many firms had trouble just staying in compliance, the exclusive emphasis on sticks over carrots made sense. As the performance of many firms has improved over the past two decades, however, it has made less sense. Seeking to reduce costs, improve their image, avoid liabilities, impress investors, and satisfy customers, many firms do far more than comply. Still, however green a company may be, regulators officially do not care, at least not in how they treat firms in permitting, enforcement, monitoring, and other regulatory functions.

The idea of distinguishing firms based on beyond-compliance performance was articulated in the mid-1990s in the Aspen Institute's Alternative Path project. Many states began to create performance tracks before EPA designed its own. In the late 1990s, New Jersey created a Gold and a two-level Silver Track program. Oregon created a Green Permits program that defined three levels of performance and offered, among other incentives, reduced permitting fees for participants. By mid-2005, the number of state programs that incorporated the performance track concept had grown to more than twenty, including Texas, Virginia, Utah, and Georgia, among others. Some offered only recognition; others reduced permit fees or gave expedited treatment to participants on administrative issues. A few of these state programs are discussed in more detail in chapter 6.

The EPA signaled an interest in performance-based regulation in July 1999 in its *Aiming for Excellence* report. It described the concept as one of "allowing top performers more flexibility in how they meet regulatory requirements if they do more to protect the environment and assure accountability."[48] To apply the concept, EPA launched its National Environmental Performance Track in June 2000. This was the final reinvention initiative of Carol Browner's term at EPA. That it was launched only six months after design work began in January 2000 was due largely to her strong personal support.[49] She was able to leave a legacy that carried over into the next administration.

The EPA solicited applications from facilities that could meet four criteria: a record of sustained compliance with environmental laws, use of an environmental management system that included several key elements, ways of identifying and responding to community issues, and a commitment to continuous improvement in environmental performance.[50] Applicants meet the last criterion by showing recent improvement in at least two indicators of environmental performance and committing to goals in four other indicators during their three years of membership. These goals are drawn from a list of some three dozen indicators falling into twelve categories of environmental performance. Some are regulated categories (such as air emissions or water discharges) while others are unregulated by EPA (such as energy, water, or materials use and product impacts). To qualify for membership, applicants commit to achieving results that exceed their existing regulatory requirements.

Some 250 facilities applied in the first round, and about 225 were accepted. Overall, by April 2005, 601 facilities had applied, of which 482 were accepted.[51] However, the number of members at any time is lower; it stood at about 400 in April 2006. Unlike most other voluntary programs, facilities that do not maintain their qualifications are dropped. Some 50 facilities have been asked to leave, typically because of deficiencies in their EMS or failure to meet other obligations, such as filing an annual performance report. Some have withdrawn or decided not to renew their membership. The EPA and state agencies visit about 10 percent of the members annually to assess their performance, seek feedback on the program itself, and build more collaborative relationships. Facilities must renew their membership every three years. As an incentive to qualify for the program and promote its goals, members receive several forms of recognition from EPA and the states and become eligible for regulatory incentives that reduce costs and increase flexibility. Other benefits include recognition by firms that rate socially responsible investments, the possibility of reduced insurance premiums, and more cooperative relationships with federal and state regulators. The strategy is to encourage environmental results from industry by providing carrots rather than threatening to use sticks.

Although interest in Performance Track has come mostly from the larger private firms, particularly those in heavily regulated sectors, members also include smaller manufacturing facilities, the service sector, federal agencies, and local government as well. Still, three-fourths of the members are from the manufacturing sector, with chemicals and electronics accounting for about one-fourth of the total. Participation is by facility, but several firms have decided to participate with multiple facilities, including Johnson & Johnson, International Paper, 3M, Dupont, Baxter, Pfizer, Rockwell-Collins, Lockheed Martin, and Bristol-Myers Squibb. In July 2004, to encourage more of such company-wide participation, EPA announced that firms that participate broadly in the facility-based program and follow certain practices at the company level could be recognized as Performance Track Corporate Leaders as an additional form of recognition. The EPA selected Johnson & Johnson, Baxter, and Rockwell-Collins as the first Corporate Leaders.

Based on lessons learned from previous reinvention experience, especially Project XL, Performance Track was designed to be low on transaction costs. Although there are discussions with facilities on their applications, especially on the performance commitments, participation is not determined through case-by-case negotiation as it was in XL. The EPA works with states in reviewing applications and consults with local officials and community representatives, but does not routinely visit an applicant's site before making a decision. Applicants certify that their EMS contains the required elements and verify that their EMS has been independently assessed. The EPA and state agencies conduct site visits with several facilities annually to verify that they are meeting the program criteria and share information. Participants must complete an annual report each year or they are removed from the program. Similarly, when serious deficiencies with respect to the EMS or other program criteria are found, as occurred especially with some of the initial members, they must be corrected within a reasonable time or the facility is asked to withdraw.

Performance Track is noteworthy in several respects. Like XL, but unlike other voluntary programs, it was designed to engage the regulatory system. From the start, the intent was to treat program members differently from other facilities. For example, EPA considers Performance Track facilities to be a "low priority for routine inspection," which means they generally will not be the subject of an EPA inspection without cause (although states still inspect them). In addition, EPA has initiated regulatory changes that will reduce routine compliance reporting and grant specific kinds of regulatory flexibility for program members.[52] The plan is to expand these regulatory incentives as the program matures. These incentives reflected the core premise of the program: Facilities with a strong compliance record, a sound EMS, community outreach, and demonstrated performance beyond what the law specifies do not require the same level of regulatory oversight as others.

Also significant was the emphasis on performance measurement. As a regulatory agency, EPA historically has been interested in performance only as it affects the compliance status of a facility. Compliance is a narrow measure of performance. Performance Track set out a much more comprehensive framework. It includes areas of performance where EPA has regulatory authority as well as those where it does not. The goal is not only to encourage beyond-compliance behavior but also to improve the ability of government and firms to measure performance. Members report not only on their absolute performance but also their results relative to changes in levels of production or other normalizing factor. The overall program results are documented in an annual progress report issued in April of each year. In addition, the applications and annual reports of each member are available to the public on the Performance Track web site. With its emphasis on measurement, Performance Track may be said to provide the most comprehensive and systematic performance reporting of any voluntary environmental program to date.[53]

Of course, the fact that members of Performance Tack have shown environmental results beyond what the law requires does not mean that they did it just because of the program. At best, government voluntary programs serve to reinforce and perhaps to exploit the many other factors that cause firms to behave in environmentally responsible ways. To some degree, Performance Track allows high-performing facilities and firms to claim credit for what they are already doing. However, membership in this kind of voluntary program may encourage firms to do more, such as strengthening their performance goals and ability to measure results, enhancing their environmental management system, or increasing their level of community outreach in order to bring themselves to the level needed to qualify for the program's benefits. In addition, once they are in, their visibility and public commitments as members places pressure on them to maintain and even improve their qualifications. To the extent that they gain more flexibility and are subject to lower regulatory transaction costs as program members, they also may be in a position to reduce their own operating costs and make other kinds of environmental improvements. Furthermore, if relationships and opportunities for dialogue and information sharing among members and with government improve, there should be other changes in behavior that may translate into better environmental results.

Unlike Project XL, which had largely run its course by the early 2000s, Performance Track was active and growing by the fall of 2005.

Although it began under administrator Browner in the Clinton administration, it was endorsed strongly by administrators Whitman, Leavitt, and Johnson in the Bush administration. In addition to maintaining a steady growth rate and demonstrating the environmental benefits that may be gained though this kind of voluntary program, EPA was working to integrate Performance Track into its planning and regulatory systems and to strengthen its relationship to state environmental agencies, especially those with similar programs. As a sign of EPA's intentions, the agency's Innovations Action Council, a group of senior officials who set policy for innovation projects, named Performance Track as a top priority for agency-wide scale-up in 2004. Still, the agency investment in the program has lagged behind expectations. In this sense, Performance Track illustrates the difficulty in institutionalizing new approaches in a complex, interdependent system that still is founded on the principles of the old regulation.

Learning from the Three Kinds of Reinvention

What lessons may be drawn from these initiatives? First, they show that cooperation is possible. Different interests may set aside old antagonisms and achieve measurable goals. Many in industry are willing to take risks and cooperate with EPA, something that was almost unthinkable thirty years ago. Moreover, their participation illustrates how government carrots may be consistent with the business interests of firms. These efforts also show that agencies may be effective by being more than just regulators. As a source of information, validator of best practices, and disseminator of ideas, agencies may play new and varied roles in environmental protection. Finally, these initiatives allow government and business to search for solutions in an extended learning process, a point that is explored more in the next chapter.

Voluntary challenge programs may take us only so far. Many of the results ascribed to them are suspect. Beginning with the claims about 33/50, advocates often were more concerned with claiming credit than establishing the validity of their programs. The reality is that sponsors of challenge programs must constantly seek participants and show results if they are to justify their continuation. As a result, there has been too little concern with holding participants accountable and documenting results. Lacking statutory grounding, often with uncertain budgets, program managers sometimes have stressed public relations over the neutral presentation of environmental results. It is difficult to find evidence that challenge programs achieved environmental results that were verifiably better than business as usual would have delivered.

Assessments of Project XL were influenced by the overblown expectations that were created from the start. With all the hyperbole about how "bold" it was and President Clinton claiming that government would "throw away the rule book" in search of commonsense solutions, probably anything EPA and industry did would have fallen short. Still, XL offers stepping-stones toward a new regulation. First, it reinforced the idea, introduced by the Amoco project and much anecdotal evidence, that regulation was so fragmented, prescriptive, and inflexible that it actually could hinder innovation and cost-effective solutions. Lessons from many of the fifty projects document the revisionist critics' claim that regulation was less effective and more costly than it could be. In this light, XL offers case studies on the limits of the old regulation.

A second lesson concerns the potential and pitfalls of negotiating environmental agreements that create legally enforceable contracts between government and industry. True, the transaction costs were high, and there was much delay and uncertainty along the way, but high transaction costs are not inevitable. A study of the first eleven XL projects by Resources for the Future found that the transaction costs per project came to $460,000, of which $350,000 was borne by the facility and $110,000 by the EPA regional office. The facilities reported that only about one-fifth of these costs were related to stakeholder interaction. A much larger source of costs (half of the total) was interacting with and gaining final approval from EPA. "Thus," the study concludes, "EPA management problems were identified by our respondents as being the most important sources of costs."[54] The meaning of superior environmental performance and the lack of coordination among regional, state, and headquarters offices were seen as the more time-consuming issues in gaining EPA approval. With more experience, clearer legal authority, and better alignment within agencies, it should be possible to negotiate agreements more economically. Experience with innovation has shown that there are learning curves, and that new approaches may be implemented more efficiently over time. Better policy alignment within agencies also may reduce the transaction costs of innovation.

A third lesson concerns how and when to involve stakeholders. Throughout the 1990s, muddled thinking and unrealistic expectations about stakeholder roles plagued reinvention. Usually defined as anyone affected by a decision, the concept of stakeholder involvement was so vague and expandable that it was used as a justification for giving nearly any disaffected interest a veto. The notion that stakeholders should have to reach consensus rather than be part of a collaborative process complicated matters even more.[55] Consensus requires the consent by all or nearly all the parties to a process. Collaboration means that affected interests are consulted but do not necessarily have to consent before action is taken. Consensus sets a very high standard for innovation because some set of interests is nearly always likely to object. The key lesson learned was the importance of being clear about who participates and their roles. Otherwise, opponents use the stakeholder issue as a tactic for blocking action, as some did with XL. In this respect, there were signs of learning. In later projects, XL did shift from a consensus model to a more collaborative one. Based on the XL experience, Performance Track was designed from the start to promote collaboration, but not to achieve consensus on every aspect of the program's design.

The primary lesson of the Performance Track is that it is possible to rationally differentiate among facilities based on their performance. To the extent that agencies had recognized differences among facilities in the past, it had been informal and focused on the absence of negatives. Now EPA was formally differentiating among them to account for the presence of positives (the EMS, performance targets, and community outreach) as well as the absence of negatives (no major compliance issues.) Although this process will become more complex as the consequences of differentiation grow, the Performance Track demonstrates that a formal tiering of regulated and other facilities is feasible. Some firms and facilities do better than others, and it is possible to analytically recognize this, based on the available information.

Performance Track also offers lessons on the role of an EMS and performance measurement. Early assessments suggested that an independent review of an EMS lends more confidence in its quality. As a consequence, in January 2004, EPA began requiring applicants to have undergone an independent assessment of their EMS, although it stopped short of requiring formal, third-party certification. Other lessons of this program, reinforced by some of the more recent EMS research, suggest that identifying one's "significant environmental aspects" provides both a process and a discipline for continuous improvement. In addition, having facilities commit to and report on performance has yielded valuable lessons on setting and measuring progress toward concrete goals. Participation in programs like Performance Track also offers another benefit by strengthening the hand of advocates within facilities and firms for progressive and innovative environmental policies.

Of course, changes were occurring at the federal and state levels beyond those discussed here. Several initiatives in the 1990s and early 2000s improved relationships among government, business, and others; created a basis for more collaboration; explored solutions on the basis of industry and economic sectors; and used technical assistance to complement the traditional stick of deterrence.[56] There were many efforts to make the old regulation more workable. In many respects, these efforts may be studied as modest stepping-stones to a new regulation. Still, except perhaps for the industry sector projects and some EMS activities, these initiatives were aimed at making incremental changes at the margins of the old regulation rather than achieving something more fundamental.[57]

Voluntary Environmental Programs and the New Regulation

Tired of the stale old debate over having more or less regulation, in the 1990s the revisionist critics called for a different kind of regulation. It would emphasize performance, cooperation, trust, and continuous improvement over bureaucratic controls, adversarialism, distrust, and compliance. In calling for change, critics envisioned a new system that would build upon and grow incrementally out of the old one. They were realistic, and they accepted the need for rules backed by government coercion. However, the limits in the old regulation, and the changes in problems, institutions, and economic relationships that had occurred, made it necessary to rethink and redesign regulation as it had existed for nearly three decades.

At the federal level in the 1990s, these efforts took the form of various reinvention initiatives, the more important of which have been discussed here. Seeing these initiatives in the context of an expanded international use of voluntary programs serves two purposes. First, it reinforces the point that dissatisfaction with the old and the search for a new regulation was not limited to the United States. Nor was it merely a superficial reaction to political events. It was part of a broader, deeper trend that is evident in many countries. Second, it links the lessons of reinvention with the lessons of voluntary programs more generally. Research on voluntary programs may help in understanding reinvention and drawing lessons for a new regulation. Despite the difficulties in evaluating the effects of voluntary programs, and there are several, more research may help to clarify the role of voluntary initiatives and their relationship to more conventional regulatory instruments. It is clear from most of the research, however, that voluntary programs are most effective when they are reinforced with or backed up by the prospect of regulation (sticks) or when government provides carrots that will encourage industry to participate and achieve results.[58] That voluntary programs have not shown impressive results on their own does not mean that they could not deliver better results when they are more effectively linked to government sticks and carrots.

Despite the several efforts to innovate, regulation in 2001 was not much different from what it had been in 1991. Behavior and relationships had changed somewhat; law and policy had changed very little. So William Ruckelshaus could write in 1998 that EPA had made progress, but "only at the margins of the agency's programs."[59] This statement was only slightly less valid by 2005. Why was change so difficult, and what lessons may be drawn from the experience?

Almost anyone who has studied reinvention in the 1990s agrees that the statutory framework posed major and probably insurmountable barriers to systemic change. The irony of reinvention was that the very system of laws and rules that was seen to require change was in fact a principal impediment to change. Fragmentation by environmental medium, a technology-based focus, and the specificity of laws and regulations created an atmosphere that was unsuited to innovation. As the next chapter argues, regulation was based on a model of what may be termed technical rather than conceptual or social learning. Put simply, there was too little play in the system to allow people to learn and adapt to what they had learned.

Of course, laws may be changed. Although there were proposals for second-generation legislation that would have allowed more legal discretion to innovate, these were not passed.[60] Even with existing laws, it may be possible to achieve enough agreement to allow more than marginal change. The EPA could have tried to stretch the limits of its authority on programs like the CSI, XL, and Performance Track more aggressively than it did, although at some legal risk. It generally did not, because there was by no means a consensus within EPA, nor among its core constituency groups, that a new regulation was workable or even desirable. Decades of distrust would not vanish overnight, as debates among industry and environmentalists revealed. Within government, many program and enforcement officials were still committed to the fundamental outlines of the old rules-and-deterrence model. Without determined leadership from the White House or Capitol Hill, these kinds of barriers are difficult to overcome.

Why the reluctance to change? A principal reason was fear of losing what had been gained over the past four decades. Many activists were convinced that loosening the fabric of the old regulation would lead to its eventual unraveling. Walter Rosenbaum has written that "many environmental organizations believe, or strongly suspect, that changes in regulatory procedures that appear to benefit industry, or other regulated interests, constitute an EPA 'sellout' to big business or its allies."[61] The old and not entirely unreasonable worries about agency capture still mattered. Add to this the concerns from enforcement and program offices and the national environmental organizations about the loss of influence that could result from a more flexible regulation, and it should not be surprising that many were reluctant to commit to change.

The view here is that EPA's innovation efforts in the 1990s, and the experience with voluntary initiatives generally, offer valuable stepping-stones toward a new regulation. Given the lack of statutory authority and conflict in the politics stream, these efforts were incremental. To be sure, realistic expectations and consistent leadership could have made XL and other programs more successful, but this should not obscure the lessons that may be drawn from the experience. Overall, these initiatives applied most of the ideas the revisionist critics had been advancing in the 1990s.

Of course, at least rhetorically, the reinvention era ended with the start of the George W. Bush administration in 2001. Still, with the exception of Project XL, many of the programs discussed here were continued under administrators Whitman, Leavitt, and Johnson. To be sure, there was always skepticism that voluntary programs could be used to forestall calls for additional regulation, especially for the issue of climate change, specifically regarding Climate Leaders. However, nearly all the efforts to address climate change had been voluntary under the Clinton administration as well. What is curious about the Bush leadership is that there was not a more concerted effort to expand on programs that offered a potential environmental and economic win-win (such as Performance Track) and enjoyed strong support from progressive firms. Such initiatives were continued and supported under Bush, but they were not embraced as a path to a more efficient and collaborative regulation. This topic is taken up the in the final chapter, which discusses the politics of a new regulation.

Before moving on to the new regulation, however, it is important to mine still other sources of ideas and experience. Our lesson drawing is not yet complete. Widespread recognition of the need for change was not unique to the federal government. It was part of a broader trend toward a postmodern regulation. Nor was the recognition of the need for change limited to the federal level, and certainly not to the United States. To explore these broader trends, the next chapter sets out elements of a conceptual framework for a new regulation and applies it to actions taken in several American states, to local watershed and ecosystem initiatives, and to environmental regulation in the Netherlands.

6

Pieces of the Puzzle: Lesson Drawing for a New Regulation

The critical issues of lesson-drawing are not whether we can learn anything elsewhere, but when, where, and how we learn.[1]

Chapters 4 and 5 examined trends in industry and the federal government that compel as well as support the transition to a new environmental regulation. Changes in at least the top-performing firms suggest a need to reconsider the regulatory strategies of the past three decades. The federal efforts to respond to these changes under the narrow banner of reinvention comprise an eclectic, often unfocused, but consistent attempt to undertake a shift toward a more flexible, performance-based, and collaborative approach that addresses the dissatisfaction with the old regulation.

This chapter expands on two themes that were introduced in chapter 5. The first is that reinvention in the 1990s was more than a superficial political response to the conservative assaults on environmental programs launched in the mid-1990s. The felt need to change regulation in this country reflected deeper social and economic changes that were visible in other nations, as well as at other levels of government in the United States. The second theme is that the 1990s offer fruitful opportunities for what Richard Rose calls lesson drawing in public policy.

The chapter considers four sources of ideas and experience. These will be used to inform the discussion in chapter 7, which outlines a new environmental regulation. The sources are:

· the social science literature on new patterns of governance, which suggests the underlying forces that are driving changes in postmodern governance (including regulation) and the forms they may take;

· innovations that are occurring in the American states, which parallel many of the ideas that have been applied at the federal level but which also offer additional sources of ideas and experience;

· illustrations of locally and community-based problem solving that have been labeled civic environmentalism and may be incorporated into the design of a new regulation; and

· experience in the Netherlands, which has shifted from a largely top-down, command-based regulation to one that is more collaborative, adaptable, and performance based.

The first source of ideas is entirely conceptual, so it offers no actual opportunity for drawing lessons. It is a valuable source of ideas on a new approach to regulation, however, because it places the topic in a historical and social context. It also suggests a conceptual foundation for drawing lessons from the other three sources and rethinking regulation more generally. The other sources reinforce the point regarding many of the perceived limitations in the old regulation and offer practical lessons for change.

Social Science Writing on Law and Governance

To invent a new environmental regulation, we need to rethink its conceptual foundations. This chapter suggests such a rethinking by discussing three perspectives from the literature on law and governance: reflexive law, social-political governance, and policy learning. These perspectives share a starting point: that the world is too complex and dynamic to be managed within a strictly modern concept of law, bureaucracy, and governance. At a theoretical level, many of the criticisms offered in this literature mirror the complaints various people have had about the weaknesses of U.S. environmental policy. If one looks carefully at the reports of the President's Council for Sustainable Development, the Aspen Institute, the Enterprise for the Environment, and the National Academy of Public Administration, they comprise an essentially postmodern critique of regulatory law and governance. Their complaints about inflexibility, legalism, hierarchy, and unresponsiveness reflect a common theme: A system that is modern in its design and operation needs to be adapted to a postmodern era.

Reflexive Law as a New Legal Rationality

Designing a new regulation means that we need to think differently about law and its place in environmental policy. The old regulation is based on a conception of law that is unsuited to the complexity and dynamism of contemporary economic and social life. This section discusses the concept of reflexive law, its relation to other forms of law, and its role in environmental regulation.

Gunther Teubner proposes reflexive law as a third and most recent stage in the evolution of legal systems. The concepts of formal and substantive law describe the first two stages. Formal law defines the relationships among private actors in society. Statutes and judicial interpretations regarding contracts and torts are examples. Formal law facilitates the growth of market economies, such as that in the United States, because it legitimates and structures private economic arrangements. A second and more recent stage, substantive law, is a legal strategy in which government intervenes in private social and economic arrangements to promote collective societal goals, such as safety and equity. It is the law of the regulatory state—environmental protection, occupational safety, food safety, and the like. Substantive law is more than just a way of structuring private relationships. It has a specific social purpose, which is why it is also called positive law. "Instead of delimiting spheres for autonomous private action, the law directly regulates social behavior by defining substantive prescriptions."[2] Substantive law is the Clean Air Act, the Clean Water Act, the Toxic Substances Control Act, and similar statutes.

Reflexive law is yet a third stage in the evolution of legal systems. How does it differ from the substantive law that is used so extensively in the old regulation? Reflexive law, Teubner writes, "seeks to design self-regulating social systems through norms of organization and procedure."[3] As a result, "legal control of social action is indirect and abstract, for the legal system only determines the organizational premises of future action."[4] The aim of reflexive law is creating incentives and procedures that induce people and organizations to assess their actions (hence the reflexivity) and adjust them to achieve socially desirable goals, rather then tell them directly what to do in all cases. Rather than relying just on negative incentives, such as penalties for noncompliance, a reflexive legal

strategy encourages behavioral change through a combination of negative and positive incentives. Positive incentives could include favorable
publicity, more collaborative relationships with regulators, more regulatory flexibility, and other measures.

Policy tools based on reflexive law have become common in the
United States and elsewhere. Consider the growing use of information
disclosure to influence behavior. The best example in the United States is
the Toxics Release Inventory. The EPA compiles and publishes TRI data
in an annual report, which often receives extensive media coverage. The
TRI does not directly require firms to install technology or otherwise
take steps to reduce their releases, but many firms have responded to the
negative publicity that may accompany the publication of TRI data by
reducing their releases of listed chemicals.[5]

Two other kinds of policy tools illustrate the concept of reflexive law.
One is environmental management systems, which were discussed in
chapter 4. The European Union incorporated EMS into public policy
through the Eco-Management and Auditing Scheme.[6] The EPA has
encouraged the greater use of EMS as well by incorporating them into
enforcement agreements and including them in voluntary programs like
the Performance Track. The combination of organizational, procedural,
and reporting provisions aims to create within firms the conditions for
self-critical reflection about behavior and how to improve it continuously. By offering incentives for firms to use an EMS, government thus
structures the behavior of business firms by "shaping both their procedures of internal discourse and their methods of coordination with other
social systems."[7]

A third illustration of reflexive law is market incentives, such as marketable permits. The emissions trading and acid rain trading programs
currently being used in the United States allocate allowances to sources
of air pollution in order to keep overall emissions at a predetermined
level. While an EMS induces reflection by specifying procedures, marketable permits do so by setting a goal and allowing firms to determine
how to reach it. Because they are used in conjunction with regulatory
standards, marketable permits should be seen as a hybrid of substantive
and reflexive law. They include a reflexive component, however, because
they create incentives and procedures that induce pollution sources

to behave in desired ways and that allow them some flexibility in making choices.

Reflexive law is playing a role in the transition to a new, more adaptable regulation. The goal of a reflexive strategy is to induce people and organizations to assess their behavior continually, so they may respond to new information, emerging technologies, and changing expectations. Used in combination with standards based on substantive law, a reflexive strategy allows a more adaptable, dynamic approach. Regulation in the United States and elsewhere has begun to incorporate reflexive law. This is one of many ways in which a new regulation has at least begun to emerge. Such mechanisms as information disclosure, management systems, and market incentives will be important elements in the new regulation.

Social-Political Governance

As noted, adversarial and distrustful relationships among government, business, and others are typically cited as weaknesses of the old regulation. A source of ideas on how relationships among government and other actors could change is the European literature on social-political governance.[8] The question these writers pose is this: How can dynamic, complex, and diverse social-political systems be governed more democratically and effectively? Their answer is to think in terms of entirely new conceptions of governance, owing to the limits of traditional, hierarchical ideas about governance in a rapidly changing world. For these writers, "the growing complexity, dynamics, and diversity of our societies, as 'caused by social, technological and scientific developments,' puts governing systems under such new challenges that new conceptions of governance are needed."[9]

Social-political governance involves new patterns of interaction among government and others in society. These patterns are not temporary, but are built into the structures and processes of governance. Distinctions between the public (the state, regulatory agencies) and the private (society, markets) are blurred as the boundaries between them become more fluid and permeable. Government acts not *on* but *with* nongovernmental and commercial entities. There is a shift from governance as one-way traffic toward a two-way traffic in which the "aspects, qualities, problems, and opportunities" of those governing and of those being governed are considered.[10]

These writers are describing the system of environmental protection that emerged in the Netherlands in the 1980s and 1990s, as well as the characteristics of the Dutch political culture that made this emergence possible. Theo de Bruijn and Kris Lulofs have written that "the environment is no longer the sole responsibility of governments. Companies and other organizations have to take up their share of responsibility."[11] This idea of sharing responsibility for environmental results was born out of a notion that none of the partners involved (governments, industry, or NGOs) has the capacity on its own to bring about the changes needed. The Dutch model is examined later in this chapter.

Several conditions support a transition to social-political governance in a society. One is the recognition that existing authority structures, relationships, or policy instruments have failed. Influential groups must have reached the conclusion that business as usual will not deliver the needed results or will involve unacceptable costs. In addition, there must be enough of a convergence of objectives and interests among groups to lead them to conclude that change will be mutually beneficial. If any set of actors decides it has more to gain from preserving the existing system than from creating a new one, a shift to a new regulation based on social-political governance is unlikely.

Other conditions that support a transition to social-political governance relate to the state of mind of key actors. They include some level of mutual trust or understanding as well as the willingness of various groups to take and share responsibility for problems and outcomes. Without a modicum of trust, actors are unwilling or unable to achieve the dialogue, sense of shared responsibility, and cooperation that are essential for the emergence of social-political governance.

Some, but not all, of these conditions currently exist in the United States. As the discussion in previous chapters indicates, there has been widespread dissatisfaction with many aspects of the old regulation. This extends beyond an awareness that it may be more costly, contentious, and intrusive than necessary, to the recognition that the existing system will not deliver the desired results. The three cases that follow (on state innovations, civic environmentalism, and the Netherlands) reinforce this point. At least so far, however, this dissatisfaction has not carried over into a consensus on what should replace the old regulation within national politics stream. It is fair to say that for many in the national environmental organizations, the less progressive companies, and in the regulatory agencies, there is a suspicion that changes in the regulatory system very likely would not be in their interests.

Nor does the state of mind of key actors auger well for the transition to a regulation based on social-political governance. Nearly every commentary about regulation in the United States emphasizes the distrust among actors. Previous chapters have argued that the design and operation of the old regulation not only reflect but also reinforce this distrust. An obsession with compliance for its own sake means everyone is a potential violator and should be treated as such; every claim must be verified and each loophole should be closed. Despite efforts to reduce distrust and improve dialogue, this compliance mind-set poses formidable barriers to building a new regulation based on social-political governance.

Policy Learning in a New Regulatory System

Another strand in the literature that will help in designing a new regulation is that of policy learning. The premise of a learning approach to public policy is the notion that governments "can learn from their experiences and that they can modify their present actions on the basis of their interpretations of how previous actions have fared in the past."[12] Conceptually, this contrasts with the view that public policy is the result of competition among groups for influence that is typically, if not inevitably, accompanied by political conflict. A learning approach does not deny the presence or even the necessity of conflict in making difficult social choices, such as those relating to the environment. Conflict is a necessary part of the political process. A learning approach does, however, mean that we should attempt to design processes and relationships with at least the goal of promoting learning through dialogue, communication, and systematic lesson drawing. A learning approach also aims to build and sustain the capacity within a policy system for incorporating what is learned into behavior and policies.[13]

Viewing environmental regulation more as a learning process than one of managing conflict and forcing conformance with rules implies

a different theory of behavior. It implies, for example, that diverse interests at some point may share similar goals, that collaboration may lead
to better outcomes, and that the accumulation and sharing of knowledge
over time may promote society's collective interests more effectively than
will adversarial relationships. Chapter 7 expands on the importance of
this alternative behavioral theory in offering a vision for a new regulation. Clearly, however, thinking of regulation as a process of learning and
not just one of managing conflict through bureaucratic processes would
lead to different model than that used now.

This approach may be further applied to environmental regulation by
distinguishing among three types of policy learning: technical, conceptual, and social.[14] Technical learning is the application of a limited number of policy instruments in the context of a relatively fixed set of policy
objectives (such as direct regulation to achieve end-of-pipe pollution
reductions). It relies on expert knowledge, bureaucratic structure, and
regulatory commands. Policy makers respond to demands for change with
"more-of-the-same" solutions: more stringent regulations, more intense
oversight, and higher penalties.

Technical learning describes the early stages of environmental policy
in industrial nations. Problems are defined narrowly, with an emphasis
on threats to human health from industrial pollution. Because problems
are compartmentalized, strategies are fragmented. Laws and agencies are
created to respond to problems as they emerge. Authority is concentrated
in pollution control agencies that are poorly connected to other policy
sectors (such as energy or transportation) and the agencies responsible
for them. Technical learning relies heavily on bureaucratic rationality:
specialized agencies, scientific experts, interaction through formal legal
processes, and hierarchical control.

Conceptual learning is a process of redefining policy goals and adjusting definitions of problems and the strategies to address them. Policy
objectives are reevaluated; perspectives on problems change; core strategies are reformulated. New concepts emerge, such as pollution prevention, ecological modernization, and sustainability. New tools, such as
life-cycle analysis or supply-chain management, are used. In conceptual
learning, environmental and economic goals are seen to complement
more than contradict each other. As the steadily diminishing returns and

increasing cost-ineffectiveness of end-of-pipe controls become apparent, people look to prevent pollution rather than control it at the point of release. Existing policy instruments come under scrutiny. For example, as deficiencies in standard regulatory instruments became clear in recent decades, policy makers complemented or replaced them with market incentives, information disclosure, and voluntary programs.

Social learning focuses on interactions and communications among actors. It builds on the cognitive capacities of technical learning and rethinking of objectives that occur in conceptual learning. However, there is more stress on developing trust, enhancing mutual competencies, and creating mechanisms for dialogue. The limits of scientific knowledge and the inevitability of multiple views on issues are explicitly recognized. Social learning reflects the tendencies of a postmodern world in which policy making is seen to be "a social process in which intersubjective information plays an important role."[15]

The argument here is that U.S. environmental policy, and more specifically what is described as the old regulation, is founded on technical learning. The institutional and legal framework still reflects that foundation. Beginning in the 1980s, however, a recognition of the deficiencies in the existing system led policy makers to search for new strategies and to rethink their policy objectives. This search, and the changes that resulted from it, constitute an effort to build a capacity for conceptual learning. By the early 1990s, continued dissatisfaction with the by-products and direct effects of regulation in the United States, reflected especially in the adversarial relations among actors and the challenges to solving problems collaboratively, led policy makers to attempt to create a capacity for social learning.

The discussion now turns to efforts at changing the old regulation or making up for its deficiencies in three settings: the American states, local problem solving, and the Netherlands. The concepts of reflexive law, social-political governance, and social learning are applied to each.

Regulatory Innovation in the American States

When it comes to innovation, environmental federalism in the United States is a blessing and a curse. It is a blessing because states offer a rich source of ideas and experience for building a new regulation. It is a curse because the sharing of authority among state and federal governments adds many sources of complexity to the challenge of actually putting a new regulation into place. This section considers regulatory innovations in the states, with two questions in mind: What do these efforts tell us about the need for a new regulation? What lessons may be drawn from them?

Until the passage of the 1970 Clean Air Act, regulation of pollution was left largely to the states. This ended when environmental regulation was nationalized in the early 1970s, which happened largely for three reasons: pollution problems often crossed state lines, requiring federal intervention; most states lacked a capacity and often the will to address environmental problems; and the fear that states would use lax pollution standards as a way to attract economic growth in an environmental "race to the bottom." As a result, as discussed in chapter 2, regulatory power steadily shifted from the states to Washington in the 1970s and 1980s.

The starting point of the federal–state relationship is that federal authority preempts that of the states when Congress determines that national action is appropriate. Some topics, such as municipal waste and groundwater, are left largely to the states. For such issues as air and water quality, drinking water, and hazardous waste management and cleanup, however, Washington sets the standards and defines the policies the states are expected to implement. Once a state has shown the capacity to manage a program in ways that meet federal expectations, it may apply for and receive delegated authority for running it. By the end of the 1990s, state agencies rather than EPA were the primary implementers. They were responsible for 90 percent of the permitting and 75 percent of the enforcement actions taken. At the same time, as state officials are quick to point out, they received on average only 25 percent of their environmental funding from Washington.[16]

The appropriate division of state and federal authority has been a source of constant tension over the years.[17] State officials complain that EPA allows states too little discretion in running their programs, stresses activity (such as number of inspections) over outcome measures, and undervalues states' commitment to and capacity for environmental protection. EPA officials argue, in turn, that national rules must be applied with consistency; all states need to maintain certain minimum standards, and activity measures are needed to exercise oversight until more reliable ones become available.

These tensions regarding state and federal authority emerged in a specific form during the 1990s, as many states undertook to adapt their own regulatory systems to the demands for change. There were variations, but typically these state initiatives stressed the themes of the revisionist critics: partnerships, collaboration, flexibility, and a focus on environmental results. Although EPA was pushing the same themes, it was reluctant to give the states much discretion to pursue their own reforms. Especially for innovative states like Massachusetts, Minnesota, and Oregon, in the 1990s EPA was viewed as a constraint on efforts to shift to a more performance-based, adaptable regulation. As one state commissioner wrote at the time: "Innovators [in the states] were becoming worn down by the seemingly endless tests and reviews to which their proposals were subjected."[18]

In response to congressional concerns about EPA–state relationships, in 2002 the General Accountability Office (GAO) prepared a report, *Overcoming Obstacles to Innovative State Regulatory Programs.*[19] The GAO studied the experiences of fifteen states, interviewed state and EPA officials, and analyzed in detail twenty innovation projects from these states (including some Project XL proposals). Although there were obstacles that had to be overcome within the states, usually related to resistance within state agencies and a lack of resources, officials from twelve of the fifteen states cited federal barriers as more significant, especially the need to comply with detailed EPA regulations, policies and guidance, as well as a perceived cultural resistance to change among EPA staff.[20] To be fair, EPA noted in response that its statutes often did not allow room for experimentation, a point many other commentators have made as well. Still, many state officials thought EPA was overly cautious and used a narrow reading of the laws as an excuse for resisting innovation proposals from states.

These recurring tensions had led in 1998 to negotiation of a joint EPA/state agreement to pursue regulatory innovation. The purpose of the agreement was to establish rules that defined roles, principles, and procedures for the two levels of government in developing, testing, and implementing innovations. Although there still have been tensions in the relationship, this has helped to clarify roles and pave the way for innovation agreements between EPA and several states.

What kinds of innovations have states pursued? What lessons do they offer? As stepping-stones toward a new regulation, this chapter looks briefly at three state programs: the Massachusetts Environmental Results Program (ERP); New Jersey's Facility-Wide Permitting pilots; and progress by several states (among them Oregon, Texas, Virginia, and Wisconsin) in developing performance tracks that are conceptually similar to the EPA program discussed in chapter 5.

The Massachusetts ERP applied the tools of self-certification and tailored technical assistance to three industry sectors made up almost entirely of small businesses: printing, dry cleaning, and photo processing.[21] Because they are small, firms in these sectors typically fall below an agency's radar screen and are effectively unregulated. Working with trade associations, the state Department of Environmental Protection (DEP) compiled a registry of firms, then conducted an extensive outreach and education process. At the start of the project, the DEP was aware of some 380 firms in these sectors; by the end of the project, its registry included about 2,200 firms. Under the ERP, each firm is required to annually certify that it is in compliance with a comprehensive set of regulations and has systems in place for maintaining compliance. To support firms in making this certification, the state provided each sector with a workbook (ranging from four pages for dry cleaners to seven for printers) that set out legal requirements for that sector and the steps necessary for meeting them. The DEP inspects a percentage of firms each year. Still, the agency's emphasis whenever possible is on enabling firms to maintain compliance, rather than on catching violators and imposing penalties.

The ERP is noteworthy because it shows government working in close cooperation with industry to expand the reach of regulators. The DEP shifted the legal burden of proof to the firm through the certification, yet it offered a practical and accessible tool to help firms meet their legal obligations. The NAPA evaluation of the program concluded that by "expanding the number of small businesses inside the state's regulatory system, DEP not only increases the scope of compliance with regulatory standards, but also levels the economic playing field among hundreds of competitors and thus reduces the incentive to ignore environmental standards."[22] In an apt illustration of lesson drawing from one jurisdiction to another, several other states began to implement their own versions of the ERP, and EPA's innovations office disseminated information about the program and provided grants for other states. By the summer of 2005, thirteen states were using the ERP model with a variety of small business sectors, such as printing and auto repair.[23]

At times the lessons learned from policy experiments differ from what people originally thought they would be. A second innovation illustrates this point. In its 1991 Pollution Prevention Act, New Jersey authorized its DEP to conduct a pilot program of facility-wide permits that would cover all regulated releases at sixteen facilities in the state. The goal was to encourage pollution prevention and simplify permitting, in part by using multimedia permits in place of medium-specific permits, and in part by using flexible permits to set caps for releases on the basis of manufacturing process. Because permitting is a core regulatory process and the conventional approach has been criticized as a source of delay, uncertainty, and costs for industry, as well as a likely barrier to technology innovation, these pilots attracted national attention.[24] By October 2001, the DEP had issued fourteen facility-wide permits to a range of facilities, including manufacturers of pharmaceuticals, chemicals, adhesive products, and air conditioners. Each facility was broken into distinct processes; this gave the permit teams a comprehensive and usually unprecedented overview of the facility and its environmental impacts.

In the NAPA evaluation, the researchers found that the pilots helped identify opportunities for preventing pollution, but not because of the permits themselves. Rather, it was the process for developing the permits that led to gains for the facility and the environment. The benefit to firms was that they were able to identify pollution prevention options that reduced environmental damage and, in many cases, increased economic efficiency. Moreover, the more flexible permits enabled firms to change their manufacturing processes without the uncertainty and costs of having to obtain permit approvals in advance. Interestingly, the researchers found little advantage in the effort to integrate permitting across media. Nearly all of the environmental and financial benefits came from changes in air permitting. They also found that a process-based approach made more sense for firms because it was more consistent with how facility managers typically approached their work.

A study by Barry Rabe reaches similar conclusions. "Perhaps the most significant discovery from the cases completed under the FWP program," he writes, "is the extent of previously undetected emissions discovered at each participating facility."[25] He adds that "the materials accounting process and comprehensive permit reviews discovered numerous emission sources that no prior permit or planning process had even identified, much less attempted to reduce or eliminate."[26] This was true even when a facility was thought to have been carefully regulated under its conventional permits. At Frigidaire, for example, the permit teams found fifty-seven separate emission sources that had not been regulated. The process also revealed sources of cross-media transfers that had simply fallen through the cracks. The close interaction between the DEP and facility staff in the permitting process generated opportunities for mutual learning as well as "transfer" benefits, where lessons from one site could be applied to others. The process led to several investments by firms and to significant reductions in their environmental impacts. In some cases, facility managers said that the added flexibility allowed them to make the investments needed to continue production at a site rather than abandon it and relocate.

The tradeoff was that, at least in this initial round, the facility-wide permits demanded more resources—both from the DEP and the facility—than did conventional permitting. However, several factors suggest that these costs could be reduced. First, as with any new activity, there is a learning curve. As more experience is gained with a process, agency staff become more proficient, and the approach spreads to more facilities, the per-unit costs typically will fall. Second, there may be ways to reduce costs by linking facility-wide permitting with a facility's EMS. The EMS involves many similar assessments of a facility's environmental impacts, as well as targets and objectives for reducing them. Both apply a more systematic approach to environmental management across the whole facility. Third, the environmental advantages of facility-wide over conventional permitting suggest that the former may offer more cost-effective ways of achieving results than the latter. And there do appear to be administrative benefits to the facility-wide approach: Where previously there were scores or hundreds of permits for each facility, there is now one consolidated document.[27]

Yet a third kind of innovation pursued in many states differentiated facilities based on their environmental performance. Illustrations are Oregon's Green Permits, Clean Texas, New Jersey's Silver and Gold tracks, and Virginia's Environmental Excellence Program.[28] Created by legislation in 1997, Oregon's Green Permits was designed to encourage use of an EMS and other innovative approaches that led to performance beyond what was legally required. It also authorized the Oregon Department of Environmental Quality (DEQ) to provide regulatory waivers that would help facilities achieve superior performance. The program created three progressively more demanding levels of qualifications, each of which would earn more recognition and flexibility from the DEQ. An entry level, called "Participants," required an EMS that covered regulated pollutants. A higher level, "Achievers," required a more elaborate EMS (usually third-party certified) that covered unregulated and regulated pollutants. The highest level, "Leaders," required a full EMS and a commitment to sustainability principles in the product life cycles, activities, and services. Benefits at the lowest level included recognition, enforcement considerations from DEQ, and technical assistance. Benefits at the higher levels included expedited or flexible permits, reduced monitoring or reporting, and regulatory waivers.

By June 2002, three facilities had been accepted for Green Permits, and three others were under review. All six applied for the achiever level; some expressed interest in moving up later to leader. No facilities applied for the participant level. However, despite strong support from its members and a public advisory group, the program was allowed to expire on its statutory sunset date at the end of 2003. Although the reasons for the demise of Green Permits lie in several political and resource issues within the Oregon DEQ, a June 2002 evaluation suggested factors that could have improved the chances for success.[29] Among these were greater efforts to build awareness, simpler criteria for the entry level to build qualifications for the higher levels, streamlined verification procedures for the EMS to reduce the time and transaction costs of applying, more regulatory flexibility as a benefit, and more standardized and consistent reporting of results. Beyond these findings, it is apparent from the evaluation that the low level of participation made it difficult to sustain support within the DEQ.

Despite the limited success in Oregon, several other states have adopted or are adopting their own versions of the performance track concept.[30] One of the more successful is Virginia's Environmental Excellence Program, which established two levels of membership. Organizations that are in the early stages of implementing an EMS may be designated an Environmental Enterprise, while those that have adopted a full EMS and demonstrate improved performance and pollution prevention measures may qualify as Exemplary Environmental Enterprises (EEE). The forty or so organizations in the second category may qualify for several kinds of regulatory flexibility, although these are still in the process of being adopted.[31] To strengthen the links between the Virginia program and EPA's national program, the state grants EEE status to facilities accepted for the EPA's Performance Track.

Tiering programs in the other states are similar in their overall design. Most include more than one level, with program benefits increasing at higher levels. Most incorporate an EMS, beyond-compliance performance, pollution prevention, and public outreach. Both the states and EPA view these programs as opportunities for cooperation. As of December 2005, ten states had signed memoranda of agreements with EPA's Performance Track program for jointly implementing their programs.

Performance tracks illustrate the practice of lesson drawing among levels of government. In designing its own Performance Track in early 2000, EPA studied the programs and experiences of states like Oregon, New Jersey, and Wisconsin. Many lessons were incorporated into the design of the national program. Similarly, several states drew on the design and experience of the national program in creating their own versions in the early 2000s. Massachusetts, Utah, and Arizona have closely modeled their programs on EPA's. They used similar EMS criteria and adopted the EPA's framework for measuring performance. In brief, the evolution of tiering programs illustrates how learning may occur among levels of government. Studies and workshops by EPA, NAPA, the Environmental Council of the States, and the Multi-State Working Group (MSWG) on Environmental Performance facilitated this learning process.[32]

The state experience illustrates the two themes of this chapter. The fact that several states were pursuing similar kinds of changes at the same time underscores the fact that reinvention was more than just a superficial political response to events in Washington, D.C. Deeper forces were at work. These brief cases also underscore the value of lesson drawing for a new regulation. In fact, systematic lesson drawing was occurring. Of the three kinds of innovations, the ERP stretched the model of the old regulation the least. What makes it noteworthy is that it signals a change in the regulatory mind-set. Instead of viewing noncompliance as a moral failure that had to be corrected, the ERP recognizes that small firms often lack the information and capacity to comply with a complex array of requirements. The ERP also reflects an appreciation of the limits of the rules-and-deterrence model for agencies, who cannot expect to be able to inspect and, if necessary, sanction tens of thousands of small firms on any consistent basis.

The New Jersey permitting pilots expanded the old regulatory model more than the ERP did. They were designed to address core weaknesses in the old regulation. Among them are the environmental medium-specific approach and the effects of inflexibility and uncertainty in environmental permitting. What is especially instructive about this case is the importance of the process rather than the permit itself. By adopting a more integrated and collaborative approach to permitting, government and industry were able to get better environmental and economic results. Of course, the disadvantage was that permitting for these pilot facilities was more resource intensive than it normally would have been. However, as noted earlier, additional experience could help reduce those costs significantly.

Performance tracking programs stretch the model of the old regulation even further. They differentiate among regulated entities based on their past and likely future performance, something that government operating under the old regulation has been reluctant to do. Moreover, agencies state publicly that they will treat facilities applying and qualifying for these performance tracks differently from those who do not. Unlike earlier voluntary programs, performance tracks are designed to change the regulatory system. They thus offer not only important lessons but a bridge to the new regulation that is discussed in the next chapter.

As was stressed at the start of this section, the blessing of federalism is that states offer a fertile source of ideas and testing grounds for innovation. The other side of the coin is that change is difficult to implement when there is extensive interdependence. Between two-thirds and three-fourths of environmental regulatory programs are delegated to states. Because they operate under delegated authority, states must seek approval for significant changes from existing policies. Similarly, because so much day-to-day authority is granted to states, EPA often has to persuade them to adopt changes it seeks to implement nationally. In effect, neither level of government may innovate without the consent of the other. Much of the flexibility EPA seeks to offer Performance Track members in such areas as permitting must be adopted by states. This is a challenge when it comes to actually implementing change.

Still, this creative tension between states and EPA may be positive overall. Barry Rabe compared regulatory innovations in four Canadian provinces (Alberta, Manitoba, Ontario, and Newfoundland) with those in four states (Arkansas, Minnesota, New Jersey, and Oklahoma). The conventional wisdom is that a decentralized regulatory system like Canada's is more conducive to innovation than a more centralized one like that of the United States. Presumably, provinces would be freer to respond to local conditions and explore innovative approaches than would states, who complain of the constraints from EPA oversight. Rabe found, however, that in four areas of innovation—pollution prevention, cross-media integration, information disclosure, and outcome-based measures of performance—the states have been much more active and effective in devising innovative policy approaches than their Canadian counterparts.[33] Federal–state relations in the United States encourage more diffusion of innovative practices and ideas through networks, associations, and grants. Rabe concludes that "for all the opprobrium heaped on American regulatory federalism, there appear to be certain dynamics that facilitate innovation not detectable in its more decentralized neighbor."[34]

These are only a few of the state initiatives of recent years that offer lessons for a new regulation. Despite their apparent benefits, there are reasons to be concerned about the history of some of these innovations. The Oregon Green Permits program was allowed to die. Similarly, New Jersey's Gold and Silver track programs languished from a lack of support and effectively were over by 2002. Despite the interest from other states, facility-wide permitting has not been adopted on a broader scale. Even in New Jersey, it has not been expanded beyond the original pilot list of sixteen. Resource constraints, changing political leadership, and lack of cooperation by main-line agency functions have hindered the success of many of these initiatives. Innovation programs are like a delicate flower; many of them "lack a firm institutional footing and could indeed disappear without much public notice or establishment of precedent."[35]

Civic Environmentalism

Many complaints about the old regulation relate to the difficulty of adapting a centralized, uniform, regulatory strategy to locally diverse situations. What DeWitt John calls civic environmentalism constitutes yet another response to these complaints. John describes civic environmentalism simply as "the process of custom-designing answers to local environmental problems."[36] It may be seen as a bottom-up approach that may supplement but not replace the top-down methods of the old regulation. Civic environmentalism emerged in the 1980s and 1990s as a loosely connected set of practices, experiences, and relationships rather than as any kind of systematic policy strategy. Most of its applications involve such issues as local and regional ecosystem protection, preservation of national forests and other natural resources, and community-level resource and pollution issues. It usually involves some combination of local activism, with a "shadow community" of interested people and a core group that exercises leadership; collaboration among business groups and community and environmental activists, as well as elected and agency officials; and outside (from government or industry) regulatory, financial, and political support.[37]

Several features distinguish civic environmentalism from a conventional regulatory approach. It is adaptive, in that it involves a series of adjustments in strategies and tactics in response to experience and new information. It is eclectic, because different policy tools may be used, including subsidies, regulation, education, emissions trading, information disclosure, and partnerships, among others. It is collaborative, because many actors join together to develop and implement solutions.

Typically, citizens, industry, nongovernmental organizations, and government are involved. Civic environmentalism also is contingent on the characteristics of the issue being addressed and the context in which it is being addressed.

One example of civic environmentalism in action is the Darby Partnership, founded in 1991 to bring stakeholders together to protect the Big and Little Darby Creeks and their 580-square-mile watershed in central Ohio. Facilitated by the Ohio Chapter of the Nature Conservancy (TNR), by 1999 the Partnership included some 100 members, representing state and federal agencies, local officials, farmers, environmental advocates, and others. In a case study of the Partnership, Katrina Korfmacher was interested in testing the proposition, drawn from the literature on ecosystem protection, that without independent funding, clear political commitment, and institutional authority to make decisions, local coordinating efforts are unlikely to succeed. The Darby Partnership lacked decision authority and resources. Its influence was based on the informal influence its members could have as a result of their information sharing, networking, and discussion at its quarterly meetings.[38]

Although the lack of decision authority and funding did limit what the Partnership could accomplish, it still accomplished a great deal. "Simply by providing a neutral forum for discussion, the partnership exposed members to ideas, information, and potential collaborators they otherwise would not have encountered."[39] Such interactions had a number of side effects. Farmers and others became aware of actions they could take to reduce environmental damage within the watershed. The positive experience with collaboration encouraged participants to apply the same techniques to other aspects of their work. The main limitation was that the Partnership was unable to influence land use in the watershed because it lacked decision authority. Still, this case shows that local organization and cooperation may achieve results, although fewer than many participants had hoped for.

Clearly, civic environmentalism as has its limits as a policy strategy. In a critical study of a community-based process to resolve a land use issue in Belmont, Massachusetts, Judith Layzer argues that the ideals of civic environmentalism were not met.[40] The process did not promote genuine deliberation, dialogue, and trust building; nor did it encourage a broad consideration of alternatives or generate creative, locally tailored solutions. To the extent that local space was protected, it was "not as a result of the town's collaborative decision-making process but as a consequence of more conventional, adversarial politics."[41] In another cautionary assessment, Troy Abel and Mark Stephan warn that participation in community-based processes may not be as broad or democratic as the advocates of civic environmentalism suggest.[42]

Denise Scheberle suggests that the determinants of success of such efforts depend on the phase of problem solving and thus the goals of the process.[43] To get community-based efforts started, for example, the key determinants are a public perception that there is a problem, a lack of public confidence in existing regulatory and governmental structures, and the presence of a local "sparkplug." To create and sustain partnerships once they are formed, key determinants are the support of elected officials and agreement among influential organizations that they will collaborate and share resources. To agree on and implement solutions, the determinants are open, inclusive, and fair stakeholder involvement; the availability of expertise; a long-term commitment of multiple, key stakeholders; and sustained community support.

In sum, the label "civic environmentalism" covers a broad and diverse range of phenomena. Evaluating them is difficult, for several reasons. First, local factors introduce substantial variation. Such variables as involvement by local officials, availability of resources, presence of a sparkplug to promote action, and degree of citizen participation, among others, will influence the results. Second, desired outcomes vary. At times, the aim is to improve coordination and communication; at other times it may be to implement a specific solution or obtain resources from government or industry. A third challenge to evaluating local efforts is their ripeness. Processes and relationships evolve over time. It is hard to say at what point they are complete and ripe for evaluation. What appears to have shown limited success one year may bear fruit a year or two later.

Still, civic environmentalism nicely illustrates our concepts from the literature. It is almost an examplar of social-political governance. It blurs the lines between public and private actors and institutions, stresses horizontal over hierarchical relationships, creates an expectation of shared responsibility, and accepts that no one set of actors possesses the authority or knowledge to solve problems on its own. The growth of civic environmentalism in the past few decades may also be seen as a response to the conditions Kooiman associates with social-political governance in other contexts. These include a dissatisfaction with existing structures, relationships, and instruments, leading to agreement among groups that change could be mutually beneficial. These cases also suggest that over time, collaboration may create the understanding and trust that promotes dialogue, shared responsibility, and new approaches to complex issues. That it is even possible to achieve these conditions is an encouraging sign for the emergence of a new regulation.

The many applications of civic environmentalism also illustrate the potential for policy learning. There is a foundation of technical learning because scientific and agency experts are involved and use existing regulatory authorities. There also is a strong element of conceptual learning because problems are approached in more integrated ways and various policy instruments (regulation, education, fees) are used in combination. What is most instructive about these local and regional initiatives, however, is the effort to develop a capacity for social learning. The literature stresses dialogue, mutual understanding, trust, and shared responsibility as necessary conditions for achieving any degree of success, as well as a benefit that may spill over into other issues.

Civic environmentalism involves issues that go well beyond the regulation of industry, which is the focus of this book. It is included in this chapter for two reasons. First, it is further evidence of the perceived limits of the old regulation. Locally and regionally, various groups have seen the need to devise more adaptive, eclectic, and collaborative ways of solving problems. In terms of my discussion of policy learning, local groups recognized that a system based primarily on technical learning had to be augmented with capacities for conceptual and social learning. Second, it documents the power as well as the limits of partnerships and collaboration. People are willing to step outside of traditional roles and relationships and engage in new ways of problem solving. Often, greater trust, understanding, and a sense of citizenship have been the result. At the same time, this literature shows that partnerships may take us only so far, especially in implementing solutions. Regulatory pressure, money, and political support also are necessary ingredients.

Environmental Regulation in the Netherlands

The Netherlands is a small country, roughly the size of New Jersey, with a population of about 16 million. It is one of the most densely populated countries in the world, with an average of 454 people per square kilometer. Most of the country is in the delta of the Rhine River on land that was reclaimed from the North Sea. About one-fourth of the land area is below sea level; it is protected from inundation by a system of natural dunes and artifical dykes. The country is highly industrialized and intensively agricultural, both of which place considerable stress on the environment. It is also one of the most economically successful countries in the world and is committed to maintaining that success.

Aside from the obvious differences in size and geographic scale, the Netherlands differs from the United States in two key respects. One is a strong tradition of cooperation and consensus-based politics. It is no accident that a leading study of the country is titled *The Politics of Accommodation.*[44] Despite the conflicts that inevitably arise, groups are able to work cooperatively to address crucial issues, in what has been termed consensual democracy. The other difference is acceptance of a strong government role in national planning. One study noted that "largely as a consequence of flood protection and land reclamation, the Dutch public has traditionally accepted the need for government intervention and has placed faith in the ability of government to plan and manage development."[45]

This combination of physical circumstances, environmental pressures, and political culture has led to a series of distinctive and innovative approaches to environmental regulation in recent years. These approaches have drawn a great deal of interest in the Dutch experience from other countries, to the extent that the title of one article describes the Netherlands as "a net exporter of environmental policy concepts."[46]

From the late 1960s to the early 1980s, like other developed economies, the Dutch relied on a top-down, technology-based regulatory system that forced the initial, necessary changes in industry's behavior.

Increasingly, however, they determined that the conventional model of top-down regulation on its own would not be sufficient over the long term to deal with the environmental pressures faced in the Netherlands. At the same time, the Dutch were committed to maintaining a high level of economic prosperity. Economic growth would not be sacrificed at the expense of the environment. The goal of Dutch policy for the past two decades has been to decouple environmental degradation from economic growth, to break what had been seen as an inevitable link between the two. In the effort to move from a zero sum to more of a win-win approach nationally, the Netherlands became a prime example of "ecological modernization," which may be described as a strategy in which environmental goals are built into the structure of the economy.[47]

The arguments that were made for a new approach in the Netherlands in the 1980s resemble those that have been made for change in the United States. It was argued that conventional regulation provided no incentive for continuous improvement, led to cost-ineffective results, failed to keep pace with technological change, and focused on end-of-pipe controls. Moreover, it failed to draw sufficiently upon industry and other sources of knowledge in devising solutions to pressing environmental issues. A government report issued in 1988 concluded, much like the NAPA reports in the United States, that the old model of regulation was "not only inadequate to the challenges of sustainability but also to some extent ineffective."[48] Also like the United States, the Dutch were determined not to trade off economic growth for the environment. A new approach was seen as necessary to sustain growth and avoid the need for more radical change that would be politically difficult and could damage the economy.

The new approach did not replace what already was in place; it grew along side of and interacted with the existing regulation. Its cornerstone is a series of National Environmental Policy Plans, the first of which (NEPP I) was adopted in 1989. It created a planning process based on multiple time frames, including short-term policies, medium-term strategic goals, and long-term (to 2010) aspirations. It defined five scales for problem solving: local, regional, fluvial, continental, and global. The NEPP framework stressed the integration of environmental concerns into all policy sectors, with many government ministries (e.g., transport, agriculture, and energy) contributing to and endorsing it. Especially in later versions, the process involved extensive consultation and cooperation with the target groups, mostly industry, whose behavior would have to change to achieve the goals.

The NEPP framework defines national goals for eight "theme" issues: climate change (the greenhouse effect, damage to the stratospheric ozone layer); acidification (acid deposition on soil, surface water, and buildings); eutrophication (nutrient buildup in surface water); dispersion (the spread of hazardous substances); waste disposal; local nuisance (effects of noise, odor, and local air pollution); water depletion (losses in water supply); and resource management (energy and materials use). The government, including the affected ministries and Parliament, set a quantitative goal for each theme. Responsibility for achieving the goals was allocated to target groups, such as industry, transport, consumers, and agriculture. Within industry, specific targets were then developed for sub-sectors or "branches," starting with chemicals, base metals, and printing. The theme goals drive the search for results: "A critical distinction between the Dutch approach and almost all other negotiated agreements is that in the case of the latter the government sets non-negotiable goals based on collective performance objectives previously established under the National Environmental Plan."[49]

In the Dutch corporatist style, trade associations and other organizations are seen as legitimate representatives of societal and economic interests. The parties involved in negotiating targets for the chemical sector, for example, included the environment and economic ministries, provincial and local governments, water boards, the Association of the Dutch Chemical Industry, and individual firms. The product of the negotiations is a covenant with targets that define the expected contribution of the industry sector in achieving the national goals. Each firm then prepares a company environmental plan (CEP) that commits it to specific targets and timetables for environmental improvement.[50] The CEP takes as a starting point the use of best available technologies. It is expected that new technologies will be developed over time, as needed, to meet the company and sector targets. As Gouldson and Murphy note, "it is anticipated that the clear framework of demanding targets may encourage such innovation."[51] In this model, the government sets goals but allows industry flexibility in determining how to meet them rather than pre-scribing technologies or other specific means that may limit firms' dis-cretion and discourage long-term innovation.

The Dutch covenants have drawn a great deal of attention in the United States and elsewhere. They represent an agreement between dif-ferent levels of government—national, provincial, and local—on what commitments industry will make with respect to meeting the national and sector targets. The covenant offers predictability to a company. The government agrees not to change the targets while the agreement is in effect, giving a company discretion in deciding how to meet them. The covenants technically are not legally binding, but their terms may be incorporated into environmental licenses (i.e., permits) and thus become binding. Although many observers have stressed the legal dimensions of the covenants, it is more useful to think of them as a management tool, even as a "communicative instrument" in which government and indus-try express and codify their expectations of each other.[52]

Officially, participation in the covenants is voluntary. As with any vol-untary effort, there are bound to be free riders who enjoy the program's benefits without incurring any obligations. The national government has worked with local licensing authorities to pressure nonparticipating firms. They may be required, through their licenses, to meet the specific provisions of the covenant but denied the opportunity to trade off reduc-tions with other firms as part of a sector agreement. In addition to this loss in flexibility, they also may not be covered by the government's com-mitment not to change the performance targets over the term of the agreement. Faced with such pressures, companies have participated in the agreements in high numbers.

The NEPP framework reflects a philosophy of shared responsibility. It was clear to government and industry in the 1980s that pollution reduc-tions in the range of 80–90 percent could not be achieved through con-ventional, technology-forcing strategies. The notion is that government should create the appropriate conditions for target groups to fulfill their responsibilities.[53] Before the mid-1980s, the Dutch relied on top-down regulation, and relationships between government and industry were dis-tant and negative. By the end of the decade, "the authoritarian style of Dutch environmental policy-makers was supplemented with a new approach designed to encourage self-regulation."[54] This more collabora-tive, goal-based approach illustrates the concept of social-political governance.

Flexibility and adaptability are built into the framework. The NEPP itself has been reviewed and revised about every four years. Every other year, the environment ministry prepares a report card regarding results achieved, problems encountered, and the implications for future policy. The company plans are also reviewed and adjusted as needed every four years. The NEPP process stresses flexibility by allowing the use of a vari-ety of policy instruments. The covenants are drawn up against the back-drop of conventional, technology-based regulation. A company that fails to meet its commitments is still subject to regulation. Economic incen-tives, such as emission fees and tax relief for innovative technology, are used. With this flexibility, government officials are able to tailor their choice of instruments to specific problems as well as to the needs and capacities of the target groups that are involved in meeting a goal. The Dutch approach also makes extensive use of networks that share infor-mation and build capacity, especially for small and medium-sized firms.[55]

To succeed, this approach requires a degree of trust among the parties. Government must trust a business to integrate environmental objectives and requirements into its planning and management in a way that will meet the targets. A business must trust the government to follow the agreements and not impose new, unanticipated requirements through legislation or regulation. Both sides gain predictability. This approach also requires a respect for the mutual competence of all of the parties. In their interviews with Dutch business managers, Gouldson and Murphy found that they much preferred dealing with government inspectors who had experience with and knowledge of their industry. Greater expertise translates into more cooperation, better information sharing, and the mutual learning that promotes continuous improvement.[56]

Of course, the critical issue is whether the Dutch achieved better envi-ronmental results than they would have under the conventional regula-tory approach. Although government and industry have mostly been pleased with the results, many environmentalists "have strong doubts whether companies, in particular the large ones, are not merely doing what they would have done under the old regulatory regime.[57] On the other hand, Neil Gunningham and Darren Sinclair observe that, "While only limited empirical study of the Dutch approach has taken place, work by the European Environment Agency suggests that the Dutch covenant with the chemical industry did achieve substantially better outcomes than a projected business-as-usual trend, and that it was environmentally effective with regard to at least 33 of the 61 chemicals studied."[58] Most, but not all, of the goals for the other sectors were being met by 2000. One area where the national goals were not being met is in carbon dioxide emissions, which have been rising steadily.[59] As for process, environmental groups were concerned in the early years about not being sufficiently involved, although the government has taken steps to expand their role. Nor has the NEPP planning process been seamless. Many local licensing authorities were reluctant to cooperate because "they were not adequately consulted on the national targets and on the VA [voluntary agreements] process itself."[60]

A more recent evaluation of the Dutch approach (referred to here as the "target group policy") assessed both the near-term environmental results and longer-term prospects for innovation. For the first, the authors found that the implementation reports summarizing the individual company reports showed that most of the 2000 pollution reduction goals had been met and there was substantial progress toward meeting the 2010 goals. In some areas there had been less progress, however, notably for emissions of nitrogen oxides, volatile organic compounds, and (in one sector) energy efficiency, as well carbon dioxide, and later agreements would have to be adjusted to account for this.[61] Interestingly, the authors cite a 2003 study by Dutch scholars who found that the covenants appear to be more effective when the firms in a sector are in a relatively strong market position, their environmental image is sensitive to the public, and there is strong competition within the sector. This suggests that chemicals as a sector might be especially well suited to this approach. As for the effects on innovation, which still are difficult to evaluate, the authors conclude that the Dutch approach is effective in stimulating nearer-term innovation, but "the consensual and target approach will generally not be conducive to innovation of a more radical kind."[62] They also suggest that evaluations of the Dutch approach by NGOs have become more positive recently. In their conclusion, Theo de

Bruijn and Vicki Norberg-Bohm rate the Dutch approach positively, at least in part, on all four of the criteria they used for evaluating the innovations studied in their book.[63]

Although there will be a need to adapt the covenants to the results of such evaluations over time, environmental policy in the Netherlands still offers a case study of a form of postmodern regulation. Reflexive law, social-political governance, and policy learning all are evident in the Dutch approach. The core of reflexivity is that government uses law to create conditions in which actors assess their behavior and continually adjust it to achieve socially desirable goals. From a policy system based largely on substantive law, the Dutch created a framework of performance targets, government–industry consultations, and accountability that encouraged reflexivity. This framework was linked with the system of licensing and monitoring that had been established under the conventional regulatory mechanisms. Regular feedback on the results of the measures taken provides a basis for adjusting the stringency of the covenants in later planning periods under the NEPP.

Environmental policy in the Netherlands is a case study in social-political governance. In the language of the new governance, the role of government is to steer rather than to row. The idea of shared responsibility is embedded in the NEPP approach. The system of mutual dependencies in the NEPP planning and implementation process reflects an awareness of the limits of government knowledge and capacities in an increasingly dynamic, diverse, and interdependent world. The value of communication and interaction among actors is a recurring theme in discussions of the NEPP. Moreover, these themes are built into the structure of government–industry relationships, through consultation committees, sector covenants, company environmental plans, and the NEPP revisions.[64]

The Dutch approach also provides an excellent illustration of a national environmental system based on policy learning. Until the mid-1980s, like most industrial nations, the Netherlands relied largely on technical learning—top-down standard setting, fragmentation by environmental medium, distant and formal relationships between government and industry, separation of environmental from other policy sectors, and so on. Within about a decade, the Dutch had achieved a largely successful transition to conceptual and social learning. They integrated policy making and implementation, both within environmental media and across policy sectors (several ministries participate in and endorse the NEPP). They created a framework that enables them to draw upon a varied range of policy instruments. Through the NEPP, the Dutch government reconceptualized environmental problems in terms of long-term sustainability and devised a system of goals that drive the planning process. Similarly, the efforts to reallocate responsibility across all sectors of Dutch society and engage industry as a "co-regulator" successfully integrated social learning into policy making.

Can the Dutch model be applied elsewhere? Certainly it cannot be transplanted whole cloth to a policy system like that in the United States, which differs from that in the Netherlands in fundamental ways. For example, given separation of powers and the institutional fragmentation in the U.S. political system, it is hard to imagine how the president, Congress, and multiple departments could unite behind one set of national environmental goals that drive national policy. Similarly, the long history of adversarial relationships and distrust among government, business, and advocacy groups poses a near-term barrier to the kind of cooperative relationships the Dutch have achieved.

Still, many elements of the Dutch approach may be adapted to the United States. The Dutch have shown that a co-regulation approach may be implemented side-by-side with a conventional one. They have shown how trade associations may be enlisted in shared efforts to develop and apply innovative technologies. They have demonstrated how measurable performance goals at a "macro" level (that of industry sectors) and a "micro" level (that of individual firms) may be used to structure and implement sector and company-level agreements. Most important, the Dutch experience has illustrated how cooperative relationships based on stable and predictable expectations among actors may have the potential to achieve better results more efficiently than the old regulation on its own.

Lessons for a New Regulation

Our three sources of ideas and experience share many characteristics. First, all may be seen as reactions to deficiencies in the old regulation. In

American states eager to innovate, there was a sense that the existing system was not only costly but overly rigid, narrowly focused, and excessively complex. Civic environmentalism, John has written, "is a widespread, genuine, democratic response to bureaucratic failure."[65] Conventional regulation, imposed from the top down, was seen to be inadequate for addressing locally diverse problems and circumstances. The Dutch experience illustrates the perceived limitations in the old approach best of all. There was a widespread perception among policy makers and others that conventional regulation, on its own, was insufficient for achieving environmental policy goals in the face of high population density, industrialization, and expectations of continued economic growth.

Second, and at the same time, all three occurred against a backdrop of conventional regulation. One could argue that innovations by the states have been pursued despite the existing constraints; the point is that even in the most innovative states there was no interest in discarding the core elements of the old regulation. Civic environmentalism was largely a response to the limitations of the existing system, but its bottom-up methods would have had limited success without the legal pressures, financial resources, and technical expertise associated with regulation. Similarly, the Dutch sector approach evolved out of and was integrated with the established system of environmental protection in the Netherlands. Even there, the old regulation stands as the default rules for firms that do not participate in the sector planning process. In each case, there was a recognition that "an underpinning of government regulation, coupled with (at least a perceived) credible threat of inspection and enforcement, is necessary to persuade the reluctant, the recalcitrant, and the incompetent that other, less coercive approaches are worth adopting."[66]

Third, all of these cases reflect the diagnoses and prescriptions offered by revisionist critics. To assert that the federal efforts at reinvention were merely a political response to the conservative assault on regulation is to ignore the widespread efforts to change regulation in the American states, in communities and watersheds across the country, and in other parts of the world. All of this reinforces the thesis that the transition from a modern to a postmodern regulation reflects deep, long-term changes in economics, society, and environmental problems far more than short-term political pressures.

More specific lessons about a new regulation may be drawn from these ideas and experiences as well. Through the efforts of organizations like the Environmental Council of the States, EPA, the Organization for Economic Co-operation and Development, and policy research (such as that commissioned by NAPA and the Brookings Institution), lessons from many innovations have been documented and the appropriate lessons have been drawn. Nearly all of these have been in the form of case studies, which at this stage is probably the most feasible approach. As the cases accumulate and the literature expands, it may be possible to conduct more systematic analyses of the cases, such as those used for research on citizen participation and environmental conflict resolution.[67]

This chapter has explored many sources from which lessons may be drawn for a new regulation. It should be clear by now that policy makers, activists, scholars, and others were saying many of the same things over the past few decades. Whether we look at the 1996 report of the PCSD, the advice of other revisionist critics, the local exercises in civic environmentalism, or the incremental changes coming from the states and EPA, the same themes emerge: We should not discard the old regulation and the capacities it created, but adapt it to changes that have been occurring in environmental problems, economic relationships, and the institutional landscape. Trends among the leading private firms, as well as among many public and nonprofit organizations, reflect a similar theme. It is time for a new environmental regulation that is more flexible, performance based, collaborative, and adaptable. Its outlines are set out in chapter 7.

7

The New Environmental Regulation

In this book, strong and effective environmental pressure is assumed; the question is whether that pressure is now channeled in the most constructive manner.[1]

This book has considered behavior, rules, and institutions as they relate to the environment from many perspectives. In the private sector, leading companies are looking well beyond their legal obligations for environmentally responsible opportunities to reduce costs, build confidence with regulators and the public, and increase market share. In government, many agencies are seeking to build flexibility and responsiveness into what has been a generally effective but increasingly antiquated system. Many at the community level are fashioning creative solutions from the diverse laws, agencies, programs, and funding sources that make up modern environmental regulation. Furthermore, as we have seen, there are many sources of ideas on a new regulation. One is the experience of other countries. Another is federal and state policy innovations in the United States. A third is the social science literature on policy learning, reflexive law, and social-political governance. Still others are the greening of industry and the advice of the revisionist critics—those friends of environmental protection who have called for change.

This book has drawn on each of these sources in making the case for a new regulation and suggesting some of its characteristics. Having considered the contributions that each of these sources of ideas, innovations, and practices may make, the book now moves to a discussion of the new regulation itself. Defining and building a new regulation is a formidable task. This final chapter takes the initial steps by offering building blocks for a new regulation. In addition, it considers how the transition from the old to the new might occur, given contemporary environmental politics. In sum, this final chapter considers the issue of what the new regulation will be as well as how we might achieve it.

Previous works have proposed several elements of a new regulatory system. In *Smart Regulation*, for example, the authors suggest a set of design principles for reforming regulation. Among these are incorporating a broader range of instruments and institutions, using less interventionist measures, and maximizing opportunities for win-win outcomes.[2] The final chapter in *Leaders and Laggards* proposes ways of "reconfiguring" environmental regulation with a framework that relies on reflexive approaches, takes advantage of environmental partnerships, and incorporates the core ideas of ecological modernization, which aims for a better integration of economic and environmental goals in society and public policy.[3] The approach taken here is conceptually similar to these, but is different in three respects. First, it aims to be more accessible to the non-social scientist. Second, it strives to offer somewhat more specific proposals that are especially suited to the U.S. context, including suggestions on how the shift to a new regulation might occur. Third, it aims to develop the contrasts between the old and the new regulations in sharper relief. Still, this chapter and these other works should be seen as going in the same general direction.

Before beginning, it is important to stress one point: Designing and implementing a new regulation does not mean that we should do away with the old one. Experience in the United States and elsewhere has shown that many elements of regulation as we know it are crucial to any system of environmental protection. Grand thinkers who argue that government's regulatory authority may be replaced with a scheme of environmental management systems, voluntary disclosure programs, or some notion of corporate social responsibility ignore the evidence about what has worked in the past. Government will play an essential role in the new regulation. Similarly, despite the barriers some activist organizations have placed in the way of change, they historically have played a critical role in maintaining pressure for environmental progress, and they will continue to do so.

For these reasons, several elements of the old regulation will be essential to the new one. First, government will need to maintain a system of core normative standards that place continuous pressure on industry for improved performance. The theory of the old regulation, for its time, was indisputably sound. Industry would not have acted to reduce or clean up pollution in the 1960s and 1970s had government not used its coercive authority to force such action. The entire series of events that make a new regulation possible—the pollution prevention movement, the greening of industry, the concern about avoiding future liabilities, the effects of the TRI, the rise of beyond-compliance programs, to name a few—would have not have occurred without the force of government regulation. The revealing study by Kagan and others on the pulp and paper industry documents the critical role that government regulation plays. "Regulation," they conclude, "has been directly responsible for the large reductions in pulp mill pollution that stem from capital investments in very costly pollution control technologies."[4] Even voluntary programs, for all their likely value, become effective only against a backdrop of regulatory pressure, in some form, from government.

Similarly, government must have the legal authority and enforcement capability to hold firms accountable for meeting the core standards. Without such authority, the environmental protection system as a whole would quickly unravel. Some firms would seek short-term advantage from not complying, by not making investments in new technologies. Even the more progressive firms would feel pressure to cut corners. The integrity of the whole system depends on government being able to hold firms accountable. Although enforcement pressures might be applied in different ways in a new regulation, and compliance would be defined differently, especially for good performers, bottom-line enforcement capability is essential.

Third, transparency matters. Studies document how information promotes environmental progress and the crucial role that nongovernmental organizations may play. Think of the conditions under which environmental degradation was allowed to occur, virtually unabated, in the former Soviet Union and Eastern Europe. The common factor was a lack of transparency—of opportunities for third-party examination and independent criticism. Even in the United States, the more serious, long-running damage occurred at federal weapons facilities. Secrecy and insulation from critical oversight effectively immunized government facilities from responsibility for many years.[5] The lesson is that democracy and the transparency associated with it are good for the environment.

A crucial part of this transparency is provided by activist groups and other nongovernmental organizations. They constitute an independent voice for bringing environmental issues to public attention and holding government as well as industry accountable. Activists have been influential in the United States for several reasons: there are no green parties that are influential enough to aggregate environmental interests; it is a decentralized policy system; and there is easy access to the courts. Over the past decade or so, the availability of information through the Toxics Release Inventory and other right-to-know laws have enhanced the watchdog role these activist groups may play. At times, to be sure, activists may go overboard in pushing uncritically for more and more disclosure, even diluting its quality and value. Still, the perspective taken here is that the value of credible, accurate information and independent advocacy is indisputable.

So building a new regulation does not mean starting from the ground up. Environmental regulation has accomplished a great deal, in the United States and elsewhere. Many of its features are necessary underpinnings for a new regulation. At the same time, it will not be sufficient simply to fine-tune the old version at the margins and hope for the best. To reduce reporting here, streamline permitting there, or write clearer regulations somewhere else may help, but it does not present a coherent vision for change. What is needed is something that falls between a grab bag of superficial change and a radical restructuring.

The next three parts of the chapter outline a foundation for a new regulation. The discussion begins with the conceptual differences between the old and the new regulation. Based on these differences, it then proposes several objectives to guide the design of a new regulation. The third part considers how institutions and actors should change. The chapter then turns to the politics of a new regulation and suggests a "mixed scanning" approach for getting from the old to the new, given the near-term political realities in the U.S. policy system.

From the Old to the New Regulation: Conceptual Differences

Where should we begin in designing a new regulation? We could start by bringing together as many plausibly good ideas as possible and applying them in any ways that are feasible. Do we reform permitting? Reduce paperwork? Make rules more flexible? Adopt market incentives for all programs? Try all of the above?

Perhaps. But there are two problems with jumping directly to specific solutions. The first is that some may not be good ideas, or they are ideas that make sense in some situations and not in others. The second problem is that this approach does not offer anything close to a coherent strategy for change. This was the purely incremental approach taken with reinvention in the 1990s, which consisted of almost random group actions and experiments that had limited long-term effects.[6] To be sure, this approach did offer a number of useful lessons on what works and what may not, as was argued in chapter 5, but the time for unfocused incrementalism has passed. Progress toward a new regulation is most likely to occur if we are able to develop a conceptual framework for guiding even a gradual transition from the old to the new.

A place to start is with the conceptual differences between the old and the new regulation. To begin with, the new regulation will reject the core behavioral theory of the old one, which is that industry will act in society's interests only under the threat of legal sanctions. The fact is that many factors other than government regulation influence behavior in the business community. This is documented by the evidence regarding firms' efforts to go beyond legal compliance, to the extent that many firms now hold themselves publicly accountable for results that are not required by law. They do this through internal corporate initiatives, industry sector programs, government partnerships, and joint efforts with advocacy groups like the Alliance for Environmental Innovation.[7] Regulatory pressure from government is necessary, but it is not the only influence on firms.

The new regulation will also reject the notion that adversarial relationships are inherently superior to collaborative ones. This is not to say that pressure on industry from government and activists is not essential for progress, nor that adversarial relationships between government and many firms in some situations are not appropriate. It does mean that the prevailing model of discourse and relationships needs to shift from finding fault and assigning blame to searching for solutions. Comparative studies of environmental policy have found that the more combative and deterrence-based style of U.S. policy makers delivers no better results than the more collaborative styles typical in other countries.[8] Changes in problems, institutions, economic relationships, and other aspects of a postmodern world make the adversarial approach outdated for all but the more unwilling and recalcitrant firms.

Related to these differences, the new regulation will reject a strategy of centralized bureaucratic control as the dominant approach. Earlier chapters discussed how the old regulation relies on a Weberian model of problem solving, characterized by hierarchy, extensive elaboration of formal rules, and emphasis on conformance. Full compliance becomes nearly impossible; most violations turn on paperwork or technical issues; conformance with and interpretations of rules take precedence over environmental results. The new regulation should reflect the principles of social-political governance and reflexive law, which stress shared responsibility and institutional arrangements that promote dialogue. A strategy of control, commands, and deterrence should give way to a strategy based more on incentives, learning, and accountability.[9] The result is a far more diverse set of tools and an appreciation of the varied roles that government may play in addition to that of "the regulator."

The new regulation will also reject the notion that firms are all the same in their intentions and capacities, or that the firm itself should be seen merely as some kind of monolithic black box. It will be designed to recognize and account for differences among firms. Many of the complaints about the old regulation derive from the practice of assuming the worst, because it was built to account for the bad apples. Extensive reporting and record keeping are justified as a way to keep the likely noncompliant sources in line. Requiring permit modifications for even minor changes in processes or materials—even when they improve environmental performance—is based on the assumption that everyone is out to game the system. A premise of the new regulation is that some facilities and firms may be trusted and relied upon more than others. Moreover, these differences should be built into our regulatory designs and incorporated into relationships between government and others in society.

Finally, the new regulation will reject the narrow focus on compliance in favor of a broader emphasis on environmental performance. Having government and industry dedicate their best efforts to ensure full conformance with a detailed set of rules has certainly shown results, but it also has had some unfortunate consequences. Many compliance issues turn on matters of process or documentation that relate more to maintaining regulatory controls than environmental protection. It is well known that regulators tend to overcontrol on some issues and undercontrol on others, leading to high costs on the former and missed opportunities on the latter. Regulated entities have little or no regulatory incentive to do better than comply because government traditionally has been concerned, not with their successes, but with their failures. The new regulation would recognize that compliance with core normative standards is essential, but that public policy should be designed to define, measure, and encourage continuous improvement. In practical terms, this means government should focus more on making progress on a set of core environmental indicators and less on catching people who deviate from the procedural and administrative checkpoints that comprise much of the current regulation.

In sum, rather than assuming industry will act responsibly only under the threat of legal sanctions, the new model would recognize the multiple factors that exert pressure on firms—such as communities, investors, insurers, and employees. The idea that adversarial relationships among government and industry are necessary or desirable would give way to a preference for collaboration that promotes dialogue, trust, and mutual learning. Rather than relying on a strategy of centralized bureaucratic control through substantive law, the new model would be based more on a reflexive legal strategy. Instead of assuming that all regulated entities are the same and should be treated as such, it is accepted that differences in performance should be formally recognized. Finally, although compliance with core standards is essential, the broader task of defining, measuring, and encouraging improved environmental performance in systematic, consistent, and comparable ways will take on more prominence in the new regulation than it did in the old.

We may use these five conceptual differences to sketch the outlines of a new regulation. Table 7.1 summarizes them and their implications. It presents them as assumptions that determine our regulatory designs; proposes design principles that flow from each; and lists conditions that should exist if we want to redesign regulation based on these assumptions.

Table 7.1
Conceptual Differences Between the Old and the New Regulation

Old vs. New: Assumptions	Design Principles	Conditions to Support Change
Old: Deterrence is the best strategy. Only rules backed by sanctions affect behavior. *New*: Rules backed by sanctions are one of many influences on behavior.	Leverage the multiple factors that influence behavior. Use reflexive law to complement substantive law. Focus negative sanctions on performance failures that matter.	Information on causes of differential performance Understanding of the richness of the institutional landscape Information on the effects of different policy tools and strategies
Old: Adversarial relationships produce the best outcomes. *New*: Collaborative relationships promote the learning and continuous improvement that leads to better outcomes.	Create opportunities for learning, dialogue, and repeated interaction. Build accountability into regulatory designs. Adapt structures and relationships to account for compliance and performance history.	Guarantees against regulatory capture Sufficient levels of trust Capacity to measure results at firm and facility levels Confidence in government's ability to act against violators
Old: Goals are best achieved through a top-down strategy of bureaucratic control. *New*: Goals are best achieved through a more diverse and decentralized strategy based on learning, pressure for results, and horizontal influence.	Recognize positives as well as negatives in firm and facility performance. Create mechanisms, procedures, and structures that encourage critical self-reflection. Maximize opportunities for learning and building capacity.	Understanding of the multiple factors that affect performance Trust to encourage dialogue and information sharing Transparency that augments government oversight Government has the capacity to be more than a regulator
Old: Regulated actors are the same in intentions and capacities. *New*: Actors vary greatly in their willingness and capacity to perform responsibly.	Create performance tiers and tailor regulatory strategies to them. Expand assistance for those with good intentions but limited capacity.	Understanding of the factors that affect performance Ability to measure performance along key indicators

Table 7.1
(continued)

Old vs. New: Assumptions	Design Principles	Conditions to Support Change
	Create pressures, tools, and incentives that leverage internal dynamics in firms.	Ability to tailor strategies based on facility, firm, and sector characteristics
Old: Conformity with a set of rules is the desired outcome.	Define core performance objectives that apply to similar actors.	Ability to measure performance along key indicators
New: Continuous improvement on a range of environmental indicators is the desired outcome.	Link voluntary programs with accountability for results.	Trust that promotes dialogue and communication
	Create networks and other mechanisms that facilitate learning.	Legal authority that allows government to negotiate outcome-based agreements with regulated actors

Take, for example, the assumption that firms will act in the interests of society only under the threat of legal sanctions. That assumption determined the approach government has taken for decades. Under this behavioral theory, the way to make continued progress is to issue more rules, exercise closer oversight, and increase penalties to maximize the deterrent effects of the rules. For a variety of reasons, this book has argued that to continue with this approach on its own would be ineffective, even counterproductive. Once we accept that government rules backed by sanctions are one of many factors that influence behavior, however, we may adopt a different set of design principles.

The new regulation incorporates a more subtle approach that reflects the economic, social, institutional, and other changes that make the old regulation increasingly obsolete. Public policy then may be used to enhance the influence of change agents within firms, increase the flow of information within them, or increase transparency for influential external parties, such as investors. Indeed, one of the benefits of the TRI has been that it forced environmental and corporate managers to account for their emissions more carefully than they had in the past. Similarly, studies have shown that a benefit of environmental management, auditing, and accounting systems has been to provide managers with better information on how to reduce environmental impacts as well as their own operating costs.

What are some of the design principles this altered view would lead us to adopt? For one, it means using strategies that incorporate the different forces that influence firms, rather than relying narrowly and solely on government regulation. It also suggests a heavier reliance on reflexive law, which is designed to encourage critical self-reflection and induce behavior that leads to continuous improvement. Doing this, of course, means that we should base our regulatory designs on what motivates firms. As for the conditions needed to support change, there should be information on the causes of different levels of performance, an understanding of the institutional landscape that influences behavior, and the capacity on the part of government to find and punish violators.

Another example is the second assumption, the need for adversarial relationships. Although a core premise of the new regulation is that government and other forces must exert constant pressure on firms for improved performance, it does not accept that institutional conflict and formalism are necessary across the board. This book argues that a fundamental shift must occur, toward the assumption that except for proven or likely bad actors, collaborative relationships backed by regulatory and other pressures for results offer the best overall outcomes for society. Indeed, the new regulation is based upon the concept of social-political governance and all that concept implies.

This shift from adversarial to collaborative relationships suggests several design principles for a new regulation. Among these are the need to create opportunities for learning, dialogue, and repeated interaction (partly as a way to build trust); to build transparency and accountability into regulatory designs; and to adapt regulatory structures and relationships to the performance history and capacities of firms. Several conditions will support a shift to a more collaborative approach. A critical one is that there be sufficient guarantees against regulatory capture, so that government will have the independence to maintain pressure for improved performance. Others are the existence of a level of trust among actors, a capacity to measure results at the facility and firm levels, and public confidence in the government's authority and willingness to act against clear violators.

The next section builds on this analysis, especially on the design principles listed in the second column of table 7.1, by suggesting objectives that may guide the design of a new regulation and proposing steps that will help in achieving them. It distills the several design principles into a list of six more specific design objectives. If we were to develop a list of objectives that should guide the design of a new regulation based on these differences, how would it look?

Design Objectives for a New Regulation

The conceptual differences between the old and the new regulations suggest objectives and mechanisms that should define the basis for policy change. Based on the contrasts presented earlier, consider the following as objectives for a new regulation. It should be designed to: (1) establish and maintain legally enforceable, demanding performance standards; (2) differentiate among regulated firms based on past and expected future performance; (3) incorporate mechanisms and incentives that promote continuous improvements in performance, including market incentives; (4) build a capacity for policy learning; (5) measure performance at the facility, firm, and sector levels; and (6) create mechanisms and relationships that build trust.

Establish and Maintain Legally Enforceable, Demanding Performance Standards

A premise of this book is that little would have been achieved over the past four decades without the coercive hand of government. The "sea change" in attitudes and behavior that we have seen in industry was driven by regulatory pressure and, at least initially, not much else. As that pressure increased the costs of industry mismanagement, forced firms onto the same competitive footing, empowered communities and other external stakeholders, provided leverage to change agents in firms, and increased the ethical imperative for responsible behavior, nonregulatory pressures became increasingly important. Still, as a variety of studies suggest, regulatory pressure is the glue that holds this entire system of norms and expectations together.

As a source of pressure on industry, the new regulation will differ from the old in several ways. In general, government should focus on setting demanding goals and leave firms more discretion in deciding how to meet them. Several studies have shown how well-defined, measurable goals may motivate high levels of performance.[10] Firms should also be able to propose and gain approval for innovative approaches that could deliver better results, through innovation agreements that help offset some of their legal risk. Sector agreements, based on the Dutch model but adapted to the U.S. system, could also be used to enlist industry on a more cooperative basis. A promising sign within government is that agencies are being pushed to gauge their success more on the basis of measures of outcomes and results than outputs or activities, as was the case in the past.[11]

Many firms would agree to more stringent performance standards in exchange for certainty in what they must accomplish and flexibility in how they may accomplish it. Experience has shown that standards may be stringent and still be met if government keeps uncertainty to a minimum. Indeed, in EPA's flexible air permit project, firms were able to commit to reducing emissions below those defined in their conventional permits, given the increased flexibility they would have. A virtue of the Dutch covenants is that they define clear expectations for industry that the government agrees not to change for specified time periods. Reduced uncertainty typically serves to promote innovation because it limits the technical and organizational risks of technological development.[12]

The question is how in the context of the U.S. policy system such stringent goals could be agreed upon and set. One way is to incorporate in environmental legislation national targets but not specify in too much detail how they are to be achieved. The National Ambient Air Quality Standards are an illustration. Another would be some version of the Dutch covenants in which stringent goals are negotiated with industry leaders as an alternative way of meeting more prescriptive technology-based standards, which would come into play if the negotiated goals are not met. Admittedly, in the context of the U.S. policy system, this is perhaps the most difficult of the design standards listed here to meet. However, with appropriate legal authority, it could be possible to devise prototypes for policies that are stringent in goals and flexible in means.

Differentiate Among Firms Based on Past and Expected Future Performance

Especially since the mid-1980s, it is clear that firms vary greatly in their willingness and ability not only to comply but to do better than the law requires. And yet, with but a few exceptions, these variations have not been recognized in regulatory law or policy. This would change under the new regulation, which should incorporate performance tracks as a design element.

As a structural innovation in regulation, performance tracks offer many advantages. They enable agencies to identify proven high performers for whom reporting, inspection, and the other oversight costs of regulation may be reduced. They define a community that is well suited to collaborative efforts with government to promote measurement, technological innovation, and information sharing. They create an environment conducive to dialogue, communication, and trust building in general. Performance tiers also allow agencies to give recognition, access, and flexibility that may translate into business value for firms. These provide carrots that may be used to induce other firms to qualify them for the higher tracks.

To incorporate performance tiers into regulation, agencies must do two things: define criteria for differentiating among firms and decide how the higher tier firms should be treated differently. The EPA's Performance Track and similar state programs offer a starting point for the first. On the second, the key is to maintain the same or higher performance expectations for better firms, but reduce oversight costs and increase the flexibility and dialogue that promote innovation. A variety of mechanisms may reduce barriers to innovation and increase internal operating efficiencies for firms; these include reduced reporting, third-party audits, and caps and other permitting innovations. Again, there is a growing body of evidence with federal and state-level performance track programs to draw upon. The challenge is to incorporate these programs more explicitly into regulatory programs and statutes.

Promote Continuous Improvements in Environmental Performance
Core normative standards that apply pressure to industry are a necessary but not a sufficient condition for effective regulation. What is most impressive in the literature on greening and voluntary programs is that firms are able to achieve more than government requires and to gain business value from doing it. Regulation should be designed to encourage such behavior by providing positive (carrots) as well as negative (sticks) incentives and encouraging reflexivity among regulated firms.[13] Regulation applies pressure for meeting core normative standards.

Beyond conventional regulation, however, government may adopt other strategies based on the use of information, incentives, and partnerships to induce firms to improve their performance.

In the new regulation, a system of core enforceable performance targets will be used in combination with reflexive instruments that enable and induce firms to continually improve their performance. Think of these as more of a "pull" strategy that is used in combination with the "push" strategy based on the more traditional substantive law. As was noted in chapter 6, many elements of a more reflexive strategy have gradually been incorporated into the old regulation. These include market incentives (such as emissions trading), information disclosure, voluntary challenge programs, and many efforts described in chapter 6 as civic environmentalism. Again, the challenge is to incorporate them more fully into the regulatory system.

Take voluntary challenge programs and market incentives as illustrations. At least in the United States, voluntary programs have been little more than creative additions at the very margins of the regulatory system. Firms typically gain no specific regulatory benefits; such programs are rarely linked strategically with regulatory goals or mechanisms. If voluntary programs could be linked more effectively with regulatory pressures and expectations, however, they could become part of an effective "sticks" and "carrots" strategy for inducing firms not only to meet core standards but also to achieve far more. In a strategy for dealing with greenhouse gases, for example, firms that achieve ambitious goals in terms of emissions reductions or energy efficiency could be exempted later from mandatory policy measures, such as technology standards or a carbon tax. Experience has shown that having the certainty of knowing what their obligations will be and flexibility in determining how to achieve them will induce firms to achieve more ambitious goals than they otherwise might.[14]

Market incentives also offer advantages as a way to encourage continuous improvement and technology innovation. Emissions trading is the approach that has been used most often in the United States. Rather than rely solely on technology requirements to achieve the desired reductions in emissions, programs like trading allowances for acid rain give firms the flexibility to exceed the standards and create an asset (the allowances) or, alternatively, to purchase allowances on the market. This gives firms an incentive to search for technology and management innovations that go beyond the prevailing techniques. There also is evidence that flexible and reflexive tools like market incentives encourage "cleaner production" measures that are superior to end-of-pipe technology controls.[15] Market incentives will play a central role in future strategies for reducing greenhouse gases. Unlike local emissions trading programs, there is little concern with the redistribution of emissions that would occur as a result of the trades. In this and other areas, market incentives will be a key element of the new regulation, especially in promoting the objective of continuous improvement.[16]

Increase Capacities for Learning
Underlying the old regulation was the assumption that solutions were known and the task of government was to compel industry to use them. As a consequence, with its legalism, distrust, and inflexibility, the old regulation was not especially well suited to learning. In contrast, the new regulation should be designed explicitly to promote and institutionalize learning as a path to innovation and better performance.

A regulatory system based on learning would have several characteristics. In his book on technology innovation, David Wallace emphasizes the capacity for dialogue and communication.[17] In the literature on policy learning, researchers also stress the need for reliable feedback mechanisms; neutral third parties and forums to document and help institutionalize lessons learned; legal protection for good-faith efforts to innovate; trust that promotes information sharing and communication; and tools in organizations (such as a well-designed EMS) that promote systematic learning. Indeed, one could argue that the more successful firms in terms of their ability to link environmental and economic success are those that have established effective internal learning systems. On a macrolevel, the efforts of NAPA, the OECD, the Multi-State Working Group on Environmental Performance, Resources for the Future, and other organizations have been valuable in documenting and evaluating the many efforts in innovations that have been made to date.[18]

A capacity for learning is of little value if there is not the ability to change behavior in response to the lessons that are learned. This is perhaps the greatest limitation of the old regulation as a learning system. For government and industry alike, inflexibility in the authorizing laws and the regulations themselves make it difficult to adapt. The complexity of a medium-specific, federal-state regulatory system adds to this effect. In this sense, reducing transaction costs and streamlining regulatory procedures could increase learning capacities under a new regulation. Similarly, legal authority that gives agencies the flexibility needed to respond to new information and opportunities would improve learning capacities. Many EPA and local efforts in the past decade (Project XL, state innovation agreements, civic environmentalism) should be seen as attempts to create the conditions that lead to flexibility and improved learning.[19] The new regulation should be explicitly designed to create opportunities for learning and allow the flexibility that will enable government and industry to change their behavior in response to what they learn.

Measure Environmental Performance

The EPA collects an astonishing array of data for determining whether or not firms are complying. Yet critics complain that there is little consistent and comparable information on environmental performance.[20] A credible and reliable set of performance indicators, at the facility, firm, and even sector levels will be an essential element of the new regulation.

As testimony to the limited data on performance, consider what researchers use when they try to explain variations in facility or firm performance in response to external regulatory or investor pressures or to internal changes, such as adopting an environmental management system. Aside from compliance data, the dependent variable in nearly all of this research is the TRI, because it is one of the few sources of comparable data on performance. This is despite the limitations in TRI data: that it excludes small firms; ignores many sources of emissions; does not account for risk; and like may self-reporting systems, includes errors. The same is true of investment firms that evaluate the performance of socially responsible firms. They lack anything like the financial indicators available for evaluating and rating a firm's financial performance. Even compliance data are difficult to evaluate without a more detailed knowledge of the issues and the regulatory setting in which the firm operates. Beyond compliance data and the TRI, researchers have begun to use other indicators. In *Shades of Green*, the authors used data on discharges of three water pollutants and number of spills as their measures of performance.[21] Researchers are trying to find better measures, but it still is difficult to devise consistent, comparable indicators for evaluating facility and corporate environmental performance.

Still, there has been progress toward better measurement at the facility, firm, and sector levels. In such efforts as the Global Reporting Initiative, EPA's Performance Track, industry codes like Responsible Care, and the actions of leading firms, there now is more emphasis on and capacity for measurement than there was even five years ago. Such efforts may contribute to building a more performance-based regulation. Agreement on a core set of facility-based environmental indicators could be used to negotiate environmental management plans with facilities as a complement or even an alternative to existing rules. Experiments with sector commitments, such as the Strategic Goals Project between EPA and the metal finishing industry, suggest a model for sector-level collaboration.[22] Although there has been little experience in the United States with bench marking at the firm level, it may be possible to allow firms (or business units within firms) to opt out of certain regulatory requirements if they can demonstrate that they are "best in class" within their sector. The Dutch energy benchmarking program offers a model for how this might be done.[23] To be sure, several issues must be faced in devising more comparable and consistent reporting frameworks, such as accounting for different kinds of products, changing levels of production, and outsourcing of manufacturing, often to other countries. Nevertheless, there is a growing body of experience that, with enough attention and resources, could be used to overcome these issues and considerably improve the capacity for measuring results.

Create Mechanisms and Relationships That Build Trust
The issue of trust or lack of it in the old regulation has come up repeatedly. Nearly every commentary on U.S. environmental policy laments the high levels of distrust, especially in comparison with other industrial nations. One former state commissioner and later an EPA regional administrator has observed that the environment "is a public policy field which is almost built on an absence of trust."[24] As Wallace, Janicke, and others have argued, this distrust has consequences. It is often a barrier to

dialogue, communication, and innovation. It increases transaction costs. It encourages a low-risk response to regulatory standards and shifts attention and resources from performance to narrower issues of compliance. Is it possible to increase trust in the U.S. regulatory system without compromising government's ability to maintain pressure on industry for better performance? Can we break what has become a vicious circle of distrust and build the basis for constructive dialogue?

Trust may be defined simply as the view that other parties in a relationship will not act against your interests, at least without warning and good reason. The social science literature suggests factors that are associated with increased trust in recurring relationships, like those between regulators and firms.[25] Three such factors stand out in the context of a new regulation. One is credibility in meeting commitments. If firms commit to achieving a result or designing a new technology, or government agrees to make regulatory changes for high-performing firms or not change requirements for a period of time, then both sides should be able to deliver on their commitments. Another factor is agreement on a set of measurable goals. These define the mutual commitments and clarify the expectations of all parties. They provide some objective indicators that the desired performance is being achieved. A third factor is a degree of transparency that assures government, industry, and the public that each party is meeting its commitments or making good faith efforts to do so. The United States rates high in transparency but lower on the other two factors. In their comparative analysis of success in reaching voluntary agreements, Delmas and Terlak see the United States as being relatively less hospitable to such agreements than other countries. They observe that "EPA can neither issue a credible threat of regulation nor credibly promise regulatory flexibility to motivate firms to go beyond compliance."[26] They attribute this to the limited discretion allowed in U.S. regulatory statutes, which itself is a reflection of the high levels of distrust.

The argument made here is that the innovation efforts of the past decade have helped to build a foundation for increased trust among the actors in the regulatory system. This is a principal justification for voluntary challenge programs and agreements, as well as for beyond-compliance programs like EPA's Performance Track. Whatever their near-term environmental effects, these programs should help in building trust by involving government, firms, and others in cooperative relationships in which all of the parties can demonstrate credibility in meeting their commitments.

Changes in Agencies and Laws

Clearly, the transition to a new regulation will require changes in government institutions and laws. To explore these, consider the outline of the new regulation that has been presented so far: Government will recognize the many factors beyond regulation that influence industry behavior; relationships will need to be less adversarial and confrontational and more collaborative; government will have to shift from a strategy based on bureaucratic control to one based on learning; variations in firms' motivations and capacities will be incorporated into regulatory designs; and the current focus on compliance will shift to a broader concern with measuring and improving environmental performance. As a consequence, the previous section argued, the new regulation should be designed to maintain core normative standards that are applied fairly to all firms, differentiate among facilities and firms based on performance, promote continuous improvement through "pull" as well as "push" strategies, increase learning capacities throughout the regulatory system, measure performance, and build trust. What does this mean for agencies and laws? Several changes come to mind.

First, agencies will need to develop more diverse skills and adaptive structures. Agencies in the United States are designed to implement a legally based control strategy fairly and efficiently. Given the constraints that are inherent in such an approach, they have been reasonably successful. Their success may be attributed to having the necessary legal, technical, and administrative skills. Although such skills will be important in the new regulation, many other skills and capabilities will also be needed. These include skills in network management, negotiation, performance measurement, collaboration, and others associated with new forms of governance.

Second, structural changes will be necessary. A long-standing issue in agency organization is whether the medium-based approach that has defined regulation for nearly four decades should be changed. In the end, such a change may merely trade off one set of strengths and weaknesses for another. What may matter more is creating structures that are suited to the characteristics of the firms being regulated. For example, it may make sense to create different organizations within agencies for dealing with high performers, for small firms, for firms unwilling or unable to meet basic legal requirements, for nonpoint and other diffuse sources, for specific sectors, and so on. This would allow agencies to develop the tools, skills, and relationships that are most appropriate for the different types of firms. The kind of relationship would be the organizing principle, rather than environmental medium or statutory authority. Knowledge of the industry across all media would also be helpful. Studies of regulation in other countries often comment on the greater respect and confidence that industry people have in government inspectors and permitting officials when they are experienced in and knowledgeable about the industry they are regulating.[27] Developing this kind of expertise within environmental agencies should be a priority in the new regulation.

Third, laws and agencies will have to incorporate more integrated, adaptive strategies. If there is a constant in the literature on the old regulation, it is that a centralized, fragmented, and rigid approach inhibits problem solving. Under a new regulation, environmental laws will allow more integration across media, use measurable goals in standard setting, authorize performance tiers, and enable agencies to respond to and encourage local and regional exercises in civic environmentalism. Whether or not that could require one integrated environmental law is a difficult question. Given current political realities, however, it will be more feasible to build additional flexibility into the existing laws as part of the incremental strategy discussed later. Indeed, second-generation legislative changes proposed in the 1990s would have given EPA authority to make exceptions from existing statutes if that would enable regulated firms to achieve better environmental results.

Observations on the current laws may be useful here. Some aspects of the current statutory framework are more suited to the demands of a new regulation than others. Consider the foundation of air pollution control, the National Ambient Air Quality Standards. The NAAQS offer the clearest example of national environmental goals that drive the regulatory system. They define ambient targets that all parts of the country must meet. It is no accident that the best trend data on environmental conditions, and the most significant improvements, are the NAAQS pollutants. One may argue with how the NAAQS are set, but their effectiveness in driving a results-based air pollution policy is clear. They have stimulated a variety of innovative approaches locally as officials devise strategies to reach or maintain air quality goals.[28]

National programs for water pollution control present an interesting picture. There is nothing comparable to the NAAQS, in the sense of uniform goals that apply nationally. The Clean Water Act does, however, incorporate a goal-oriented approach, through water quality standards adopted by states and approved by EPA. The theory of the water program is that states will work backward from these goals to determine what kinds of control measures are needed in different locations. A series of court decisions in the 1990s reinforced this link, holding that the Clean Water Act required the states to set total maximum daily loads (TMDLs) for dischargers into a water body. Indeed, the TMDL program offers interesting opportunities for testing ideas for a new regulation. It could combine many elements discussed here: strategies tailored to situations, incentives and mechanisms that encourage critical self-reflection, negotiated agreements based on measurable goals, and shared responsibility for results.

Falling at the bottom in its relevance for a new regulation is hazardous waste. Devised in a hurry under the apparent crisis conditions of the late 1970s and early 1980s, and fueled by public fears about "ticking time bombs" like Love Canal, programs established under RCRA and HSWA embody some of the worst characteristics of the old regulation. They provide little information about results, rely almost entirely on process controls, and demand costly reporting and record keeping. Furthermore, they are complex and difficult to implement for the hundreds of thousands of small-quantity generators to which they apply. They are also a constant source of friction between government and industry and, many would argue, a distraction from more substantive activities. A product of the contentious environmental politics of the early 1980s, HSWA in particular offers a model for how *not* to design a new regulation. For these reasons, reform and streamlining of the RCRA regulations has been a major EPA effort for the past several years.

Of course, an important part of the equation is the several key environmental issues that current laws fail to address. If, as Ken Geiser argues, the future of environmental management lies in managing materials rather than simply controlling pollution, current laws fall considerably short.[29] They largely ignore and sometimes exacerbate the need for greater efficiency in materials, energy, and water use. They provide little incentive for more sustainable product design, use, or disposal. Although these broader issues are not addressed in this book, a more complete transition to a new regulation will require a broader conception of the environmental "problem" along the lines suggested by Geiser and others.

In the meantime, in line with the mixed scanning approach described later, a pragmatic legislative strategy would be to authorize agencies such as EPA and its state counterparts to grant exceptions to existing requirements with appropriate justification. These exceptions could allow agencies to implement cross-media permitting and other more integrated approaches, provide technology waivers with "soft landing" provisions for promising innovations, negotiate alternative environmental contracts with specific facilities or firms when they can deliver significant results for a set of core environmental indicators, and implement performance tracks that allow varied oversight and permitting requirements.

The appropriate justification for these incremental steps toward a new regulation has been a matter of debate. Should legal exceptions be granted only if they promise "superior" environmental performance, anything better than what the current system delivers, or simply greater efficiency in getting the same result? These questions came up repeatedly in Project XL and would be a central issue in proposals for legislative change. Given the arguments made here about the need for systematic change, it would make sense for Congress to authorize exceptions that provide a reasonable assurance of at least the current level of environmental protection, so long as they promote the objectives set out for a new regulation.

For all of these changes, there are questions of resources and priorities. Many people think that we cannot afford to change. They argue that the day-to-day demands of managing the current regulatory system necessarily will crowd out efforts to innovate. They point to the reportedly high costs of such innovations as EPA's Project XL and Common Sense Initiative, New Jersey's facility-wide permitting, and federal–state efforts to develop flexible air permits in an era of tight government budgets as a barrier to change. In an age of limited resources, some people argue, government cannot afford to invest in these kinds of innovations, which at least initially could require more resources.

However valid they may be, there are several responses to these concerns. First, with all of these innovations, there is a learning curve. In the case of both XL and the flexible air permits, each additional transaction typically has cost less in time and resources than earlier ones. Second, some of the initial costs of these innovations grew out of the lack of policy alignment within agencies and disputes about the role of outside groups. This was especially the case with Project XL. As these issues are resolved and agencies align internally, the costs of the innovations should fall. Third, the old regulation is so full of transaction costs and administrative complexities that a new model will surely offer opportunities for simplification. In the innovative permit projects, for example, what had been sixty to eighty separate permits at one facility were consolidated into one integrated permit, which allowed more efficiency by the facility and the agencies. Finally, the changes that are associated here with a new regulation will involve a greater sharing of responsibility and work between business and government. With a chance at more flexibility and lower regulatory transaction costs, firms will be in a position to share more of the regulatory process burdens with government.

One of the principal challenges for innovators is to draw upon the many sources of experience presented here but apply them in ways that are consistent with American institutions and culture. Drawing on the experience of the Netherlands does not mean that what worked reasonably well there could be applied whole cloth here. As Theo de Bruijn and Vicki Norberg-Bohm concluded in their collection of essays comparing innovations in several western democracies, new approaches need to have a good fit with the existing national policy style if they are to be closely embedded in the larger policy system.[30] This is why so much attention has been given in this book to the characteristics of the U.S. policy system, to the effect this has had on our regulatory designs, and to the comparisons with other countries. Context matters, in environmental regulation as in any other policy area. Those who would lead the transition to a new regulation must first do their homework. Understanding that context and what it means for a new regulation has been a principal goal of this book.

The Politics of a New Environmental Regulation

The political debate for the past four decades has been dominated by the two old story lines. In this debate, the scope and stringency of regulation is seen as the measure of society's commitment to the environment. Those who resent the intrusion of the state into markets and fear the economic effects of stringent programs demand less regulation. On the other side, environmental advocates see a strong regulatory and enforcement presence along lines of the old model as essential for progress. The notion that there is a third way—a different regulation made up of new relationships, structures, and roles—typically has been lost in the debate.

This is not to say that people did not appreciate the need for change, or that changes did not occur. Legislatively, the incorporation of emissions trading in air programs, the use of information disclosure, and greater attention to nonpoint sources constituted important changes in the old model. Administratively, more use of consensus-based methods, improved programs for compliance assistance and self-auditing, and the modest progress in building pollution prevention strategies into regulation have had positive, if limited, effects. Conceptually, there is wide agreement, even among strong defenders of environmental programs, that regulation should change. Overall, however, there has not been a political consensus that could deliver legislative authority for regulatory change.

The mid-1990s should have been the right time for the transition to a new regulation. There was a Democratic administration that generally supported environmental values and would not immediately be suspected of wanting to roll back standards. A number of prominent defenders of environmental programs (e.g., NAPA, E4E, and PCSD) were offering thoughtful critiques of the old system and setting out arguments and principles for a new one. Well-known firms were showing results beyond what government required. Federal and state agencies were trying to adopt more flexible, collaborative, performance-based approaches. Proposals for change involved the kinds of potential win-wins for the environment and the economy that the Clinton administration might have welcomed. Still, in the end, the reinvention era of the 1990s left little by way of lasting effects in law, policy, and institutions. The reasons are varied: a lack of commitment and perhaps resources at EPA, a sensitivity to the criticisms of the national environmental groups, nervousness about appearing to reduce enforcement, or the distractions of having to defend regulation in the face of the Republican onslaught of 1995. Whatever the reasons, the politics stream could not accommodate the demands for change churning in the policy and problem streams.

The results of the 2000 elections could have opened the door to a new era. It did not. Why has the Bush administration not picked up and pushed the innovation agenda more aggressively? After all, many leading firms are calling for the kinds of changes the revisionist critics wrote about in the 1990s. Politically, innovation projects from the previous administration that were continued in the Bush years provide political cover for a more rapid transition to a new regulation. True, EPA's Performance Track and some other Browner-era initiatives were endorsed by Administrator Christine Whitman and her successors, Michael Leavitt and Stephen Johnson. But they have not been embraced, in the sense of expanding and institutionalizing them in as part of an effort toward building a new system. Although there have been controversial efforts to reform regulation or introduce what firms see as more rationality into regulatory processes, the goal of building a more flexible, performance-based regulation has not been taken as a priority. Like its predecessor, the Bush administration has focused more on fine-tuning the old regulation than making the transition to a new one.

The situation in Congress is even less promising. In the 1990s, the proposals for second- and third-generation legislation that would have authorized incremental change were discussed seriously, but none were adopted. Since 2001, even this modest degree of legislative interest and consensus has dissipated. On environmental topics, partisan differences on Capitol Hill are as striking as they have ever been. Issues of homeland security and war pushed environmental reform even further down the legislative agenda in the early 2000s. Certainly, the realistic chances of substantive change in the environmental statutes in the foreseeable future range from very low to nonexistent. However promising many innovations that have been discussed in this book, the reality is that "policy change can succeed at the federal level . . . only with the active assistance of Congress."[31]

Within the states, where many promising efforts have been under way, the picture is bleak as well. Leaders in regulatory innovation in the 1990s faced massive budget deficits in the early 2000s. This highlights the challenge for state innovators. It is abundantly clear that state governments will not have the permitting, inspection, and enforcement resources to implement the old regulation. A top-down, compliance-based approach is simply not feasible with the resources that will be available to states in the coming years. Like the federal government, states need to innovate to find ways to meet environmental goals with constant or fewer resources. When tough budget times hit, however, innovation programs in the states are seen as fluff and often are cut.

What about industry leaders as drivers for change? The political dynamics within industry are complex. A visible cadre of major firms has been making the case for a new regulation not just rhetorically but in action. These include firms from the pharmaceutical and healthcare sectors (e.g., Baxter, Pfizer, Bristol-Myers Squibb, Johnson & Johnson), chemicals and energy (e.g., Dupont, Dow, or BP-Amoco), computers and electronics (Hewlett-Packard, IBM, Texas Instruments, and Intel come to mind), among others. It is these and many other firms that are setting and reporting on corporate goals, thinking about product design and stewardship, and participating in EPA and NGO voluntary programs. They take high environmental standards as a given and seek business value from top environmental performance. To be sure, they may criticize regulation for its transaction costs, uncertainty, and cost-ineffectiveness, but they accept regulation as a necessary fact of life and have learned to manage it and derive strategic value from their environmental policies.

Others within industry present a different picture. Among most large firms, compliance is seen as legally and politically necessary. Beyond this, many firms do not make a case for leadership and actively oppose new requirements across the board. In some sectors, such as mining, there are large gaps in regulatory coverage that firms do not want to see closed. For most small and medium-sized firms, it is a daily struggle to cope with existing requirements, especially given the complexity of the rules and the several layers of government they must deal with. Talk of a new environmental regulation is a vague and distant prospect, obscured by the demands of maintaining compliance. Moreover, even among larger firms, there is talk of a "green arthritis" that could threaten the progress made to date when economic conditions are less favorable.[32]

National environmental groups generally have been skeptical of proposals that involve more flexibility or less oversight for industry. The NRDC was highly critical of Project XL, especially Intel's and 3M's permitting plans.[33] In part, they viewed flexible regulation as a wolf in sheep's clothing that would lead to relaxed standards and collusion with industry. Poorly designed and implemented, flexible regulation could have this result, as discussed in chapter 6. Well designed and with adequate safeguards, however, the new regulation could promise better results in more areas than the old one. Even among the national activist organizations, there is a growing recognition that a newer generation of environmental issues and a political reluctance to expand conventional regulatory controls make it necessary to think creatively about changing the regulatory system along that lines that are discussed here.[34] The test of their support will be the ability to demonstrate that a new regulation can still deliver measurable environmental results.

However, several political realities also may explain environmentalists' frequent opposition to these proposals. First, national organizations derive their political clout from stringent, top-down federal regulation. This is where they are able to use their influence with Congress, to leverage national fund raising, and to litigate. Second, activist groups typically have more success in attracting members and raising money when they stress contrasts and raise fears than when they work quietly to find a middle way. Third, activist groups may take a hard line on innovation projects to increase their negotiating leverage. That flexibility will make a firm more efficient or competitive may be of little direct interest to many activists. Their interests may lie in maintaining stringent national rules and exercising close oversight over industry, without regard to the larger financial implications. The political dynamics of environmental advocacy have encouraged continued support for the old rules-and-deterrence model of regulation.

Among the national groups, Environmental Defense has taken a slightly different path. It played a key role in incorporating acid rain allowance trading into the 1990 Clean Air Act. Through its Alliance for Environmental Innovation, it also has entered into successful partnerships with companies like McDonald's and Federal Express. Another promising trend is the emergence of bridge-builders like CERES. Formed by leaders from the socially responsible investment community in 1989, CERES enlists firms as "endorsers" of sustainability principles and asks them to report on a range of corporate environmental indicators. CERES also led in creating the Global Reporting Initiative, discussed in chapter 4. Although the more traditional activist groups play a crucial role in environmental protection by keeping the pressure on both industry and government and pushing for transparency, these newer organizations that are committed to partnerships and collaboration may play a different kind of role in supporting the transition to a new regulation.

The politics of a new regulation in the early 2000s come down to this: The forces that built momentum toward a new regulation are still in play, but are less visible than they were before. The political leadership at EPA has taken a generally moderate, reformist approach to regulation, within an administration that is highly suspect and criticized on many environmental issues. Leading firms still want to engage government and others, as their continued participation in a range of voluntary government, NGO, and industry initiatives shows. On the other hand, less progressive elements in industry may see the current political situation as an opportunity to reduce standards rather than evolve toward a different kind of regulation. In this they have had some success. Whatever momentum existed in many states is at least slowed by budgetary constraints. Environmental groups approach the topic cautiously, especially given their distrust of the administration. Within Congress, partisan conflict and the press of other issues make broad legislative change unlikely. Given all of this, how do we make the transition from an old to a new regulation?

Getting There from Here

This book has given mixed views on the prospects for a new environmental regulation. On the positive side, there has been incremental progress toward creating a more adaptable, performance-based learning system. There are emerging islands of trust in the larger sea of adversarial legalism. At federal and state levels, regulatory agencies have gained experience with a variety of innovative approaches, although few have advanced much beyond the pilot or small-scale implementation stage. Influential companies are demonstrating the business value of environmental excellence. Partnerships among communities, activists, and businesses are showing measurable results at the ecosystem level. Compare a snapshot of 2005 with one of 1975, and it is clear that much has changed.

Still, these changes are occurring at the margins. The old regulation remains largely intact. The problem stream is changing and the policy stream struggles to adapt, but the politics stream is still locked in a debate over the pro- and antiregulatory story lines. The task now is getting from here to there: from an old regulation designed for a earlier time to one that recognizes the changes in problems, institutions, behavior, and relationships that have occurred, as well as one that takes advantage of the learning that has taken place over the past nearly four decades of modern environmental regulation.

There are two ways to change the world—in a large number of small steps whose effects accumulate over time, or in a few big leaps. In public administration theory, Charles Lindblom has presented this as a contrast between the incremental and rational-comprehensive models of policy change.[35] Relative to many other systems, policy making in the United States has been described as incremental, a variation on the British style of "muddling through." Policy makers set limited goals that are vague, sometimes contradictory, and subject to negotiation over time, in a process of successive mutual adjustments. Policies change in small steps, each of which builds upon those that precede it.

Proponents of a new regulation in the 1990s were mostly incrementalists. Their pragmatic view of the world is captured in Bill Ruckelshaus' statement about his Enterprise for the Environment project:

Participants agreed, he wrote, "rather than to leap all at once, to proceed . . . in an incremental, evolutionary way—cautiously placing one stepping stone at a time, moving forward, then testing its stability before moving to the next."[36] This is a classic expression of an incremental strategy.

Still, what Ruckelshaus and others were advocating was more than just classic muddling through. Their approach was piecemeal, but it also was intended to be systematic. It called for a set of carefully documented policy experiments that would lead to long-term change. Even EPA's reinvention projects in the 1990s adopted this learn-by-experimentation approach. The goal of Project XL, for example, was to document the results of fifty pilots and determine which to adopt more widely. As it turned out, it was difficult to apply this strategy to a system that was not well suited to policy learning, but the notion of deliberately creating opportunities for learning was sound.

The strategy proposed here is similar to Amitai Etzioni's model of mixed scanning. As a change strategy, mixed scanning "combines higher order, fundamental decision making with lower order, incremental decisions that work and/or prepare for the higher order ones."[37] Mixed scanning is more strategic and planned than a purely incremental approach, but more pragmatic and adaptable than what Charles Lindblom terms a rational-comprehensive approach to change. It offers a strategic middle path, in which a conceptual framework and set of design objectives guide a more pragmatic process of experimentation on the ground. This chapter has set out such a conceptual framework. A mixed scanning approach means that incremental steps should be taken in the context of the kind of conceptual framework that has been presented in this chapter.

The first step a mixed-scanning strategy would require is changing the laws. Nearly every assessment of the policy system in the 1990s concluded that a prescriptive and fragmented legal framework posed major barriers to innovation. In theory, these barriers would be overcome with an integrated and performance-based environmental protection statute that replaced its medium-focused predecessors. In practice, although proposals for such a law have been made in the United States, and versions have been adopted in other countries, wholesale revisions are unlikely here. A basis for a mixed scanning approach, however, would be legislative changes that would give regulators more discretion to innovate and government and industry the chance to create more opportunities for learning.

A second step in a mixed-scanning strategy would be to begin to implement aspects of a new regulation with the better, proven environmental performers. Proposals for alternative tracks that treat high performers differently from lesser ones are compelling, for many reasons. It is with high performers that government may begin to build relationships based on trust and dialogue. It is the high performers who are in a position to generate information about new technologies or best practices that may be diffused more broadly. For facilities with good track records, government may, with more confidence, offer flexibility as well as delegate more oversight authority to third parties. The EPA's Performance Track and some twenty state programs similarly designed are a step in this direction.

A third step in a mixed-scanning strategy would be to replace existing regulatory provisions with environmental management contracts at selected sites, based on core performance indicators. The most effective way to move from a largely process-based to a performance-based system is to identify important performance indicators for a facility, industry sector, or geographic area, measure them regularly, and hold sources accountable for the results. Except for environmental indicators that necessarily are process based (such as procedures for preventing chemical accidents), legal obligations would be based on outcomes. These contracts would combine elements of integrated permitting, environmental management systems, and performance measurement to define an alternative, but legally enforceable set of requirements for regulated entities that choose this route.

A fourth step would be to take a dramatically different approach to regulating small facilities, based on experience gained in the Massachusetts Environmental Results Program and similar efforts. Given the growing importance of small and diffuse sources and limits in the oversight capacities of regulators, the rules-and-deterrence model has become less effective for most small facilities. The constraints on their resources, information, and flexibility in responding to diverse regulations mean that they will often evade compliance. As the ERP revealed, many are not even included on the lists of regulated facilities. In place of the top-down, deterrence model of the old regulation, agencies should adopt a more facilitative approach that defines key areas for improvement and provides the needed tools. For those who still evade compliance, the enforcement model then becomes entirely appropriate.

A fifth near-term step would be to establish performance agreements with industry organizations. These would draw their inspiration from the Dutch sector covenants, with adjustments to the American regulatory system and culture. Combining elements of EPA's sector projects, voluntary challenge programs, performance tracks, the agreements used in Project XL, and industry efforts like Responsible Care, these agreements would commit firms to achieving measurable results for performance indicators that are significant for a sector, especially for those that currently are unregulated. These sector agreements would substitute for more conventional technology-based rules, at least for a time. To avoid the problem of free riders within a sector, nonparticipants would be subject to conventional regulation. Similarly, an inability to meet the industry commitments could justify the imposition of conventional regulatory controls.

These near-term steps serve longer-term purposes. They add to the list of lessons about what does and does not work. They gradually build new relationships as actors gain experience with each other and with new ways of doing business. They expand our capacities in environmental management systems, performance measurement, community engagement, sharing of best practices, public–private dialogue, and other tools of the new regulation. Finally, they keep the spirit of innovation alive until the larger political conditions for fundamental change are achieved.

In a mixed-scanning strategy, typically long periods of incremental learning and adaptation (for testing, trust building, and experimentation) are punctuated with more intense periods of rapid and comprehensive change. In the context of environmental regulation, this could include statutory authority for a modified regulatory approach, basic shifts in resources and priorities at federal and state levels, agency reorganization (from a media-based to some other organizing principle), and a fundamental restructuring of relationships between government and outside organizations. This would involve both a speeding up of the process of change as well as the incorporation of the many lessons learned and relationships forged during the less eventful period of incremental change.

The conditions for such a period of more intense and comprehensive change are not easy to imagine in the context of contemporary American politics. They would include a consensus from all or most sides of the environmental debate that a new regulation could improve economic efficiency and environmental progress. They also would include strong commitment from the White House and the congressional leadership and the support or acquiescence of national environmental organizations. Because many people still are locked into the largely symbolic debate over the two old story lines, it may take some time for these conditions to come about. The gridlock in the politics stream is the main barrier to change. This gridlock is not necessarily inevitable in environmental politics, however. The experience of the 1970s demonstrates convincingly that "the U.S. political system is capable of developing major environmental policies in fairly short order under the right conditions."[38] Whether or not the right conditions will exist in the near future is uncertain, to be sure. In the meantime, an incremental but conceptual and learning-based strategy for change offers the best alternative for speeding up the transition to a new environmental regulation.

Two Visions for the Future

Consider the two visions of environmental regulation that have been presented in this book. In the first, measures to protect the environment are seen to present a nearly inevitable tradeoff with economic growth and competitiveness. As rational economic actors, business entities are presumed to reduce the adverse environmental effects of their behavior only when they are compelled to do so by government, under threat of legal sanctions. Any deviations from government specifications are undesirable; not only may such deviations increase pollution, they also undermine government's authority to prescribe and enforce the system of rules on which environmental quality is thought to depend.

This vision of regulation assumes a high degree of bureaucratic control over economic entities. It relies almost entirely on sticks over carrots as a way of influencing behavior. Over time, it leads to situations in which the coercive powers of the state are applied to minute aspects of behavior. Because there is a concern that the economic power of industry may co-opt government and use the authority of the state to promote industry's narrow interests over society's broader concerns, there are clear lines between government and industry. Fairly high levels of adversarial relationships are assumed to be healthy and necessary to maintain government's autonomy from industry influence. Indeed, underlying the theory of the old regulation is an assumption that adversarial combat produces the best outcomes for society.

This vision of environmental regulation involves heroic assumptions about government and what it may accomplish. Government must perform three kinds of tasks: determine what society's goals should be, decide what specific steps should be taken to achieve them, and ensure that large numbers of entities conform. This first is an inherently governmental role that only government may perform. The second and third are more complex tasks in which government, on its own, may have limited capacity. In this vision of regulation, however, government is expected to take the lead in determining how goals are to be achieved and in ensuring conformance with a complex system of rules and standards.

Now consider the second vision of environmental regulation. Government plays an essential role, to be sure, in deciding what society's environmental goals should be and maintaining a system of core normative standards and accountability. However, it allows far more discretion for regulated entities to determine how they will achieve those standards. It also involves more delegation of responsibility to industry and third parties to see that regulated firms meet their performance expectations.

Society's interests in environmental quality and economic efficiency are not necessarily incompatible. The traditional zero sum of regulation is seen as a potential, but not an inevitable, win-win. Regulation is designed to maximize the opportunities for win-win solutions by granting firms the flexibility to discover least-cost solutions, keeping the transaction costs of permitting and documentation to a minimum, and promoting the integration of environmental decision making into long-term business planning. Government uses factors other than regulation to influence behavior. It relies on both substantive and reflexive legal strategies, depending on the problem and situation. In addition to regulation, government uses strategies based on information, incentives, and partnerships to get results.

In this second vision, carrots are seen to be as effective as sticks. Positive reinforcement through recognition and different treatment for good performers is combined with negative reinforcement through penalties and "shaming" for poor performers. The idea that adversarial relations lead to the best outcomes is replaced by the idea of social-political governance—that cooperation, sharing of responsibility, and a collaborative search for solutions will deliver better results. Rather than trying to control every aspect of behavior, government focuses more on creating incentives and procedures that will encourage actors to continually evaluate and improve their performance. Although government must sustain a capacity to deter irresponsible behavior, its punitive powers are used strategically for regulated firms that are unwilling to meet their core regulatory obligations.

Most important, this second vision is designed to incorporate and build a capacity for policy learning. It recognizes that solutions are not always known, especially by government. It relies on the problem-solving abilities of regulated firms to discover and apply solutions—always under pressure from government for measurable results. It relies on legal instruments and policy strategies that encourage self-critical reflection among firms, with more use of reflexive legal strategies. In this vision of regulation, there is room to adapt to new opportunities and information.

At a broad level, these two visions differentiate the old from a new environmental regulation. The old one is based on bureaucratic oversight, compulsion, and deterrence. The new one reflects a more complex and dynamic view of relationships and of the factors that shape behavior. The old regulation assumes an inherent incompatibility between environmental and economic success at both the macro (societal) and micro (firm) levels. The new one is designed to make environmental and economic success more compatible. By assuming that industry will subvert the public good at any opportunity, the old regulation reinforces distrust among actors. The new regulation is realistic; it accepts that there will always be cheaters, and that credible enforcement is necessary. At the same time, it is designed to encourage collaboration and to create the social capital that promotes trust.

Our goal in the next decade or two should be to move from the first to the second vision. To be sure, as argued throughout this book, such a transition is already under way Still, progress has been slow. The statutory basis of the old regulation remains intact, virtually untouched by the experience of the past two decades. The "gotcha" mentality of enforcement officials is well entrenched, with corrosive effects on relationships and environmental performance. Agency innovations have rarely progressed beyond the status of pilots and experiments. Groups like the Enterprise for the Environment have been unable to agree on more than vague principles. The transition to a new environmental regulation is incomplete. Indeed, in most respects, it has stalled.

The question now is whether we will continue to muddle through with an anachronistic policy system or take advantage of the forces that are pushing us toward a new regulation. Each additional year of muddling adds to the list of lost opportunities: to the innovations that are not adopted because of costly and uncertain permitting processes, to the talent and resources that are diverted from preventing pollution or redesigning products to doing low-value paperwork, to the distrust that encourages small firms to stay below the regulatory screen rather than seek help.

The old environmental regulation has brought us reasonably well through the first in what will surely be several developmental phases in environmental policy. It was suited to a specific time, for a particular set of issues, in an early phase of institutional development. What is needed now is a more dynamic, adaptive approach that creates capacities for learning, a sharing of responsibility, and continuous improvement. Like many other countries for whom these changes are already under way, it is time for the United States to build a new environmental regulation on the foundations of the old.

Notes

Preface

1. Lon Fuller, *The Morality of Law* (New Haven, CT: Yale University Press, 1965), 181.

Chapter 1

1. Mary Graham, *The Morning After Earth Day: Practical Environmental Politics* (Washington, DC: Brookings Institution, 1999), 118.

2. This is roughly the projection for annual costs by 2000 in EPA's 1990 report, *Environmental Investments: The Cost of a Clean Environment* (Washington, DC: EPA, 1990). This also is discussed in a 1999 report by Frank S. Arnold, "Environmental Protection: Is It Bad for the Economy?" Available at the web site of EPA's National Center for Environmental Economics (www.epa.gov/economics).

3. This estimate is based on an extrapolation from estimates in the 1990 *Environmental Investments* report. A reasonable estimate in 2004 dollars would be about $3.4 billion.

4. As is argued by Gregg Easterbrook in *A Moment on the Earth: The Coming Age of Environmental Optimism* (New York: Viking, 1995), xiii–xxi.

5. These critics are discussed in detail throughout this book, especially chapter 5. For general discussions of their critiques, see Daniel A. Mazmanian and Michael Kraft, eds., *Toward Sustainable Communities: Transition and Transformations in Environmental Policy* (Cambridge, MA: MIT Press, 2001); and Robert A. Durant, Daniel J. Fiorino, and Rosemary O'Leary, eds., *Environmental Governance Reconsidered: Challenges, Choices, and Opportunities* (Cambridge, MA: MIT Press, 2004).

6. An example is the Environmental Law Institute's *Barriers to Environmental Technology and Use* (Washington, DC: Environmental Law Institute, 1998).

7. This point about the similarities in initial national responses to pollution problems is made in the comparative literature, but most clearly in Martin

Janicke and Helmut Weidner, eds., *National Environmental Policies: A Comparative Study of Capacity Building* (Berlin: Springer, 1997). Also see Martin Janicke, "Democracy as a Condition for Environmental Policy Success: The Importance of Non-institutional Factors," in William M. Lafferty and James Meadowcroft, eds., *Democracy and the Environment: Problems and Prospects* (Cheltenham, UK: Edward Elgar, 1996), 71–85.

8. There is an extensive literature on this. For illustrations, see J. Clarence Davies and Jan Mazurek, *Pollution Control in the United States: Evaluating the System* (Washington, DC: Resources for the Future, 1998); Marian R. Chertow and Daniel C. Esty, eds., *Thinking Ecologically: The Next Generation of Environmental Policy* (New Haven, CT: Yale University Press, 1997); Daniel J. Fiorino, "Environmental Policy as Learning: A New View of an Old Landscape," *Public Administration Review*, 61 (May/June 2001), 322–344; and Robert W. Hahn, ed., *Risks, Costs, and Lives Saved: Getting Better Results from Regulation* (New York: Oxford University Press, 1996).

9. For comparisons of the approaches taken in these countries, see William M. Lafferty and James Meadowcroft, eds., *Implementing Sustainable Development: Strategies and Initiatives in High-Consumption Societies* (Oxford: Oxford University Press, 2000).

10. A useful review is Michael E. Kraft and Norman J. Vig, "Environmental Policy from the 1970s to the Twenty-First Century," in Norman J. Vig and Michael E. Kraft, eds., *Environmental Policy: New Directions for the Twenty-First Century*, 6th ed. (Washington, DC: CQ Press, 2006), 1–33.

11. See Daniel J. Fiorino, *Making Environmental Policy* (Los Angeles: University of California Press, 1995), 25–30.

12. The best exposition of this view is Eugene Bardach and Robert Kagan, *Going by the Book: The Problem of Regulatory Unreasonableness* (Philadelphia: Temple University Press, 1982).

13. From Bill Clinton and Al Gore, *Reinventing Environmental Regulation* (Washington, DC, White House, 1996), 2. This was part of the White House announcement of several initiatives in March 1995, including Project XL.

14. Jonathan Lash and David T. Buzzelli, "Beyond Old-Style Regulation," *Journal of Commerce* (Feb. 28, 1995), 8a. They wrote this article in their capacity as co-chairs of the President's Council on Sustainable Development, whose 1996 report also reflected the revisionist critique of regulation; see *Sustainable America: A New Consensus for Prosperity, Opportunity, and a Healthy Environment for the Future* (Washington, DC: PCSD, 1996), 25–55.

15. The three reports, all published by the National Academy of Public Administration in Washington, DC, are *Setting Priorities, Getting Results: A New Direction for EPA* (1995); *Resolving the Paradox of Environmental Protection: An Agenda for Congress, EPA, and the States* (1997); and *environment.gov: Transforming Environmental Protection for the 21st Century* (2000).

16. NAPA, *environment.gov*, 11.

17. Ibid., 18.

18. Discussed in William D. Ruckelshaus, "Stepping Stones," *Environmental Forum*, 15 (March–April 1998), 30–36. The environmentalist point of view is presented in that same issue by Linda Greer, "Why We Didn't Sign," 37–38.

19. Discussed in Daniel J. Fiorino, "Rethinking Environmental Regulation: Perspectives on Law and Governance," *Harvard Environmental Law Review*, 23 (1999), 441–469.

20. Davies and Mazurek, *Pollution Control in the United States*, 68–77. Good discussions of changes in environmental problems also may be found in Graham, *The Morning After Earth Day*, 12–26; and U.S. Environmental Protection Agency, *Reducing Risk: Setting Priorities and Strategies for Environmental Protection* (Washington, DC: EPA Science Advisory Board, 1990).

21. Daniel A. Mazmanian, "Los Angeles' Transition from Command-and-Control to Market-Based Clean Air Policy Strategies and Implementation," in Daniel A. Mazmanian and Michael E. Kraft, eds., *Toward Sustainable Communities: Transitions and Transformation in Environmental Policy* (Cambridge, MA: MIT Press, 2001), 77–112.

22. www.socialinvesting.org (accessed July 5, 2005). On the potential influence of investment generally, see Stephan Schmidheiny and Federico Zorraquin, *Financing Change: The Financial Community, Eco-Efficiency, and Sustainable Development* (Cambridge, MA: MIT Press, 1996).

23. Christopher J. Bosso and Deborah Lynn Gruber, "Maintaining Presence: Environmental Advocacy and the Permanent Campaign," in Vig and Kraft, eds., *Environmental Policy*, 78–99. Also see DeWitt John, "Civic Environmentalism," in Durant et al., *Environmental Governance Reconsidered*, 220–254.

24. David W. Rejeski and James Salzman, "Changes in Pollution and the Implications for Policy," in National Research Council, *New Tools for Environmental Protection: Education, Information, and Voluntary Measures* (Washington, DC: National Academy of Sciences, 2002), 17–42, quote on 37.

25. The last two examples are from EPA's report on its flexible air permits pilot projects: *Evaluation of Implementation Experiences with Innovative Air Permits* (prepared by the EPA's Office of Air Quality Planning and Standards and Office of Policy, Economics, and Innovation, 2004), 6.

26. For the structure of the computer industry and regulatory implications, see Jan Mazurek, *Making Microchips: Policy, Globalization, and Economic Restructuring in the Semiconductor Industry* (Cambridge, MA: MIT Press, 1999).

27. Peter Drucker, "The Next Society: A Survey of the Near Future," *The Economist* (November 3, 2001), 11. Another discussion of the rise of the service economy and the environment are Bruce Guile and Jared Cohon, "Sorting Out a Service-Based Economy," in Marian R. Chertow and Daniel C. Esty, eds., *Thinking Ecologically: The Next Generation of Environmental Policy* (New Haven: Yale University Press, 1997), 76–90.

28. Discussed in Rejeski and Salzman, "Changes in Pollution and the Implications for Policy," 17.

29. At the same time, it should be recognized that many environmental investments will only be made when government forces them to be made. This is one of the conclusions in Neil Gunningham, Robert A. Kagan, and Dorothy Thornton, *Shades of Green: Business, Regulation, and the Environment* (Palo Alto, CA: Stanford University Press, 2003), 60–74.

30. Kathryn Harrison, "Talking with the Donkey: Collaborative Approaches to Environmental Protection," *Journal of Industrial Ecology*, 2 (1999), 51–72.

31. For discussions of information-based approaches, see Mary Graham, *Democracy by Disclosure* (Washington, DC: Brookings Institution, 2002); Mary Graham and Catherine Miller, "Disclosure of Toxic Releases in the United States, in Theo de Bruijn and Vicki Norberg-Bohm, eds., *Industrial Transformation: Environmental Policy Innovation in the United States and Europe* (Cambridge, MA: MIT Press, 2005), 307–333; and National Research Council, *New Tools for Environmental Protection.*

32. Discussed in "Resolving Environmental Disputes," in Rosemary O'Leary, Robert F. Durant, Daniel J. Fiorino, and Paul S. Weiland, *Managing for the Environment: Understanding the Legal, Organizational, and Policy Challenges* (San Francisco: Jossey-Bass, 1999), 192–220.

33. Gunther Teubner, "Substantive and Reflexive Elements in Modern Law," *Law and Society Review*, 17 (1983), 253–254. Eric Orts first applied these concepts to environmental regulation in "Reflexive Environmental Law," *Northwestern University Law Review*, 89 (1995), 1227–1340.

34. Jan Kooiman, ed., *Modern Governance: New Government–Society Interactions* (London: Sage, 1993). Also see Gunther Teubner, Lindsay Farmer, and Declan Murphy, eds., *Environmental Law and Ecological Responsibility: The Concept and Practice of Ecological Responsibility* (New York: Wiley, 1994).

35. Martijn Van Vliet, "Environmental Regulation of Business: Options and Constraints for Communicative Governance," in Kooiman, *Modern Governance*, 105–118, quote on 108.

36. For the theoretically minded, the distinctions between social-political governance and the "new public administration" are discussed in B. Guy Peters and John Pierre, "Governance Without Government? Rethinking Public Administration," *Journal of Public Administration Research and Theory*, 8 (1998), 223–243, especially pp. 231–234.

37. United Nations Industry and Environment Programme, *Cleaner Production Program* (Paris: UNEP, 1992), 1–5. This is quoted and discussed in Ken Geiser, "Pollution Prevention," in Durant et al., *Environmental Governance Reconsidered*, 427–454, quote on 438.

Chapter 2

1. J. Clarence Davies and Jan Mazurek, *Pollution Control in the United States: Evaluating the System* (Washington, DC: Resources for the Future, 1998), 14.

2. For comparisons, see Lennart J. Lundqvist, *The Hare and the Tortoise: Clean Air Policies in the United States and Sweden* (Ann Arbor, MI: University of Michigan Press, 1980); David Vogel, *National Styles of Regulation: Environmental Policy in Great Britain and the United States* (Ithaca, NY: Cornell University Press, 1986); Ronald Brickman, Sheila Jasanoff, and Thomas Ilgen, *Controlling Chemicals: The Politics of Regulation in Europe and the United States* (Ithaca, NY: Cornell University Press, 1985); Martin Janicke and Helmut Weidner, eds., *National Environmental Policies: A Comparative Study of Capacity Building* (Berlin: Springer, 1996); Neil Gunningham, Robert A. Kagan, and Dorothy Thornton, *Shades of Green: Business, Regulation, and the Environment* (Palo Alto, CA: Stanford University Press, 2003); Robert A. Kagan and Lee Axelrod, eds., *Regulatory Encounters: Multinational Corporations and American Adversarial Legalism* (Berkeley, CA: University of California Press, 2000); Andrew Gouldson and Joseph Murphy, *Regulatory Realities: The Implementation and Impact of Industrial Environmental Regulation* (London: Earthscan, 1998); William M. Lafferty and James Meadowcroft, eds., *Implementing Sustainable Development: Strategies and Initiatives in High-Consumption Societies* (Oxford: Oxford University Press, 2000); and Uday Desai, ed., *Environmental Politics and Policy in Industrialized Countries* (Cambridge, MA: MIT Press, 2002).

3. R. Shep Melnick, "Administrative Law and Bureaucratic Reality," *Administrative Law Review*, 28 (Spring 1992), 245–259.

4. See the country studies in Lafferty and Meadowcroft, *Implementing Sustainable Development*, and Janicke and Weidner, *National Environmental Policies*.

5. Robert A. Kagan, "Introduction: Comparing National Styles of Regulation in Japan and the United States," *Law and Policy*, 22 (October 2000), 225–244, quote on 229.

6. Eugene Bardach and Robert Kagan, *Going by the Book: The Problem of Regulatory Unreasonableness* (Philadelphia: Temple University Press, 1982), 119.

7. For the European experience with packaging waste and energy efficiency, see the discussion in Arthur P. J. Mol, Volkmar Lauber, and Duncan Liefferink, eds., *The Voluntary Approach to Environmental Policy: Joint Environmental Approach to Environmental Policy Making in Europe* (Oxford: Oxford University Press, 2000). Another European illustration is Helge Jorgens and Per-Olof Busch, "Voluntary Approaches in Waste Management: The Case of the German ELV Program," in Theo de Bruijn and Vicki Norberg-Bohm, eds., *Industrial Transformation: Environmental Policy Innovation in the United States and Europe* (Cambridge, MA: MIT Press, 2005), 93–117.

8. Lundquist, *The Hare and the Tortoise*.

9. An example is the study of pulp and paper mills in Gunningham et al., *Shades of Green*.

10. Discussed in Robert A. Kagan, "Introduction: Comparing National Styles of Regulation in Japan and the United States," *Law and Policy*, 22 (October 2000), 225–244, quote on 236.

11. See James L. Regens, Barry L. Seldon, and Euel Elliot, "Modeling Compliance to Environmental Regulation: Evidence from Manufacturing Industries," *Journal of Policy Modeling*, 19 (1997), 683–696; and Kathryn Harrison, "Is Cooperation the Answer? Canadian Environmental Enforcement in Comparative Context," *Journal of Policy Analysis and Management*, 14 (1995), 221–224.

12. Nigel Haigh and Frances Irwin, eds., *Integrated Pollution Control in Europe and North America* (Washington, DC: Conservation Foundation, 1990); Davies and Mazurek, *Pollution Control in the United States*, 18–19; 220–222; 284–285.

13. Magali Delmas and Ann Terlak, "Regulatory Commitment to Negotiated Agreements: Evidence from the United States, Germany, the Netherlands, and France," *Journal of Comparative Policy Analysis: Research and Practice*, 4 (2002), 5–29.

14. Ibid., 19.

15. Lafferty and Meadowcroft, *Implementing Sustainable Development*, 425.

16. Ibid., 415.

17. Jeremy Richardson, ed., *Policy Styles in Western Europe* (London: Allen and Unwin, 1982).

18. For a discussion, see Lawrence S. Rothenburg, *Environmental Choices: Policy Responses to Green Demands* (Washington, DC: CQ Press, 2002), 15–19.

19. The classic work on incrementalism is Charles E. Lindblom, "The Science of Muddling Through," *Public Administration Review* 19 (Spring 1959), 79–88.

20. The incremental aspects of environmental policy are discussed in Daniel J. Fiorino, *Making Environmental Policy* (Los Angeles: University of California Press, 1995), 134–135.

21. John S. Dryzek, *The Politics of the Earth: Environmental Discourses* (Oxford: Oxford University Press, 1997), 61.

22. This is the focus of the country comparisons in Lafferty and Meadowcroft, *Implementing Sustainable Development*.

23. Alexis de Tocqueville, *Democracy in America* (New York: Doubleday, 1969), 270.

24. Robert A. Kagan, "Adversarial Legalism in American Government," in Marc K. Landy and Martin A. Levin, eds., *The New Politics of Public Policy* (Baltimore: Johns Hopkins University Press, 1995), 88–118, quote on 90.

25. David Wallace, *Environmental Policy and Industrial Innovation: Strategies in Europe, the US and Japan* (Earthscan: London, 1995).

26. Cass Sunstein, *After the Rights Revolution: Reconceiving the Regulatory State* (Cambridge, MA: Harvard University Press, 1990).

27. For the effects of a rights-based strategy in another policy area, see R. Shep Melnick, "Separation of Powers and the Strategy of Rights: The Expansion of Special Education," in Landy and Levin, *The New Politics of Public Policy*, 23–46.

28. Marver Bernstein, *Regulating Business by Independent Commission* (Princeton, NJ: Princeton University Press, 1955.) For more on regulatory capture, see Marc Allen Eisner, *Regulatory Politics in Transition* (Baltimore: Johns Hopkins University Press, 1993).

29. Ronald Inglehart, "Public Support for Environmental Protection: The Impact of Subjective Problems and Subjective Values in 43 Societies," *PS: Political Science and Politics*, 28 (1995), 57–71.

30. David B. Spence, "Paradox Lost: Logic, Morality, and the Foundations of Environmental Law in the 21st Century," *Columbia Journal of Environmental Law*, 20 (1995), 171–172.

31. The term "amoral calculator" is from Robert A. Kagan and John T. Scholz, "The Criminology of the Corporation and Regulatory Enforcement Strategies," in Keith Hawkins and John M. Thomas, eds., *Enforcing Regulation* (Boston: Kluwer-Nijhoff, 1984), 67–95.

32. A classic statement is Woodrow Wilson, "The Study of Public Administration," reprinted in Louis C. Gawthrop, ed., *The Administrative Process and Democratic Theory* (New York: Houghton Mifflin, 1970), 77–85.

33. Daniel J. Fiorino, "Strategies for Regulatory Reform: Forward Compared to Backward Mapping," *Policy Studies Journal*, 25 (1997), 249–265.

34. For a historical analysis of regulation, see Eisner, *Regulatory Politics in Transition*.

35. Dryzek, *The Politics of the Earth*, 63.

36. Melnick, "Administrative Law and Bureaucratic Reality," 245–259.

37. John W. Kingdon, *Agendas, Alternatives, and Public Policies*, 2nd ed. (New York: Harper Collins, 1995), 84–88.

38. Michael E. Kraft, "Environmental Policy in Congress," in Norman J. Vig and Michael E. Kraft, eds., *Environmental Policy: New Directions for the Twenty-First Century*, 6th ed. (Washington, DC: CQ Press, 2006), 124–147.

39. For the shift in authority from state to national levels, see Richard N. L. Andrews, *Managing the Environment, Managing Ourselves: A History of American Environmental Policy* (New Haven, CT: Yale University Press, 1999), 201–226. For the system that emerged, see J. Clarence Davies, *The Politics of Pollution* (New York: Pegasus, 1970); Alfred A. Marcus, *Promise and Performance: Choosing and Implementing an Environmental Policy* (Westport, CT: Greenwood Press, 1980); Paul R. Portney and Robert N. Stavins, eds., *Public Policies for Environmental Protection*, 2nd ed. (Washington, DC: Resources for the Future, 2000).

40. These periods are presented in terms of a learning model in Daniel J. Fiorino, "Environmental Policy as Learning," *Public Administration Review*, 61 (May/June 2001), 322–334.

41. Mary Graham, *The Morning After Earth Day: Practical Environmental Politics* (Washington, DC: Brookings Institution, 1999), 29.

42. Ibid., 29.

43. Denise Scheberle, *Federalism and Environmental Policy: Trust and the Politics of Implementation* (Washington, DC: Georgetown University Press, 1997); Evan Ringquist, *Environmental Protection at the State Level: Politics and Progress in Controlling Pollution* (Armonk, NY: M.E. Sharpe, 1993); Barry G. Rabe, "Power to the States: The Promise and Pitfalls of Decentralization," in Vig and Kraft, *Environmental Policy*, 6th ed., 34–56.

44. For the uses of economic analysis, see Fiorino, *Making Environmental Policy*, 124–128.

45. For these criticisms, see Marc K. Landy, Marc J. Roberts, and Stephen R. Thomas, *The Environmental Protection Agency: Asking the Wrong Questions* (New York: Oxford University Press, 1990); U.S. Environmental Protection Agency, *Unfinished Business: A Comparative Assessment of Environmental Problems, Overview Report* (Washington, DC: EPA Science Advisory Board, 1987); U.S. Environmental Protection Agency, *Reducing Risk: Setting Priorities and Strategies for Environmental Protection* (Washington, DC: EPA Science Advisory Board, 1990).

46. An excellent analysis of this topic is Mary Graham's *The Morning After Earth Day*.

47. On this point see Landy et al., *The Environmental Protection Agency: Asking the Wrong Questions*.

48. For an assessment of ADR at EPA, see Rosemary O'Leary and Susan Summers Raines, "Lessons Learned from Two Decades of Dispute Resolution at the U.S. Environmental Protection Agency," *Public Administration Review*, 61 (November/December 2001), 682–692. Also see Edward P. Weber, *Pluralism by the Rules: Conflict and Cooperation in Environmental Regulation* (Washington, DC: Georgetown University Press, 1998) and Daniel J. Fiorino, "Regulatory Negotiation as a Policy Process," *Public Administration Review*, 48 (July/August 1988) 764–772.

49. For next-generation problems and solutions, see Marian R. Chertow and Daniel C. Esty, eds., *Thinking Ecologically: The Next Generation of Environmental Policy* (New Haven, CT: Yale University Press, 1997).

50. Jeanne Herb, Susan Helms, and Michael J. Jenson, "Harnessing the 'Power of Information': Environmental Right to Know as a Driver of Sound Environmental Policy," in National Research Council, *New Tools for Environmental Protection: Education, Information, and Voluntary Measures* (Washington, DC: National Academy Press, 2002), 253–262.

51. U.S. Environmental Protection Agency, *The United States Experience with Economic Incentives to Protect the Environment* (Washington, DC: EPA Office of the Administrator, 2001).

52. A valuable source on the thinking about integrated pollution control at the time is "Integrated Pollution Control: A Symposium," *Environmental Law*, 22 (1992), 1–279.

53. Quoted by Marc K. Landy, in "The New Politics of Environmental Policy," in Landy and Levin, *The New Politics of Public Policy*, 207–227, quote on 219.

54. Ibid.

55. Discussed in Robert Paehlke, "Sustainability," in Robert F. Durant, Daniel J. Fiorino, and Rosemary O'Leary, eds., *Environmental Governance Reconsidered: Challenges, Choices, and Opportunities* (Cambridge, MA: MIT Press, 2004), 35–67.

56. Kraft, "Environmental Policy in Congress," 133–136.

57. The recommendations of these groups are discussed in more detail in chapter 5.

58. For a review of the Bush administration record, see Douglas Jehl, "On Rules for the Environment, Bush Sees a Balance, Critics a Threat," *New York Times*, February 23, 2003. An interesting point of view is presented by Gregg Easterbrook, "Everything You Know About the Bush Environmental Record is Wrong" (Washington, DC: AEI–Brookings Joint Center for Regulatory Studies, Working Paper 02-6, 2002). For a general review and assessment, see Norman J. Vig, "Presidential Leadership and the Environment," in Vig and Kraft, *Environmental Policy*, 6th ed., 111–117.

59. For a balanced yet critical view of the New Source Review program, see the National Academy of Public Administration's report, *A Breath of Fresh Air: Reviving the New Source Review Program* (Washington, DC: NAPA 2003). For the Bush administration policies, see Juliet Eilperin, "New Rules Could Allow Power Plants to Pollute More," *Washington Post*, August 31, 2005, A-1.

60. William D. Ruckelshaus, "Stepping Stones," *Environmental Forum*, 15 (March–April 1998), 30–36, quote on 30.

61. Ibid., 30.

Chapter 3

1. Eugene Bardach and Robert A. Kagan, *Going by the Book: The Problem of Regulatory Unreasonableness* (Philadelphia: Temple University Press, 1982), 58.

2. Patterns in public support are summarized in Lawrence S. Rothenberg, *Environmental Choices: Policy Responses to Green Demands* (Washington, DC: CQ Press, 2002), 9–12.

3. J. Clarence Davies and Jan Mazurek, *Pollution Control in the United States: Evaluating the System* (Washington, DC: Resources for the Future, 1998), 55. These numbers were current as of 1995. For 2001, the numbers were a 161 percent increase in GDP and a 149 percent increase in vehicle miles traveled. The updated numbers are from the EPA's *Draft Report on the Environment 2003* (www.epa.gov/indicators/roe/index.htm) issued in June 2003.

4. Richard N. L. Andrews, *Managing the Environment, Managing Ourselves: A History of American Environmental Policy* (New Haven, CT: Yale University Press, 1999), 280.

5. Michael E. Kraft and Norman J. Vig, "Environmental Policy from the 1970s to 2000: An Overview," in Norman J. Vig and Michael E. Kraft, eds.,

Environmental Policy: New Directions for the Twenty-First Century, 4th ed. (Washington, DC: CQ Press, 2000), 1–31, quote on 27.

6. Gregg Easterbrook, *A Moment on the Earth: The Coming Age of Environmental Optimism* (New York: Viking, 1993), 471–472.

7. Michael E. Kraft and Norman J. Vig, "Environmental Policy from the 1970s to the Twenty-First Century," in Vig and Kraft, *Environmental Policy*, 5th ed. (Washington, DC: CQ Press, 2003), 1–32.

8. Ibid., 25.

9. Davies and Mazurek, *Pollution Control in the United States*, 53–100. Other summaries of results are in Kraft and Vig, "Environmental Policy from the 1970s to 2000," 20–24; Paul R. Portney and Robert N. Stavins, eds., *Public Policies for Environmental Protection*, 2nd ed. (Washington, DC: Resources for the Future, 2000); and EPA's *Draft Report on the Environment 2003*. The report remains in draft form as of September 2005. The EPA plans to issue the next version in FY 2006 and has sought public comment on a list of proposed indicators for the 2006 report.

10. Davies and Mazurek, *Pollution Control in the United States*, 57–59.

11. EPA, *Draft Report on the Environment 2003*, 1–8.

12. Davies and Mazurek, *Pollution Control in the United States*, 55.

13. Mary Graham, *The Morning After Earth Day: Practical Environmental Politics* (Washington, DC: Brookings Institution, 1999), 16.

14. Davies and Mazurek, *Pollution Control in the United States*, 70.

15. Graham, *The Morning After Earth Day*, 17.

16. EPA, *Draft Report on the Environment 2003*, 2–17.

17. Ibid., 2–7.

18. Ibid., 3–15.

19. Ibid., 3–14.

20. Davies and Mazurek, *Pollution Control in the United States*, 88.

21. EPA, *Draft Report on the Environment 2003*, 3–9.

22. Mary Graham and Catherine Miller, "Disclosure of Toxic Releases in the United States," in Theo de Bruijn and Vicki Norberg-Bohm, eds., *Industrial Transformation: Environmental Policy Innovation in the United States and Europe* (Cambridge, MA: MIT Press, 2005), 307–333. However, releases in some categories also increased in later time periods or did not decline as rapidly. Although a useful source, remember that the TRI has a number of design limitations. Because it fails to account for small and scattered sources, for example, it may identify less than 10 percent of emissions of hazardous air pollutants. There also is evidence of reporting errors and other problems that limit the usefulness of the TRI as a source of overall data on environmental performance. Nor do the TRI data tell us much about the relative risk of various emissions, which vary considerably.

23. Davies and Mazurek, *Pollution Control in the United States*, 199–205.

24. Ibid., 95.

25. Martin Janicke, "The Political System's Capacity for Environmental Policy," in Martin Janicke and Helmut Weidner, eds., *National Environmental Policies: A Comparative Study of Capacity Building* (Berlin: Springer, 1996), 1–24. See, by the same authors, *Successful Environmental Policy: A Critical Evaluation of 24 Cases* (Berlin: Ed. Sigma, 1995). Also see, on capacity, Lawrence S. Rothenberg, *Environmental Choices: Policy Responses to Green Demands* (Washington, DC: CQ Press, 2002), 3.

26. A starting point is David Shaman and David Wheeler, "Controlling Industrial Pollution in the Developing World," *Environmental Quality Management*, 69 (1998), 69–75.

27. Barry G. Rabe, "Power to the States: The Promise and Pitfalls of Decentralization," in Vig and Kraft, *Environmental Policy*, 6th ed., 34–37. State air requirements often exceed federal ones; see Matthew Potoski, "Clean Air Federalism: Do States Race to the Bottom?" *Public Administration Review*, 61 (May/June 2001), 335–342. Also see Denise Scheberle, "Devolution," in Robert F. Durant, Daniel J. Fiorino, and Rosemary O'Leary, eds., *Environmental Governance Reconsidered: Challenges, Choices, and Opportunities* (Cambridge, MA: MIT Press, 2004), 361–392. States also are showing more initiative on greenhouse gases. See Barry G. Rabe, *Statehouse and Greenhouse: The Emerging Politics of American Climate Change Policy* (Washington, DC: Brookings Institution, 2004).

28. Andrews, *Managing the Environment, Managing Ourselves*, 358.

29. Rothenberg, *Environmental Choices*, 9–12; Christopher J. Bosso and Deborah Lynn Gruber, "Maintaining Presence: Environmental Advocacy and the Permanent Campaign," in Vig and Kraft, *Environmental Policy*, 6th ed., 80–86; Everett C. Ladd and Karlyn H. Bowman, *Attitudes Toward the Environment: Twenty-Five Years After Earth Day* (Washington, DC: American Enterprise Institute, 1995).

30. For an early example of TRI research, see Shameek Konar and Mark A. Cohen, "Information as Regulation: The Effect of Community Right to Know Laws on Toxic Emissions," *Journal of Environmental Economics and Management*, 32 (1997), 109–124. For a recent one, see Graham and Miller, "Disclosure of Toxic Releases on the United States." A recent study suggests that the effects of the TRI on firms may be subsiding over time. See Mark Stephan, Michael E. Kraft, and Troy D. Abel, "Information Politics and Environmental Performance: The Impact of the Toxics Release Inventory on Corporate Decision Making." Paper presented at the annual meeting of the American Political Science Association, September 1–4, 2005.

31. Bosso and Gruber, "Maintaining Presence."

32. For costs and benefits, see A. Myrick Freeman III., "Economics, Incentives, and Environmental Policy," in Vig and Kraft, *Environmental Policy*, 6th ed., 194–203; Portney and Stavins, *Public Policies for Environmental Protection*; and

Robert W. Hahn, ed., *Risks, Costs, and Lives Saved: Getting Better Results from Regulation* (New York: Oxford University Press, 1996).

33. U.S. Environmental Protection Agency, *The Benefits and Costs of the Clean Air Act: 1970–1990* (Washington, DC: EPA, 1997).

34. Davies and Mazurek, *Pollution Control in the United States*, 19.

35. Michael Porter and Claas van der Linde, "Green and Competitive: Ending the Stalemate," *Harvard Business Review* 13 (1995), 120–134.

36. "End-of-Pipe or Cleaner Production? An Empirical Comparison of Environmental Innovation Decisions Across OECD Countries," presented to the Organization for Economic Co-operation and Development, Washington, DC, June 14–15, 2005, 21.

37. Environmental Law Institute, *Barriers to Environmental Technology and Use* (Washington, DC: ELI, 1998), 5. Also discussed in Cass R. Sunstein, "Paradoxes of the Regulatory State," *University of Chicago Law Review*, 57 (1990), 407–441.

38. ELI, *Barriers to Environmental Technology and Use*, 5.

39. Ibid., 6.

40. Ibid., 5.

41. Ibid., 5–6.

42. David Wallace, *Environmental Policy and Industrial Innovation: Strategies in Europe, the US, and Japan* (London: Earthscan, 1995).

43. Ibid., 16.

44. Dennis D. Hirsch, "Bill and Al's XL-ent Adventure: An Analysis of the EPA's Legal Authority to Implement the Clinton Administration's Project XL," *University of Illinois Law Review* (1998), 129–172, quote on 138–139.

45. Barry Rabe, "Integrated Environmental Permitting: Experience and Innovation at the State Level," *State and Local Government Review* 27 (Fall 1995), 209–220.

46. U.S. Environmental Protection Agency (in conjunction with the Chemical Manufacturers Association, or CMA), *EPA/CMA Root Cause Analysis Pilot Project: An Industry Survey* (Washington, DC: EPA Office of Enforcement and Compliance, 1999), 11.

47. Bardach and Kagan, *Going by the Book*, 67.

48. Ibid., 20.

49. Ibid., 119.

50. See National Academy of Public Administration, *Setting Priorities, Getting Results: A New Direction for the Environmental Protection Agency* (Washington, DC: NAPA, 1995), 97–98 and U.S. Environmental Protection Agency, *Amoco-U.S. EPA Pollution Prevention Project, Yorktown, Virginia, Project Summary*, Office of Policy, Planning, and Evaluation, EPA, 1992.

51. Michael Porter and Claas van der Linde, "Toward a New Conception of the Environment-Competitiveness Relationship," *Journal of Economic Perspectives*, 9 (1995), 119–132; Andrew J. Hoffman, *Competitive Environmental Strategy: A Guide to the Changing Business Landscape* (Washington, DC: Island Press, 2000), 79–80.

52. James P. Lester, "Federalism and State Environmental Policy," in James P. Lester, ed., *Environmental Politics and Policy: Theories and Evidence*, 2nd ed. (Durham, NC: Duke University Press, 1995), 49–53.

53. Maarten A. Hajer, *The Politics of Environmental Discourse: Ecological Modernization and the Policy Process* (Oxford: Oxford University Press, 1995).

54. Paul R. Portney, "Air Pollution Policy," in Portney and Stavins, *Public Policies for Environmental Protection*, 77–123. The cost-effectiveness of emissions trading programs is discussed in Winston Harrington and Richard D. Morgenstern, "Economic Incentives versus Command and Control: What's the Best Approach for Solving Environmental Problems?" *Resources* (Fall/Winter 2004), 13–17.

55. U.S. Environmental Protection Agency, *The United States Experience with Economic Incentives for Protecting the Environment* (Washington, DC: EPA, 2001); Robert N. Stavins, *Experience with Market-Based Environmental Policy Instruments* (Washington, DC: Resources for the Future, 2000, Discussion Paper 00-09); and Daniel J. Fiorino, "Flexibility," in Durant et al., *Environmental Governance Reconsidered*, 393–425.

56. The value chain discussion is adapted from the Global Environmental Management Initiative, *Environment: Value to the Top Line* (Washington, DC: GEMI, 2001), 6–7. The concept is from Michael Porter, *Competitive Advantage* (New York: Free Press, 1985).

57. Dryzek, *The Politics of the Earth*, 79.

58. U.S. Environmental Protection Agency, *Enforcement and Compliance Assurance: FY98 Accomplishments Report* (Washington, DC: EPA Office of Enforcement and Compliance Assurance, 1999).

59. Davies, *Reforming Permitting*, 21–22.

60. Ibid., 42.

61. National Academy of Public Administration, *environment.gov: Transforming Environmental Protection in the 21st Century* (Washington, DC: NAPA, 2000), 18.

62. Ibid., 18.

Chapter 4

1. Neil Gunningham, Robert A. Kagan, and Dorothy Thornton, *Shades of Green: Business, Regulation, and Environment* (Palo Alto, CA: Stanford University Press, 2003), 26.

2. Richard MacLean and Frank Friedman, "Green Arthritis," *Environmental Forum* (November–December 2000) 18, 37–49.

3. See Kathryn Harrison, "Challenges in Evaluating Voluntary Environmental Programs," in National Research Council, *New Tools for Environmental Protection: Education, Information, and Voluntary Measures* (Washington, DC: National Academy Press, 2002), 263–282, quote on 270.

4. This point is made in some detail in Andrew J. Hoffman, *Competitive Environmental Strategy: A Guide to the Changing Business Landscape* (Washington, DC: Island Press, 2000).

5. For examples of typical complaints, see "Hazardous Waste Industries Urge EPA to Clarify, Ease, Regulations on Accumulating, Storing Waste," *Daily Environment Report* (Washington, DC: Bureau of National Affairs, August 11, 2004).

6. An example is Stephan Schmidheiny, *Changing Course: A Global Business Perspective on Development and the Environment* (Cambridge, MA: MIT Press, 1992).

7. Nigel Roome, ed., *Sustainability Strategies for Industry: The Future of Corporate Practice* (Washington, DC: Island Press, 1998).

8. Examples are Jennifer Nash and John Ehrenfeld, "Codes of Environmental Management Practice: Assessing Their Potential as Tools for Change," *Annual Review of Energy and the Environment*, 22 (1997), 487–535; Cary Coglianese and Jennifer Nash, eds., *Regulating from the Inside: Can Environmental Management Systems Achieve Policy Goals?* (Washington, DC: Resources for the Future, 2001); Joseph Rees, "The Development of Industry Self-Regulation in the Chemical Industry," *Law and Policy*, 19 (1997), 447–528; Neil Gunningham and Joseph Rees, "Industry Self-Regulation: An Institutional Perspective," *Law and Policy*, 19 (1997), 363–414. On the greening literature generally, at an earlier stage, see Doris A. Fuchs and Daniel A. Mazmanian, "The Greening of Industry: Needs of the Field," *Business Strategy and the Environment*, 7 (1998), 193–203.

9. Johan Schot and Kurt Fischer, "Introduction: The Greening of the Industrial Firm," in Kurt Fischer and Johan Schot, eds., *Environmental Strategies for Industry: International Perspectives on Research Needs and Policy Implications* (Washington, DC: Island Press 1993), 3–33.

10. Ibid., 8.

11. Michael Porter and Claas van der Linde, "Green and Competitive: Ending the Stalemate," *Harvard Business Review*, 73 (September–October 1995), 120–134. See by the same authors, "Toward a New Conception of the Environment-Competitiveness Relationship," *Journal of Economic Perspectives*, 9 (Fall 1995), 97–118.

12. Ibid, 120.

13. Ibid.

14. Ibid, 129.

15. Ibid.

16. Stuart L. Hart, "Beyond Greening: Strategies for a Sustainable World," *Harvard Business Review*, 75 (January–February 1997), 67–76.

17. Ibid., 76. A similar case is made in a business and environment text by Andrew J. Hoffman, who observes: "Rather than denying or lamenting environmental pressures, managers must now consider how environmentalism and business strategy overlap" (*Competitive Environmental Strategy*, 10).

18. Forest Reinhardt, *Down to Earth: Applying Business Principles to Environmental Management* (Boston: Harvard Business School Press, 2000), x.

19. Ibid., 3.

20. Ibid., 3–4.

21. Noah Walley and Bradley Whitehead, "It's Not Easy Being Green," *Harvard Business Review*, 72 (May–June 1994), 46–52, quote on 46.

22. Karen L. Palmer, Wallace E. Oates, and Paul R. Portney, "Tightening Environmental Standards: The Benefit-Cost or the No-Cost Paradigm?" *Journal of Economic Perspectives*, 9 (Fall 1995), 119–132.

23. Michele Ochsner concludes: "In studies of facilities across the country, researchers have consistently found that regulatory compliance is important in motivating companies to investigate pollution prevention alternatives and in shaping their assessment of the key benefits of the projects which they have implemented" ["Pollution Prevention: An Overview of Regulatory Incentives and Barriers," *New York University Environmental Law Journal*, 3 (1998), 596–597].

24. That firms should strive to create business value through their environmental actions is also a central part of the Walley and Whitehead article. They recommend that firms take a long-term, integrated, and strategic perspective, much as writers like Reinhardt and Hart argued later. See "It's Not Easy Being Green," 50–52.

25. For a summary of these "event" studies, see Andrew A. King and Michael Lenox, "Does It *Really* Pay to Be Green?" *Journal of Industry Ecology*, 5 (2001), 105–116. They cite the results of one study which concluded that Union Carbide lost 28 per cent of its market capitalization (some $1 billion) after the 1984 catastrophe in Bhopal, India [W. G. Blacconiere and D. M. Patton, "Environmental Disclosures, Regulatory Costs, and Changes in Firm Value," *Journal of Accounting and Economics*, 8 (1994), 357–377].

26. An example is M. Khanna, W. R. Quimo, and D. Bojilova, "Toxic Release Information: A Policy Tool for Environmental Protection," *Journal of Environmental Economics and Management*, 36 (1998), 243–266.

27. King and Lennox, "Does It *Really* Pay to Be Green?"

28. Ibid., 106.

29. U.S. Environmental Protection Agency, *Green Dividends? The Relationship Between Firms' Environmental Performance and Financial Performance*

(Washington, DC: EPA Office of Cooperative Environmental Management, 2000, EPA-100-R-00-021), 6.

30. Organization for Economic Co-operation and Development, "The Firm, the Environment, and Public Policy" (Paris: OECD, 2001), 34.

31. Nicole Darnell, Jason Jolley, and Bjarne Ytterhus, "Does a Facility's Environmental Performance Predict Its Financial Performance?" Paper presented at the OECD Conference on Public Environmental Policy and the Private Firm, Washington, DC, June 14–15, 2005, 3.

32. *The U.S. Electric Utility Industry: Uncovering Hidden Value Potential for Strategic Investors* (New York: Innovest Strategic Advisors, 2002), 8. Available at www.innovestgroup.com (accessed August 3, 2005).

33. Ibid., 8.

34. KPMG, *International Survey of Corporate Environmental Reporting* (Amsterdam: KPMG, 1999). On the early issues in environmental reporting, see the Global Environmental Management Initiative, *Measuring Environmental Performance: A Primer and Survey of Metrics in Use* (Washington, DC: GEMI, 1997).

35. KPMG, *International Survey of Corporate Responsibility Reporting 2005* (Amsterdam: KPMG, 2005). Available at www.kpmg.com/Rut2000_prod/Documents/9/Survey. (accessed August 22, 2005).

36. See www.bms.com/EHS.html.

37. R. Scott Marshall and Darrell Brown, "Corporate Environmental Reporting: What's In a Metric?" *Business Strategy and the Environment*, 12 (2002), 87–106.

38. www.globalreporting.org.

39. KPMG, *Intentional Survey 2005*, 5.

40. Marshall and Brown, "Corporate Environmental Reporting," 88.

41. www.facilityreporting.org.

42. Richard N. L. Andrews et al., "Environmental Management Systems: History, Theory, and Implementation Research," in Coglianese and Nash, eds. *Regulating from the Inside*, 31–60, quote on 32.

43. Nicole Darnall and Alexei Pavlichev, *Environmental Policy Tools and Firm-level Management Practices in the U.S.* (Raleigh: North Carolina State University, 2004).

44. Cary Coglianese and Jennifer Nash, "Environmental Management Systems and the New Policy Agenda," in Coglianese and Nash, eds. *Regulating from the Inside*, 1–25, quote on 10.

45. Andrews et al. "Environmental Management Systems," 42. This view is strongly reinforced by the results of the Darnall and Pavlichev survey of U.S. business firms.

46. Kristina Dahlstrom, Chris Howes, Paul Leinster, and Jim Skea, "Environmental Management Systems and Company Performance: Assessing the

Case for Extending Risk-Based Regulation," *European Environment*, 13 (2003), 187–203.

47. Matthew Potoski and Aseem Prakash, "Green Clubs and Voluntary Compliance: ISO 14001 and Firms' Regulatory Performance," *American Journal of Political Science*, 49 (2005), 235–248.

48. Wilma Rose Q. Anton, George Deltas, and Madhu Khanna, "Incentives for Environmental Self-Regulation and Implications for Environmental Performance," *Journal of Environmental Economics and Management*, 48(July 2004), 632–654, quote on 634. Matthew Potoski and Assem Prakash reach a similar conclusion with respect to reduced air emissions at ISO-certified facilities in "Covenent with Weak Swords: ISO 14001 and Firms' Environmental Performance," *Journal of Policy Analysis and Management*, 49 (2005), 745–769.

49. University of North Carolina at Chapel Hill, *Environmental Management Systems: Do They Improve Performance?* Project Final Report: Executive Summary (January 30, 2003), ES-25.

50. Ibid.

51. Richard Florida and Derek Davison, "Why Do Firms Adopt Advanced Environmental Practices (And Do They Make a Difference)?" in Coglianese and Nash, eds., *Regulating from the Inside*, 82–104.

52. Gunningham et al., *Shades of Green*, 95–134.

53. Mikeal Hilden, Jukka Lepola, Per Mickwitz, Aard Mulders, and Marika Palosaari, *Evaluation of Environmental Policy Instruments: A Case Study of the Finnish Pulp and Paper and Chemical Industries* (Helsinki: Finnish Environmental Institute, 2002. 113.

54. Ibid., 115.

55. Gunningham et al., *Shades of Green*, 146.

56. Nash and Ehrenfeld, "Codes of Environmental Management Practice," 498.

57. This discussion is based on information on the ACC's web site (www .americanchemistry.org).

58. Neil Gunningham and Peter Grabosky, *Smart Regulation: Designing Environmental Policy* (Oxford: Oxford University Press, 1998), 161.

59. For assessments of Responsible Care, see Neil Gunningham, "Environment, Self-Regulation, and the Chemical Industry: Assessing Responsible Care," *Law and Policy*, 17 (January 1995), 57–109; Joseph V. Rees, "The Development of Communitarian Regulation in the Chemical Industry," *Law and Policy*, 19 (1997), 477–528; and Neil Gunningham and Darren Sinclair, *Leaders and Laggards: Next-Generation Environmental Regulation* (Sheffield, UK: Greenleaf, 2002), 139–145.

60. Terry F. Yosie, "Responsible Care at Fifteen Years," *Environmental Science and Technology*, 37 (November 1, 2003), 401A.

61. Andrew King and Michael Lenox, "*The Academy of Management Journal*," 43 (2000), 698–716. It should be noted that this study focused on TRI emissions,

a fairly narrow set of performance indicators, and not on the broader range of behaviors that Responsible Care was designed to influence.

62. Gunningham et al., *Shades of Green*, 18. (This and the following three quotes are from the April 2002 draft of the manuscript rather than the published version.) Also see Robert A. Kagan, Neil Gunningham, and Dorothy Thornton, "Explaining Corporate Environmental Performance: How Does Regulation Matter?" *Law and Society Review*, 37 (2003), 51–89.

63. Ibid, 43–44 (April 2002 draft).

64. Ibid, 22.

65. Ibid, 117.

66. Reinhardt, *Down to Earth*, 19–22.

67. Richard Elliot Benedick, *Ozone Diplomacy: New Directions in Safeguarding the Planet* (Cambridge, MA: Harvard University Press, 1991).

68. Aseem Prakash, *Greening the Firm: The Politics of Corporate Environmentalism* (Cambridge: Cambridge University Press, 2000), 3–6.

69. Reinhardt, *Down to Earth*, 79.

70. James Boyd, *Searching for the Profit in Pollution Prevention: Case Studies in the Corporate Evaluation of Environmental Opportunities* (Washington, DC: Resources for the Future, 1998), 2.

71. Ibid., 40.

72. Porter and van der Linde, "Toward a New Conception of the Environment-Competitiveness Relationship," 98–100.

73. Reinhardt, *Down to Earth*, 103.

74. Aseem Prakash, *Greening the Firm*, 59–70.

75. Quoted in Prakash, *Greening the Firm*, 79.

76. Ibid., 119.

77. Terry Davies, *Reforming Permitting* (Washington, DC: Resources for the Future, 2001).

78. U.S. Environmental Protection Agency, *Evaluation of Implementation Experiences with Innovative Air Permits* (Washington, DC: EPA Office of Air Quality Planning and Standards and Office of Policy, Economics, and Innovation, 2004).

79. Reinhardt, *Down to Earth*, 162.

80. Porter and van der Linde, "Green and Competitive," 129.

81. Gunningham et al., *Shades of Green*, 2.

Chapter 5

1. William D. Ruckelshaus, "Stepping Stones," *Environmental Forum*, 15 (March-April 1998), 30–36. The quote is from p. 31.

2. Richard Rose, *Lesson-Drawing in Public Policy: A Guide to Learning Across Time and Space* (Chatham, NJ: Chatham House, 1993), 50.

3. Marian R. Chertow and Daniel C. Esty, *Thinking Ecologically: The Next Generation of Environmental Policy* (New Haven, CT: Yale University Press, 1997), 2.

4. Although the term "voluntary" is used here because this is consistent with the broader literature, few government programs are truly voluntary. The research suggests that the more effective ones are usually accompanied by some other pressure or threat of pressure from government or others.

5. Organization for Economic Co-operation and Development, *Voluntary Approaches for Environmental Policy: An Assessment* (Paris, OECD, 1999).

6. Another example is the Chicago Climate Exchange, which is a voluntary yet legally binding trading system for greenhouse gases. See www.chicagoclimatex .com (accessed August 29, 2005).

7. Keith Brouhle, Charles Griffiths, and Ann Wolverton, "The Use of Voluntary Approaches for Environmental Policymaking in the U.S." in Edoardo Croce, ed., *The Handbook of Environmental Voluntary Agreements: Design, Implementation, and Evaluation Issues* (New York: Springer-Verlag, 2005), 107–134.

8. Cited in Kathryn Harrison, "Challenges in Evaluating Voluntary Environmental Programs," in National Research Council, *New Tools for Environmental Protection: Education, Information, and Voluntary Measures* (Washington, DC: National Academy of Sciences, 2002), 263–282.

9. Eric Welch and A. Hibiki, "Japanese Voluntary Agreements: Bargaining Power and Reciprocity as Contributors to Effectiveness," *Policy Sciences*, 35 (2002), 401–424.

10. Organization for Economic Co-operation and Development, *Voluntary Approaches in Environmental Policy: Environmental Effectiveness, Economic Efficiency, and Usage in Policy Mixes* (Paris: OECD, Draft Final Report, 2002), 4.

11. Brouhle et al., "The Use of Voluntary Approaches for Environmental Policy Making in the U.S."

12. Ibid.

13. Ibid., 130.

14. See Karl Hausker, *The Convergence of Ideas on Improving the Environmental Protection System* (Washington, DC: Center for Strategic and International Studies, 1999). Responding to the criticism from environmentalists, Hausker wrote "it would be supremely ironic if the hundreds of participants in the next generation policy forums had come up with a recipe for environmental disaster, despite their commitments to, and credentials in, environmental protection" (n. 4).

15. Linda E. Greer, "Why We Didn't Sign," *Environmental Forum*, 15 (March–April 1998), 37–38.

16. President's Council for Sustainable Development, *Sustainable America: A New Consensus for Prosperity, Opportunity, and a Healthy Environment for the Future* (Washington, DC: PSCD, 1996), 25–43, quote on 28.

17. National Academy of Public Administration, *Setting Priorities, Getting Results: A New Direction for the Environmental Protection Agency* (Washington, DC: NAPA, 1995), 97–98.

18. Aspen Institute, *A Call to Action to Build a Performance-Based Environmental Management System* (Washington, DC: Aspen Institute, 2000).

19. Chertow and Esty, *Thinking Ecologically*, 4.

20. Neil Gunningham and Peter Grabosky, *Smart Regulation: Designing Environmental Policy* (Oxford: Oxford University Press, 1998), 11.

21. In addition to the sources already given, examples are Cass R. Sunstein, "Paradoxes of the Regulatory State," *Chicago Law Review*, 57 (1990), 407–441; Ian Ayres and John Braithwaite, *Responsive Regulation: Transcending the Deregulation Debate* (New York: Oxford University Press, 1992); Donald F. Kettl, ed., *Environmental Governance: A Report on the Next Generation of Environmental Policy* (Washington, DC: Brookings Institution, 2002); Alfred A. Marcus, Donald A. Geffen, and Ken Sexton, *Reinventing Environmental Regulation: Lessons from Project XL* (Washington, DC: Resources for the Future, 2002); and Daniel J. Fiorino, "Toward a New System of Environmental Regulation: The Case for an Industry Sector Approach," *Environmental Law*, 26 (1996), 457–488.

22. For a more detailed analysis of EPA and its institutional setting, see Daniel J. Fiorino, *Making Environmental Policy* (Los Angeles: University of California Press, 1995).

23. Walter A. Rosenbaum, "Escaping the 'Battered Agency Syndrome': EPA's Gamble with Regulatory Reinvention," in Norman J.Vig and Michael E. Kroft, eds., *Environmental Policy: New Directions for the Twenty-First Century*, 4th ed. (Washington, DC: CQ Press, 2000), 165–189.

24. U.S. Environmental Protection Agency, *Administrator's Update No. 12, Common Sense Initiative* (Washington, DC: EPA, 1994). Also see "Common Sense Initiative Council Federal Advisory Committee; Establishment," 59 *Federal Register* (November 3, 1994) 55,117. The EPA later issued a final report on the CSI as *The Common Sense Initiative: Lesson Learned About Protecting the Environment in Common Sense, Cost-Effective Ways* (Washington, DC: Office of Reinvention, 1998).

25. The limits in the CSI stakeholder model are discussed in Daniel J. Fiorino, "Regulatory Policy and the Consensus Trap: An Agency Perspective," *Analyse & Kritik*, 19 (1997), 64–76.

26. U.S. Environmental Protection Agency, *Sustainable Industry: Promoting Strategic Environmental Protection in the Industrial Sector, Phase I Report* (Washington, DC: EPA Office of Policy, 1993). Discussed in Daniel J. Fiorino,

"Strategies for Regulatory Reform: Forward Compared to Backward Mapping," *Policy Studies Journal*, 25 (1997), 249–265.

27. Jan Mazurek, *The Use of Voluntary Agreements in the United States: An Initial Survey* (Paris: OECD, 1998), 30–31.

28. For an assessment, see Cary Coglianese and Laurie K. Allen, "Building Sector-Based Consensus: A Review of the US EPA's Common Sense Initiative," in Theo de Bruijn and Vicki Norberg-Bohm, eds., *Industrial Transformation: Environmental Policy Innovation in the United States and Europe* (Cambridge, MA: MIT Press, 2005), 65–92.

29. 63 *Federal Register* (April 15, 1998) 18507.

30. U.S. Environmental Protection Agency, *Evaluation of Implementation Experiences with Innovative Air Permits* (Washington, DC: EPA Office of Air Quality Planning and Standards and Office of Policy, Economics, and Innovation, 2004).

31. For voluntary programs, see Jan Mazurek, *The Use of Voluntary Agreements in the United States*.

32. Listed at www.epa.gov/partners (accessed August 4, 2005).

33. For 33/50 and similar programs, see Daniel Press and Daniel Mazmanian, "Understanding the Transition to a Sustainable Economy," in Vig and Kraft, eds., *Environmental Policy*, 5th ed., 275–298. Terry Davies and Jan Mazurek, *Industry Incentives for Environmental Improvement: An Evaluation of U.S. Federal Initiatives* (Washington, DC: Resources for the Future, 1996); and Mazurek, *The Use of Voluntary Agreements in the United States*. Mazurek reports that, measured from 1991 to 1994, the reductions linked to the program actually amounted to 27 percent, not the 51 percent that was claimed (p. 18). The evidence on 33/50 is also reviewed in Brouhle et al., "The Use of Voluntary Approaches for Environmental Policy Making in the U.S.," and in Harrison, "Challenges in Evaluating Voluntary Environmental Programs."

34. www.epa.gov/climateleaders.

35. This was one of the conclusions reached in Davies and Mazurek, *Industry Incentives for Environmental Improvement*.

36. An example is Magali A. Delmas and Ann Terlak, "Voluntary Agreements for the Environment: Institutional Constraints and Potential for Innovation," in Kurt Deketelaere and Eric Orts, eds., *Environmental Contracts: Comparative Approaches to Innovation in the United States and Europe* (Boston: Kluwer Law International, 2000), 349–367.

37. U.S. Environmental Protection Agency, *Amoco-U.S. EPA Pollution Prevention Project, Yorktown, Virginia: Project Summary* (Washington, DC: EPA Office of Policy, Planning, and Evaluation, 1992). Discussed in Fiorino, "Toward a New System of Environmental Regulation."

38. Philip K. Howard, *The Death of Common Sense: How Law Is Suffocating America* (New York: Random House, 1994), 7.

39. "Regulatory Reinvention (XL) Pilot Projects," 60 *Federal Register* (May 23, 1995), 27,283.

40. The concern among companies was that even though EPA had promised not to enforce the letter of the law, a citizens lawsuit could make them liable. See National Academy of Public Administration, "Excellence, Leadership, and the Intel Corporation: A Study of EPA's Project XL," in *Resolving the Paradox of Environmental Protection: An Agenda for Congress, EPA, and the States* (Washington, DC: NAPA, 1997), 88.

41. From the Intel case study in NAPA, *Resolving the Paradox of Environmental Protection*, 86. For 3M, see Alfred A. Marcus, Donald A. Geffen, and Ken Sexton, "The Quest for Cooperative Environmental Management: Lessons from the 3M Hutchison Project XL in Minnesota," in Deketelaere and Orts, *Environmental Contracts*, 143–164, and by the same authors, *Reinventing Environmental Regulation*.

42. Bradford C. Mank, "The Environmental Protection Agency's Project XL and Other Regulatory Reform Initiatives: The Need for Legislative Authorization," *Ecology Law Quarterly*, 25 (1998), 1–88, quote on 13. Also see Dennis B. Hirsch, "Bill and Al's XL-Ent Adventure: An Analysis of the EPA's Legal Authority to Implement the Clinton Administration's Project XL," *University of Illinois Law Review*, 1998 (1998), 129–172.

43. EPA efforts to learn from the experience and resolve issues are described in Marcus et al., *Reinventing Environmental Regulation*, 179–184.

44. Alan Blackmun and Jan Mazurek, "The Cost of Developing Site-Specific Environmental Regulations: Evidence from EPA's Project XL," *Environmental Management*, 27 (2001), 109–121.

45. Magali Delmas and Jan Mazurek, "A Transaction Cost Perspective on Negotiated Agreements: The Case of the U.S. EPA XL Program," in A. Baranzini and P. Thalman, eds., *Voluntary Approaches to Climate Protection: An Economic Assessment of Private–Public Partnerships* (Cheltenham, UK: Edward Elgar, 2003).

46. For a comparison of three projects that were successfully negotiated and the evidence of better results, see Marcus et al., *Reinventing Environmental Regulation*, 111–144.

47. U.S. Environmental Protection Agency, *Project XL Comprehensive Report* (Washington, DC: EPA Office of Policy, Economics, and Innovation, 2002), 4. Available at epa.gov/projectxl/xlcompreport00.htm (accessed August 22, 2005).

48. U.S. Environmental Protection Agency, *Aiming for Excellence: Actions to Encourage Stewardship and Accelerate Environmental Progress* (Washington, DC: Office of the Administrator, 1999), 13. Another influence on the design of the Performance Track was EPA's StarTrack, which had been implemented in its New England Region. See Jennifer Nash, "Tiered Environmental Regulation: Lessons from the StarTrack Program," in de Bruijn and Norberg-Bohm, *Industrial Transformation*, 253–278.

49. For a brief description of the program, see Daniel J. Fiorino, "Performance Track Places Trust in the Carrot over the Stick," *Environmental Quality Management*, 11 (Spring 2001), 9–22. The author was a principal designer and the first national director of EPA's Performance Track.

50. The original program notice and description may be found at "National Environmental Achievement Track Program," 69 *Federal Register* (July 6, 2000). 41655–41663. The initial design envisioned a two-level program, the first of which was labeled the achievement track. Later it was kept to one level and the entire program was called the performance track.

51. The numbers are from EPA's *Performance Track Third Annual Progress Report: Growth and Renewal* (Washington, DC: EPA Office of Policy, Economics, and Innovation, 2005), 7. This report is available on the program web site at epa.gov/performancetrack, as is information on members, program benefits, application materials, state programs, and other aspects of Performance Track.

52. The first rule granting regulatory benefits may be found at "National Environmental Performance Track Program," 69 *Federal Register* (April 22, 2004) 21737–21754. This included a provision allowing members to store hazardous waste for longer time periods and reducing the frequency of specific categories of air compliance reporting.

53. The annual progress reports provide an analysis of results achieved by members. Members have shown results in such areas as energy efficiency; water and materials use; air, water, and waste releases; and habitat preservation and restoration, among others. They have improved in most, but not all of the indicators. There is limited information on member performance more generally, but research on this topic by the Regulatory Policy Program of the Kennedy School of Government will be available sometime in 2006.

54. Allen Blackmun, James Boyd, Alan Krupnick, and Janice Mazurek, *The Economics of Tailored Regulation and the Implications for Project XL* (Washington, DC: Resources for the Future, 2001), 8.

55. Cary Coglianese, "Is Consensus an Appropriate Basis for Regulatory Policy?" in Deketelaere and Orts, *Environmental Contracts*, 93–113.

56. Examples are in U.S. Environmental Protection Agency, *Innovating for Better Environmental Results: A Report on Progress from the Innovation Action Council* (Washington, DC: EPA 2004, EPA 100-R-04-001).

57. For the Sector Strategies Program, which pursues collaborative and innovative approaches with key industry sectors, see EPA, *Innovating for Better Environmental Results*, 27–29 and www.epa.gov/sectors. For the EMS initiatives, see the same report, 26–27 and www.epa.gov/ems. There were also notable efforts to provide compliance assistance, especially to small firms, and to make regulation more workable.

58. This is a principal conclusion of the 2002 OECD study, *Voluntary Approaches in Environmental Policy* and of the several sources cited earlier in

this chapter. Also see Neil Gunningham and Darren Sinclair, *Leaders and Laggards: Next-Generation Environmental Regulation* (Sheffield, UK: Greenleaf, 2002), 148–150.

59. Ruckelshaus, "Stepping Stones," 36.

60. The Progressive Policy Institute was active in promoting proposals for a second generation statute. For more background, see its web site at www .ppionline.org. In the Senate, Senator Lieberman of Connecticut introduced the Innovative Environmental Strategies Act of 1997. In the House, Representatives Greenwood of Pennsylvania and Dooley of California co-sponsored the Second Generation Environmental Improvement Act of 1999. Both would have authorized EPA to enter into innovative agreements to encourage better environmental performance.

61. Rosenbaum, "EPA's Gamble with Regulatory Reinvention," in Vig and Kraft, eds. *Environmental Policy*, 4th ed. 165–189, quote on 184.

Chapter 6

1. Richard Rose, *Lesson-Drawing in Public Policy: A Guide to Learning Across Time and Space* (Chatham, NJ: Chatham House, 1993), 157.

2. Gunther Teubner, "Substantive and Reflexive Elements in Modern Law," *Law and Society Review*, 17 (1983), 253–254. Eric Orts applied this concept to regulation in "Reflexive Environmental Law," *Northwestern University Law Review*, 89 (1995), 1227–1340.

3. Teubner, "Substantive and Reflexive Elements in Modern Law," 254–255.

4. Ibid., 255.

5. On the effects of the TRI, see Mark Stephan, "Environmental Information Disclosure Programs: They Work, But Why?" *Social Science Quarterly*, 83 (2002), 190–205; 155; Shameek Konar and Mark A. Cohen, "Information as Regulation: The Effect of Community Right to Know Laws on Toxic Emissions," *Journal of Environmental Economics and Management*, 32 (1997), 109–124. James T. Hamilton, "Pollution as News: Media and Stock Market Reactions to the Toxics Release Inventory Data," *Journal of Environmental Economics and Management*, 28 (1995), 98–113.

6. The EMAS was adopted by the European Union in September 1993 as Council Regulation 1836/93. For a more detailed discussion of the EMAS as reflexive law, see Orts, "Reflexive Environmental Law," 1227; and Andrew Gouldson, "Voluntary Regulation and Industrial Capacities for Environmental Improvement: The Case of the EU Eco-Audit Regulation in the United Kingdom," in Theo de Bruijn and Vicki Norberg-Bohm, eds., *Industrial Transformation: Environmental Policy Innovation in the United States and Europe* (Cambridge, MA: MIT Press, 2005), 229–252.

7. Teubner, "Substantive and Reflexive Elements in Modern Law," 255.

8. For excellent essays on social-political governance, see Jan Kooiman, ed., *Modern Governance: New Government–Society Interactions* (London: Sage, 1993) and Gunther Teubner, Lindsay Farmer, and Declan Murphy, eds., *Environmental Law and Ecological Responsibility: The Concept and Practice of Ecological Responsibility* (New York: Wiley, 1994).

9. Jan Kooiman, in Kooiman, ed., *Modern Governance*, "Social-Political Governance: An Introduction," 1–6, quote on 6.

10. Ibid., 4.

11. Theo de Bruijn and Kris Lulofs, "Promoting Environmental Management in Dutch SMEs: Policy Implementation Networks." Paper presented at a workshop on voluntary, collaborative, and information-based policies, Kennedy School of Government, Cambridge, MA, May 11–12, 2001.

12. Colin J. Bennett and Michael Howlett, "The Lessons of Learning: Reconciling Theories of Policy Learning and Policy Change," *Policy Sciences*, 25 (1992), 275–294, quote on 276.

13. Hugh Heclo, *Modern Social Politics in Britain and Sweden: From Relief to Income Maintenance* (New Haven, CT: Yale University Press, 1974), 306.

14. Pieter Glasbergen, "Learning to Manage the Environment," in William M. Lafferty and James Meadowcroft, eds., *Democracy and the Environment: Problems and Prospects* (Cheltenham, UK: Edward Elgar, 1996), 175–193. A learning model is applied to the United States in Daniel J. Fiorino, "Environmental Policy as Learning: A New View of an Old Landscape," *Public Administration Review*, 61 (May/June 2001), 322–334.

15. Glasbergen, "Learning to Manage the Environment," 193.

16. National Academy of Public Administration, *environment.gov: Transforming Environmental Protection in the 21st Century* (Washington, DC: NAPA, 2000), 136.

17. For discussions, see Barry Rabe, "Power to the States: The Promise and Pitfalls of Decentralization," in Norman J. Vig and Michael E. Kraft, *Environmental Policy: New Directions for the Twenty-First Century*, 6th ed. (Washington, DC: CQ Press, 2006), 34–56; Denise Scheberle, "Devolution," in Robert F. Durant, Daniel J. Fiorino, and Rosemary O'Leary, eds. *Environmental Governance Reconsidered: Challenges, Choices, and Opportunities* (Cambridge, MA: MIT Press, 2004), 361–392.

18. Peder Larson, "A Culture of Innovation," *Environmental Forum*, 15 (September–October 1998), 20–28, quote on 28.

19. U.S. General Accountability Office, *Environmental Protection: Overcoming Obstacles to Innovative State Regulatory Programs* (Washington, DC: GAO, 2002, GAO-02-268).

20. Ibid., 3.

21. NAPA, *environment.com*, 34–39.

22. Ibid., 35.

23. For updated information, see www.epa.gov/permits/erp/states.htm (accessed July 17, 2005).

24. NAPA, *environment.gov*, 53–56. This discussion is based on the background report to the NAPA study and on Barry G. Rabe, "Permitting, Prevention, and Integration: Lessons from the States," in Donald F. Kettl, ed., *Environmental Governance: A Report on the Next Generation of Environmental Policy* (Washington, DC: Brookings Institution, 2002), 14–57. The NAPA background report is Susan Helms, Jennifer Sullivan, and Allen White, "The Potential and Pitfalls of Innovative Permits: Learning from New Jersey's Facility-Wide Permitting Program." Washington, DC: National Academy of Public Administration, 2000 (available at www.napawash.org/pc_economy_environment). accessed December 27, 2005.

25. Rabe, "Permitting, Prevention, and Integration," 33.

26. Ibid.

27. Ibid., 38.

28. For an overview, see Jerry Speir, "EMSs and Tiered Regulation: Getting the Deal Right," in Cary Coglianese and Jennifer Nash, eds., *Regulating from the Inside: Can Environmental Management Systems Achieve Policy Goals?* (Washington, DC: Resources for the Future, 2001), 198–219. Illustrative state web sites are Clean Texas (www.cleantexas.org) and Virginia's Environmental Excellence Program (www.deq.state.va.us/veep).

29. This discussion is based on an evaluation of Green Permits commissioned by the Oregon DEQ: *The Status of Innovative Permitting to Encourage Beyond-Compliance Environmental Performance: An Evaluation of Oregon's Green Permits Program* (prepared by the firm of Kerr, Greiner, Anderson, and April in June 2002).

30. State leadership programs are listed at epa.gov/performancetrack/states/programs.htm.

31. Described at www.deq.state.va.us/veep (accessed July 17, 2005).

32. The Multi-State Working Group on Environmental Performance is an organization of states and other interested parties that sponsors and disseminates information on innovative approaches to environmental performance and management (www.mswg.org).

33. Barry Rabe, "Federalism and Entrepreneurship: Explaining American and Canadian Innovation in Pollution Prevention and Regulatory Innovation," *Policy Studies Journal*, 27 (1999), 288–306, quote on 289.

34. Ibid., 292.

35. Rabe, "Prevention, Permitting, and Integration," 25.

36. DeWitt John, "Civic Environmentalism," in Durant et al. *Environmental Governance Reconsidered*, 219–254, quote on 219. Also see Dewitt John, *Civic*

Environmentalism: Alternatives to Regulation in States and Communities (Washington, DC: CQ Press, 1994).

37. John, "Civic Environmentalism," in Durant et al., 230–242.

38. Katrina Smith Korfmacher, "What's the Point of Partnering? A Case Study of Ecosystem Management in the Darby Creek Watershed," *American Behavioral Scientist*, 44 (December 2000), 548–564, quote on 550.

39. Ibid., 558.

40. Judith Layzer, "Citizen Participation and Government Choice in Local Environmental Controversies," *Policy Studies Journal*, 30 (2002), 193–207.

41. Ibid., 203.

42. Troy D. Abel and Mark Stephan, "The Limits of Civic Environmentalism," *American Behavioral Scientist*, 44 (December 2000), 614–628.

43. Denise Scheberle, "Moving Toward Community-Based Environmental Management: Wetland Protection in Door County," *American Behavioral Scientist* 44 (December 2000), 565–579.

44. A. Lijphart, *The Politics of Accommodation: Pluralism and Democracy in the Netherlands*, 2nd ed. (Berkeley: University of California Press, 1975).

45. Andrew Gouldson and Joseph Murphy, *Regulatory Realities: The Implementation and Impact of Industrial Environmental Regulation* (London: Earthscan, 1998), 105.

46. D. Liefferink, "The Netherlands: A Net Exporter of Environmental Policy Concepts," in M. S. Anderson and D. Liefferink, eds., *European Environmental Policy: The Pioneers* (Manchester, UK: Manchester University Press, 1997), 210–250.

47. The most complete discussion of this concept may be found in Maarten Hajer, *The Politics of Environmental Discourse: Ecological Modernization and the Policy Process* (Oxford: Oxford University Press, 1995). Also see John Dryzek, *The Politics of the Earth: Environmental Discourses* (Oxford: Oxford University Press, 1997).

48. Theo de Bruijn and Kris Lulofs, "The Dutch Policy Program on Environmental Management: Policy Implementation in Networks," in de Bruijn and Norberg-Bohm, *Industrial Transformation*, 203–228, quote on p. 219. The reasons for changing their approach are discussed on pp. 217–220.

49. Neil Gunningham and Darren Sinclair, *Leaders and Laggards: Next-Generation Environmental Regulation* (Sheffield, UK: Greenleaf, 2002), 106.

50. For sectors with large numbers of small sources, such as printing, companies do not prepare individual environmental plans. For these sectors, in which production processes are generally similar, the covenants are implemented through a handbook that describes the relevant standards and technologies that companies should follow. This is similar to the approach that has been used in the Massachusetts Environmental Results Program in the United States.

51. Gouldson and Murphy, *Regulatory Realities*, 108.

52. Marie Louise Van Muijen, "The Netherlands: Ambitious on Goals— Ambivalent on Action," in William M. Lafferty and James Meadowcroft, eds., *Implementing Sustainable Development: Strategies and Initiatives in High Consumption Societies* (Oxford: Oxford University Press, 2000), 154–155; Martin Van Vliet, "Environmental Regulation of Business: Options and Constraints for Communicative Governance," in Kooiman, ed., *Modern Governance*, 105–118, quote on 108.

53. Gouldson and Murphy, *Regulatory Realities*, 107.

54. Hans Bressers and Loret A. Plethenburg, "The Netherlands," in Martin Janicke and Helmut Weidner, eds., *National Environmental Policies: A Comparative Study of Capacity-Building* (Berlin: Springer, 1997), 109–131, quote on 116.

55. Assessed in de Bruijn and Lulofs, "The Dutch Policy Program on Environmental Management," 203–228.

56. Gouldson and Murphy, *Regulatory Realities*, 112–113.

57. Peter S. Hofman and Geerten J. I. Schrama, "Innovations in the Dutch Environmental Policy for the Industry Target Group." Paper presented at the Eighth Greening of Industry Network Conference, Chapel Hill, NC, November 15–18, 1999, 15.

58. Gunningham and Sinclair, *Leaders and Laggards*, 106.

59. Discussed in Van Muijen, "The Netherlands," 168–169.

60. David Wallace, *Environmental Policy and Industrial Innovation: Strategies in Europe, the US, and Japan* (London: Earthscan, 1995), 53.

61. Peter S. Hofman and Geerten J. I. Schrama, "Dutch Target Group, Policy," in de Bruijn and Norberg-Bohm, *Industrial Transformation*, 39–63.

62. Ibid., 57.

63. Theo de Bruijn and Vicki Norberg-Bohm, "Conclusion: Lessons for the Design and Use of Voluntary, Collaborative, and Information-Based Approaches to Environmental Policy," in de Bruijn and Norberg-Bohm, *Industrial Transformation*, 361–387. They rate the Dutch target approach as "notable" in terms of "substantially improved environmental performance" and "private sector leadership" and as uncertain at this point on "development and diffusion of environmentally superior technologies" and "patterns of changing behavior at levels beyond individual firms" (363).

64. The mechanics of the covenant process are discussed in Wallace, *Environmental Policy and Industrial Innovation*, 48–54.

65. John, "Civic Environmentalism," 221.

66. Gunningham and Sinclair, *Leaders and Laggards*, 39.

67. An example of citizen participation is Thomas C. Beierle and Jerry Crawford, *Democracy in Practice: Public Participation in Environmental*

Decisions (Washington, DC: Resources for the Future, 2002). For environmental disputes, an example is Rosemary O'Leary, Tina Nabatchi, and Lisa Bingham, "Environmental Conflict Resolution," in Durant et al., *Environmental Governance Reconsidered*, 323–354.

Chapter 7

1. Gregg Easterbrook, *A Moment on the Earth: The Coming Age of Environmental Optimism* (New York: Viking, 1995), 369–370.

2. Neil Gunningham and Peter Grabosky, *Smart Regulation: Designing Environmental Policy* (Oxford: Oxford University Press, 1998), 375–426.

3. Neil Gunningham and Darren Sinclair, *Leaders and Laggards: Next-Generation Environmental Regulation* (Sheffield, UK: Greenleaf, 2002), 189–204.

4. Robert A. Kagan, Neil Gunningham, and Dorothy Thornton, "Explaining Corporate Environmental Performance: How Does Regulation Matter?" *Law and Society Review*, 37 (2003), 51–89, quote on 83. In *Shades of Green* they observe that "Surveys of environmental and corporate managers suggest that regulation is the single most important driver of improved environmental performance" [Neil Gunningham, Robert A. Kagan, and Dorothy Thornton, *Shades of Green: Business, Regulation, and the Environment* (Palo Alto, CA: Stanford University Press, 2003, 45.]

5. For an illustration, see Judith A. Layzer's chapter, "Government Secrets at Rocky Flats," in her book, *The Environmental Case: Translating Values Into Public Policy* (Washington, DC: CQ Press, 2002), 78–101.

6. Discussed further in Daniel J. Fiorino, "Rethinking Environmental Regulation: Perspectives on Law and Governance," *Harvard Environmental Law Review*, 23 (1999), 441–469.

7. www.environmentaldefense.org/alliance.

8. For a cautionary note on cooperation, see Kathryn Harrison, "Is Cooperation the Answer? Canadian Environmental Enforcement in Comparative Perspective," *Journal of Policy Analysis and Management*, 14 (1995), 221–244.

9. On this point see, Daniel J. Fiorino, "Flexibility," in Robert A. Durant, Daniel J. Fiorino, and Rosemary O'Leary, eds., *Environmental Governance Reconsidered: Challenges, Choices, and Opportunities* (Cambridge, MA: MIT Press 2004), 393–425.

10. For measurement driving performance, see Shelley H. Metzenbaum, "Measurement That Matters: Cleaning Up the Charles River," in Donald F. Kettl, ed., *Environmental Governance: A Report on the Next Generation of Environmental Policy* (Washington, DC: Brookings Institution, 2002), 58–117. Also see the discussion in Durant et al., *Environmental Governance Reconsidered*, 497–501.

11. For example, EPA reported in its 2004 *Annual Report* that the percentage of annual performance goals that track environmental or related outcomes as opposed to outputs (such as issuing permits or taking enforcement actions) rose from 44 percent in 2004 to 60 percent in 2005. U.S. Environmental Protection Agency, *Fiscal Year 2004 Annual Report* (Washington, DC: EPA Office of the Chief Financial Officer, 2004), 17.

12. Magali A. Delmas and Ann Terlaak, "Voluntary Agreements for the Environment: Institutional Constraints and Potential for Innovation," in Kurt Deketelaere and Eric Orts, eds., *Environmental Contracts: Comparative Approaches to Regulatory Innovation in the United States and Europe* (Boston: Kluwer Law International, 2000), 349–357, quote on 357.

13. This is also recommended in Gunningham and Grabosky, *Smart Regulation*, 387–391.

14. The experience with flexible air permits is an example.

15. So an OECD seven-country study concludes. See "End-of-Pipe or Cleaner Production? An Empirical Comparison of Environmental Innovation Decisions Across OECD Countries." Paper presented at the Organization for Economic Co-operation and Development's Conference on Public Environmental Policy and the Private Firm (Washington, DC: April 14–15, 2005).

16. Like information disclosure and other reflexive mechanisms, market incentives should be used carefully. They are far more suited to greenhouse gases, where the distribution of emissions is not important, than to hazardous air pollutants, where the distribution of emissions and risks is important.

17. David Wallace, *Environmental Policy and Industrial Innovation: Strategies in Europe, the USA, and Japan* (London: Earthscan, 1995).

18. These include not only written studies, but also workshops and conferences that are used to evaluate and diffuse information about innovations among countries and across levels of government.

19. Daniel J. Fiorino, "Environmental Policy as Learning: A New View of an Old Landscape," *Public Administration Review*, 61 (May/June 2001), 322–334.

20. For an example, see J. Clarence Davies and Jan Mazurek, *Pollution Control in the United States: Evaluating the System* (Washington, DC: Resources for the Future, 1998), 27–100.

21. Gunningham et al., *Shades of Green*, 9–10.

22. For more on measuring performance on a sector basis, see the U.S. Environmental Protection Agency's *Sector Strategies Performance Report* (Washington, DC: EPA National Center for Environmental Innovation, 2004, EPA 100-R-04-002) or www.epa.gov/sectors.

23. Martin Enevoldsen, "Industrial Energy Efficiency," in Arthur P. J. Mol, Volkmar Lauber, and Duncan Liefferink, eds., *The Voluntary Approach to*

Environmental Policy: Joint Environmental Approach to Environmental Policy-Making in Europe (Oxford: Oxford University Press, 2000), 62–103.

24. Robert E. Roberts, quoted in Kettl, *Environmental Governance*, 184.

25. For trust in environmental regulation, see Christopher H. Foreman, Jr., "The Civic Sustainability of Reform," in Kettl, *Environmental Governance*, 160–162. More generally, see Francis Fukuyama, *Trust: The Social Virtues and the Creation of Prosperity* (New York: Free Press, 1995) and Robert D. Putnam, *Making Democracy Work: Civic Traditions in Modern Italy* (Princeton, NJ: Princeton University Press, 1993).

26. Magali Delmas and Ann Terlak, "Regulatory Commitment to Negotiated Agreements: Evidence from the United States, Germany, the Netherlands, and France," *Journal of Comparative Policy Analysis: Research and Practice*, 4 (2002), 5–29, quote on 14.

27. Gouldson and Murphy make this point in a study of the United Kingdom and the Netherlands: "Regulated companies prefer regulatory staff with recent industrial experience as they understand the processes that they regulate" [Andrew Gouldson and Joseph Murphy, *Regulatory Realities: The Implementation and Impact of Industrial Environmental Regulation* (London: Earthscan, 1998), 113].

28. Daniel A. Mazmanian, "Los Angeles' Transition from Command-and-Control to Market-Based Clean Air Policy Strategies and Implementation," in Daniel A. Mazmanian and Michael E. Kraft, eds., *Toward Sustainable Communities: Transition and Transformations in Environmental Policy* (Cambridge, MA: MIT Press, 2001), 77–112.

29. Ken Geiser, *Materials Matter: Toward a Sustainable Materials Policy* (Cambridge, MA: MIT Press, 2001).

30. "Conclusion: Lessons for the Design and Use of Voluntary, Collaborative, and Information-Based Approaches to Environmental Policy," in Theo de Bruijn and Vicki Norberg-Bohm, *Industrial Transformation: Environmental Policy Innovation in the United States and Europe* (Cambridge, MA: MIT Press, 2005), 361–387, quote on 365.

31. Michael E. Kraft, "Environmental Policy in Congress: From Consensus to Gridlock," in Norman J. Vig and Michael E. Kraft, eds., *Environmental Policy: New Directions for the Twenty-First Century*, 5th ed. (Washington DC: CQ Press, 2003), 146.

32. Richard MacLean and Frank Friedman, "Green Arthritis," *Environmental Forum* (November-December 2000), 17, 36–49.

33. Alfred Marcus, Donald A. Geffen, and Ken Sexton, *Reinventing Environmental Regulation: Lessons from Project XL* (Washington, DC: Resources for the Future, 2002), 85–86; 119–120.

34. Environmental Defense is the best example, but other national organizations may be more open to these kinds of approaches as well.

35. Charles E. Lindblom, "The Science of Muddling Through," *Public Administration Review,* 19 (Spring 1959), 79–88; Charles E. Lindblom, *The Policy Making Process* (Englewood Cliffs, NJ: Prentice-Hall, 1968).

36. William D. Ruckelshaus, "Stepping Stones," *Environmental Forum,* 15 (March–April 1998), 30.

37. Amitai Etzioni, "Mixed Scanning Revisited," *Public Administration Review,* 19 (January/February 1986), 8–14, quote on 8.

38. Kraft, "Environmental Policy in Congress," 133.

Bibliography

Abel, Troy D. and Mark Stephan. "The Limits of Civic Environmentalism." *American Behavioral Scientist*, 44 (December 2000), 614–628.

Andrews, Richard N. L. *Managing the Environment, Managing Ourselves: A History of American Environmental Policy*. New Haven, CT: Yale University Press, 1999.

Andrews, Richard N. L., Nicole Darnall, Deborah Rigling Gallagher, Suellen Terrill Keiner, Eric Feldman, Matthew L. Mitchell, Deborah Amaral, and Jessica D. Jacoby. "Environmental Management Systems: History, Theory, and Implementation Research." In Cary Coglianese and Jennifer Nash, eds., *Regulating from the Inside: Can Environmental Management Systems Achieve Policy Goals?* Washington, DC: Resources for the Future, 2001, 31–60.

Anton, Wilma Rose Q., George Deltas, and Madhu Khanna. "Incentives for Environmental Self-Regulation and Implications for Environmental Performance." *Journal of Environmental Economics and Management*, 48 (July 2004), 632–654.

Aspen Institute. *A Call to Action to Build a Performance-Based Environmental Management System*. Washington, DC: Aspen Institute, 2000.

Ayres, Ian and John Braithwaite. *Responsive Regulation: Transcending the Deregulation Debate*. New York: Oxford University Press, 1992.

Bardach, Eugene and Robert Kagan. *Going by the Book: The Problem of Regulatory Unreasonableness*. Philadelphia: Temple University Press, 1982.

Beierle, Thomas C. and Jerry Crawford. *Democracy in Practice: Public Participation in Environmental Decisions*. Washington, DC: Resources for the Future, 2002.

Benedick, Richard Elliot. *Ozone Diplomacy: New Directions in Safeguarding the Planet*. Cambridge, MA: Harvard University Press, 1991.

Bennett, Colin J. and Michael Howlett. "The Lessons of Learning: Reconciling Theories of Policy Learning and Policy Change." *Policy Sciences*, 25 (1992) 275–294.

Bernstein, Marver. *Regulating Business by Independent Commission*. Princeton, NJ: Princeton University Press, 1955.

Blacconiere, W. G. and D. M. Patton. "Environmental Disclosures, Regulatory Costs, and Changes in Firm Value." *Journal of Accounting and Economics*, 8 (1994), 357–377.

Blackman, Alan and Jan Mazurek. "The Cost of Developing Site-Specific Environmental Agreements: Evidence from EPA's Project XL." *Environmental Management*, 27 (2001), 109–121.

Bosso, Christopher J. and Deborah Lynn Guber. "Maintaining Presence: Environmental Advocacy and the Permanent Campaign." In Norman J. Vig and Michael E. Kraft, eds., *Environmental Policy: New Directions for the Twenty-First Century*, 6th ed. Washington, DC: CQ Press, 2006, 78–99.

Boyd, James. *Searching for the Profit in Pollution Prevention: Case Studies in Corporate Evaluation of Environmental Opportunities*. Washington, DC: Resources for the Future, 1998.

Bressers, Hans and Loret A. Plethenburg, "The Netherlands." In Martin Janicke and Helmut Weidner, eds., *National Environmental Policies: A Comparative Study of Capacity Building*. Berlin: Springer, 1996, 109–132.

Brickman, Ronald, Sheila Jasanoff, and Thomas Ilgen. *Controlling Chemicals: The Politics of Regulation in Europe and the United States*. Ithaca, NY: Cornell University Press, 1985.

Brouhle, Keith, Charles Griffiths, and Ann Wolverton. "The Use of Voluntary Approaches for Environmental Policymaking in the U.S." In Edoardo Croce, ed., *The Handbook of Voluntary Environmental Agreements: Design, Implementation, and Evaluation Issues*. New York: Springer-Verlag, 2005, 107–134.

Chertow, Marian R. and Daniel C. Esty. *Thinking Ecologically: The Next Generation of Environmental Policy*. New Haven, CT: Yale University Press, 1997.

Coglianese, Cary. "Is Consensus an Appropriate Basis for Regulatory Policy?" In Kurt Deketelaere and Eric Orts, eds., *Environmental Contracts: Approaches to Regulatory Innovation in the United States and Europe*. Boston: Kluwer Law International, 2000, 93–113.

Coglianese, Cary and Laurie K. Allen. "Building Sector-Based Consensus: A Review of the USEPA's Common Sense Initiative." In Theo de Bruijn and Vicki Norberg-Bohm, eds., *Industrial Transformation: Environmental Policy Innovation in the United States and Europe*. Cambridge, MA: MIT Press, 2005, 65–92.

Coglianese, Cary and Jennifer Nash. "Environmental Management Systems and the New Policy Agenda." In Cary Coglianese and Jennifer Nash, eds., *Regulating from the Inside: Can Environmental Management Systems Achieve Policy Goals?* Washington, DC: Resources for the Future, 2001, 1–25.

Coglianese, Cary and Jennifer Nash, eds. *Regulating from the Inside: Can Environmental Management Systems Achieve Policy Goals?* Washington, DC: Resources for the Future, 2001.

Dahlstrom, Kristina, Chris Howes, Paul Leinster, and Jim Skea. "Environmental Management Systems and Company Performance: Assessing the Case for Extending Risk-Based Regulation." *European Environment*, 13 (2003), 187–203.

Darnall, Nicole and Alexei Pavlichev. *Environmental Policy Tools and Firm-Level Management Practices in the U.S.* Raleigh: North Carolina State University, 2004.

Davies, J. Clarence. *The Politics of Pollution.* New York: Pegasus, 1970.

Davies, J. Clarence and Jan Mazurek. *Pollution Control in the United States: Evaluating the System.* Washington, DC: Resources for the Future, 1998.

Davies, Terry. *Reforming Permitting.* Washington, DC: Resources for the Future, 2001.

Davies, Terry and Jan Mazurek. *Industry Incentives for Environmental Improvement: An Evaluation of U.S. Federal Initiatives.* Washington, DC: Resources for the Future, 1996.

de Bruin, Theo and Vicki Norberg-Bohm, eds. *Industrial Transformation: Environmental Policy Innovation in the United States and Europe.* Cambridge, MA: MIT Press, 2005.

de Bruijn, Theo and Vicki Norberg-Bohm. "Conclusion: Lessons for the Design and Use of Voluntary, Collaborative, and Information-Based Approaches to Environmental Policy. In Theo de Bruijn and Vicki Norberg-Bohm, eds., *Industrial Transformation: Environmental Policy Innovation in the United States and Europe.* Cambridge, MA: MIT Press, 2005, 361–387.

de Bruijn, Theo and Kris Lulofs. "The Dutch Policy Program on Environmental Management: Policy Implementation in Networks." In Theo de Bruijn and Vicki Norberg-Bohm, eds. *Industrial Transformations: Environmental Policy Innovation in the United States and Europe.* Cambridge, MA: MIT Press, 2005, 203–228.

Delmas, Magali and Jan Mazurek. "A Transaction Cost Perspective on Negotiated Agreements: The Case of the U.S. EPA XL Program." In A. Baranzini and P. Thalman, eds., *Voluntary Approaches to Climate Protection: An Economic Assessment of Private–Public Partnerships.* Cheltenham, UK: Edward Elgar, 2003.

Delmas, Magali and Ann Terlak. "Voluntary Agreements for the Environment: Institutional Constraints and Potential for Innovation." In Kurt Deketelaere and Eric Orts, eds., *Environmental Contracts: Approaches to Regulatory Innovation in the United States and Europe.* Boston: Kluwer Law International, 2000, 349–367.

Delmas, Magali and Ann Terlak. "Regulatory Commitment to Negotiated Agreements: Evidence from the United States, Germany, the Netherlands, and

France."*Journal of Comparative Policy Analysis: Research and Practice*, 4 (2002), 5–29.

Desai, Uday, ed. *Environmental Politics and Policy in Industrial Countries.* Cambridge, MA: MIT Press, 2002.

de Tocqueville, Alexis. *Democracy in America.* New York: Doubleday, 1969.

Dryzek, John S. *The Politics of the Earth: Environmental Discourses.* Oxford: Oxford University Press, 1997.

Durant, Robert F., Daniel J. Fiorino, and Rosemary O'Leary, eds., *Environmental Governance Reconsidered: Challenges, Choices, and Opportunities.* Cambridge, MA: MIT Press, 2004.

Easterbrook, Gregg. *A Moment on the Earth: The Coming Age of Environmental Optimism.* New York: Viking, 1993.

Eisner, Marc Allen. *Regulatory Politics in Transition.* Baltimore: Johns Hopkins University Press, 1995.

Environmental Law Institute. *Barriers to Environmental Technology and Use.* Washington, DC: ELI, 1998.

Etzioni, Amitai. "Mixed Scanning Revisited." *Public Administration Review*, 46 (January February, 1986), 8–14.

Fiorino, Daniel J. "Regulatory Negotiation as a Policy Process." *Public Administration Review*, 48 (July/August 1988), 764–772.

Fiorino, Daniel J. *Making Environmental Policy.* Los Angeles: University of California Press, 1995.

Fiorino, Daniel J. "Toward a New System of Environmental Regulation: The Case for an Industry Sector Approach." *Environmental Law*, 26 (1996), 457–498.

Fiorino, Daniel J. "Strategies for Regulatory Reform: Forward Compared to Backward Mapping." *Policy Studies Journal*, 25 (1997), 249–265.

Fiorino, Daniel J. "Regulatory Policy and the Consensus Trap: An Agency Perspective," *Analyse & Kritik*, 19 (1997), 64–76.

Fiorino, Daniel J. Rethinking Environmental Regulation: Perspectives on Law and Governance." *Harvard Environmental Law Review*, 23 (1999), 441–469.

Fiorino, Daniel J. "Environmental Policy as Learning: A New View of an Old Landscape." *Public Administration Review*, 61 (May/June 2001), 322–334.

Fiorino, Daniel J. "Flexibility." In Robert F. Durant, Daniel J. Fiorino, and Rosemary O'Leary, eds., *Environmental Governance Reconsidered: Challenges, Choices, and Opportunities.* Cambridge, MA: MIT Press, 2004, 393–425.

Fischer, Kurt and Johan Schot, eds. *Environmental Strategies for Industry: International Perspectives on Research Needs and Policy Implications.* Washington, DC: Island Press, 1993.

Florida, Richard and Derek Davison. "Why Do Firms Adopt Advanced Environmental Management Practices (And Do They Make a Difference?)" In

Cary Coglianese and Jennifer Nash, eds., *Regulating from the Inside: Can Environmental Management Systems Achieve Policy Goals?* Washington, DC: Resources for the Future, 2001, 82–104.

Foreman, Christopher H. "The Civic Sustainability of Reform." In Donald F. Kettl, ed., *Environmental Governance: A Report on the Next Generation of Environmental Policy.* Washington, DC: Brookings Institution, 2002, 146–176.

Freeman, A. Myrick III. "Economics, Incentives, and Environmental Policy." In Norman J. Vig and Michael E. Kraft, eds., *Environmental Policy: New Directions for the Twenty-First Century,* 6th ed. Washington, DC: CQ Press, 2006, 193–238.

Fuchs, Doris and Daniel A. Mazmanian. "The Greening of Industry: Needs of the Field." *Business Strategy and the Environment,* 7 (1998), 193–203.

Fukuyama, Francis. *Trust: The Social Virtues and the Creation of Prosperity.* New York: Free Press, 1995.

Geiser, Ken. *Materials Matter: Toward a Sustainable Materials Policy.* Cambridge, MA: MIT Press, 2001.

Geiser, Ken. "Pollution Prevention." In Robert F. Durant, Daniel J. Fiorino, and Rosemary O'Leary, eds., *Environmental Governance Reconsidered: Challenges, Choices, and Opportunities.* Cambridge, MA: MIT Press, 2004, 427–454.

Glasbergen, Pieter. "Learning to Manage the Environment." In William M. Lafferty and James Meadowcroft, eds., *Democracy and the Environment: Problems and Prospects.* Cheltenham, UK: Edward Elgar, 1996, 175–193.

Gouldson, Andrew. "Voluntary Regulation and Capacities for Environmental Improvement: The Case of the EU Eco-Audit Regulation in the United Kingdom." In Theo de Bruijn and Vicki Norberg-Bohm, eds. *Industrial Transformation: Environmental Policy Innovations in the United States and Europe.* Cambridge, MA: MIT Press, 2005, 229–252.

Gouldson, Andrew and Joseph Murphy. *Regulatory Realities: The Implementation and Impact of Industrial Environmental Regulation.* London: Earthscan, 1998.

Graham, Mary. *The Morning After Earth Day: Practical Environmental Politics.* Washington, DC: Brookings Institution, 1999.

Greer, Linda E. "Why We Didn't Sign." *Environmental Forum,* 18 (March–April 1998), 37–38.

Guile, Bruce and Jared Cohen. "Sorting Out a Service-Based Economy." In Marian R. Chertow and Daniel C. Esty, eds. *Thinking Ecologically: The Next Generation of Environmental Policy.* New Haven: Yale University Press, 1997, 76–90.

Gunningham, Neil and Joseph Rees. "Industry Self-Regulation: An Institutional Perspective." *Law and Policy,* 19 (1997), 363–414.

Gunningham, Neil and Peter Grabosky. *Smart Regulation: Designing Environmental Policy.* Oxford: Oxford University Press, 1998.

Gunningham, Neil and Darren Sinclair. *Leaders and Laggards: Next-Generation Environmental Regulation.* Sheffield, UK: Greenleaf, 2002.

Gunningham, Neil, Robert A. Kagan, and Dorothy Thornton. *Shades of Green: Business, Regulation, and the Environment.* Palo Alto, CA: Stanford University Press, 2003.

Hahn, Robert W., ed. *Risks, Costs, and Lives Saved: Getting Better Results from Regulation.* New York: Oxford University Press, 1996.

Haigh, Nigel and Frances Irwin, eds. *Integrated Pollution Control in Europe and North America.* Washington, DC: Conservation Foundation, 1990.

Hajer, Maarten J. *The Politics of Environmental Discourse: Ecological Modernization and the Policy Process.* Oxford: Oxford University Press, 1995.

Hamilton, James T. "Pollution as News: Media and Stock Market Reactions to the Toxics Release Inventory Data." *Journal of Environmental Economics and Management*, 28 (1995), 98–113.

Harrison, Kathryn. "Is Cooperation the Answer? Canadian Environmental Enforcement in Comparative Context." *Journal of Policy Analysis and Management*, 14 (1995), 221–224.

Harrison, Kathryn. "Challenges in Evaluating Voluntary Environmental Programs." In National Research Council, *New Tools for Environmental Protection: Education, Information, and Voluntary Measures.* Washington, DC: National Academy Press, 2002, 263–282.

Hart, Stuart. "Strategies for a Sustainable World." *Harvard Business Review*, 75 (1997), 66–76.

Hausker, Karl. *The Convergence of Ideas on Improving the Environmental Protection System.* Washington, DC: Center for Strategic and International Studies, 1999.

Hawkins, Keith and John M. Thomas, eds. *Enforcing Regulation.* Boston: Kluwer-Nijhoff, 1984.

Heclo, Hugh. *Modern Social Politics in Britain and Sweden: From Relief to Income Maintenance.* New Haven, CT: Yale University Press, 1974.

Herb, Jean, Susan Helms, and Michael J. Jensen. "Harnessing the 'Power of Information': Environmental Right to Know as a Driver of Sound Environmental Policy." In National Research Council, *New Tools for Environmental Protection: Education, Information, and Voluntary* Measures. Washington DC: National Academy Press, 2002, 253–262.

Hilden, Mikeal, Jukka Lepola, Per Mickwitz, Aard Mulders, and Marika Palosaari. *Evaluation of Environmental Policy Instruments: A Case Study of the Finnish Pulp and Paper and Chemical Industries.* Helsinki: Finnish Environmental Institute, 2002.

Hirsch, Dennis D. "Bill and Al's XL-ent Adventure: An Analysis of the EPA's Legal Authority to Implement the Clinton Administration's Project XL." *University of Illinois Law Review* (1998), 129–172.

Hoffman, Andrew J. *Competitive Environmental Strategy: A Guide to the Changing Business Landscape.* Washington, DC: Island Press, 2000.

Hofman, Peter S. and Geerten J. Schrama. "Dutch Target Group Policy." In Theo de Bruijn and Vicki Norberg-Bohm, eds., *Industrial Transformation: Environmental Policy Innovation in the United States and Europe*. Cambridge, MA: MIT Press, 2005, 39–63.

Howard, Philip K. *The Death of Common Sense: How Law Is Suffocating America*. New York: Random House, 1994.

Inglehart, Ronald. "Public Support for Environmental Protection: The Impact of Subjective Problems and Subjective Values in 43 Societies." *PS: Political Science and Politics*, 28 (1995), 57–71.

Janicke, Martin. "Democracy as a Condition for Environmental Policy Success: The Importance of Non-institutional Factors." In William M. Lafferty and James Meadowcroft, eds., *Democracy and the Environment: Problems and Prospects*. Cheltenham, UK: Edward Elgar, 1996, 71–85.

Janicke, Martin and Helmut Weidner. *Successful Environmental Policy: A Critical Evaluation of 24 Cases*. Berlin: Ed. Sigma, 1995.

Janicke, Martin and Helmut Weidner, eds. *National Environmental Policies: A Comparative Study of Capacity Building*. Berlin: Springer, 1996.

John, DeWitt. *Civic Environmentalism: Alternatives to Regulation in States and Communities*. Washington, DC: CQ Press, 1994.

John, DeWitt. "Civic Environmentalism." In Robert F. Durant, Daniel J. Fiorino, and Rosemary O"Leary, eds. *Environmental Governance Reconsidered: Challenges, Choices, and Opportunities*. Cambridge, MA: MIT Press, 2004, 219–254.

Kagan, Robert A. "Adversarial Legalism in American Government." In Marc K. Landy and Martin Levin, eds., *The New Politics of Public Policy*. Baltimore: Johns Hopkins University Press, 1995, 23–46.

Kagan, Robert A. "Introduction: Comparing National Styles of Regulation in Japan and the United States. *Law and Policy*, 22 (October 2000), 225–244.

Kagan, Robert and Lee Axelrod, eds. *Regulatory Encounters: Multinational Corporations and American Adversarial Legalism*. Berkeley: University of California Press, 2000.

Kagan, Robert A. and John T. Scholz. "The Criminology of the Corporation and Regulatory Enforcement Strategies." In Keith Hawkins and John M. Thomas, eds., *Enforcing Regulation*. Boston: Kluwer-Nijhoff, 1984, 67–95.

Kagan, Robert A., Neil Gunningham, and Dorothy Thornton. "Explaining Corporate Environmental Performance: How Does Regulation Matter?" *Law and Society Review*, 37 (2003), 51–89.

Kettl, Donald F., ed. *Environmental Governance: A Report on the Next Generation of Environmental Policy*. Washington, DC: Brookings Institution, 2002.

Khanna, M., W. R. Quimo, and D. Bojilova. "Toxic Release Information: A Policy Tool for Environmental Protection." *Journal of Environmental Economics and Management*, 36 (1998), 243–266.

King, Andrew and Michael Lenox. "Industry Self-Regulation without Sanctions: The Chemical Industry's Responsible Care Program," *Academy of Management Journal*, 43 (2000), 698–716.

King, Andrew and Michael Lenox. "Does It Really Pay to Be Green? *Journal of Industrial Ecology*, 5 (2001), 105–116.

Kingdon, John W. *Agendas, Alternatives, and Public Policies*, 2d ed. New York: Harper Collins, 1995.

Kooiman, Jan, ed. *Modern Governance: New Government–Society Interactions*. London: SAGE, 1993.

Konar, Shameek and Mark A. Cohen. "Information as Regulation: The Effects of Community Right to Know Laws on Toxic Emissions." *Journal of Environmental Economics and Management*, 32 (1997), 109–124.

Korfmacher, Katrina Smith. "What's the Point of Partnering? A Case Study of Ecosystem Management in the Darby Creek Watershed." *American Behavioral Scientist*, 44 (December 2000), 548–564.

KPMG. *International Survey of Corporate Environmental Reporting*. Amsterdam: KPMG, 1999.

KPMG. *International Survey of Corporate Environmental Reporting*. Amsterdam: KPMG, 2005.

Kraft, Michael E. "Environmental Policy in Congress." In Norman J. Vig and Michael E. Kraft, eds., *Environmental Policy: New Directions for the Twenty-First Century*, 6th ed. Washington, DC: CQ Press, 2006, 124–147.

Kraft, Michael and Norman J. Vig. "Environmental Policy from the 1970s to 2000: An Overview." In Norman J. Vig and Michael E. Kraft, eds., *Environmental Policy: New Directions for the Twenty-First Century*, 4th ed. Washington, DC: CQ Press, 2000, 1–31.

Lafferty, William M. and James Meadowcroft, eds. *Democracy and the Environment: Problems and Prospects*. Cheltenham, UK: Edward Elgar, 1996.

Lafferty, William M. and James Meadowcroft, eds. *Implementing Sustainable Development: Strategies and Initiatives in High-Consumption Societies*. Oxford: Oxford University Press, 2000.

Landy, Marc K. "The New Politics of Environmental Policy," In Marc K. Landy and Martin Levin, eds., *The New Politics of Public Policy*. Baltimore: Johns Hopkins University Press, 1995.

Landy, Marc K., Marc J. Roberts, and Stephen R. Thomas. *The Environmental Protection Agency: Asking the Wrong Questions*. New York: Oxford University Press, 1990.

Larson, Peder. "A Culture of Innovation," *Environmental Forum*, 15 (September-October 1998), 20–28.

Layzer, Judith. "Citizen Participation and Government Choice in Local Environmental Controversies." *Policy Studies Journal*, 30 (2002), 193–207.

Layzer, Judith A. *The Environmental Case: Translating Values Into Policy.* Washington, DC: CQ Press, 2002.

Lester, James P., ed. *Environmental Politics and Policy: Theories and Evidence*, 2nd ed. Durham, NC: Duke University Press, 1995.

Lijphart, A. *The Politics of Accommodation: Pluralism and Democracy in the Netherlands*, 2nd ed. Berkeley, CA: University of California Press, 1975.

Lindblom, Charles. "The Science of Muddling Through." *Public Administration Review*, 19 (Spring 1959), 79–88.

Lindblom, Charles. *The Policy Making Process*. Englewood Cliffs, NJ: Prentice-Hall, 1968.

Lundqvist, Lennart J. *The Hare and the Tortoise: Clean Air Policies in the United States and Sweden*. Ann Arbor: University of Michigan Press, 1980.

MacLean, Richard and Frank Friedman. "Green Arthritis." 17 *Environmental Forum* (November-December 2000), 36–49.

Mank, Bradford C. "The Environmental Protection Agency's Project XL and Other Regulatory Reform Initiatives: The Need for Legislative Authorization." *Ecology Law Quarterly*, 25 (1998), 1–88.

Marcus, Alfred A., Donald A. Geffen, and Ken Sexton. *Reinventing Environmental Regulation: Lessons from Project XL*. Washington, DC: Resources for the Future, 2002.

Marshall, R. Scott and Darrell Brown. "Corporate Environmental Reporting: What's In a Metric?" *Business Strategy and the Environment*, 12 (2002), 87–106.

Mazmanian, Daniel A. "Los Angeles' Transition from Command-and-Control to Market-Based Clean Air Policy Strategies and Implementation." In Daniel A. Mazmanian and Michael E. Kraft, eds., *Toward Sustainable Communities: Transition and Transformations in Environmental Policy*. Cambridge, MA: MIT Press, 2001, 77–112.

Mazmanian, Daniel A. and Michael E. Kraft, eds. *Toward Sustainable Communities: Transition and Transformations in Environmental Policy*. Cambridge, MA: MIT Press, 2001.

Mazurek, Jan. *The Use of Voluntary Agreements in the United States: An Initial Survey*. Paris: Organization for Economic Co-operation and Development, 1998.

Mazurek, Jan. "Third-Party Auditing of Environmental Management Systems." In Robert F. Durant, Daniel J. Fiorino, and Rosemary O'Leary, eds., *Environmental Governance Reconsidered: Challenges, Choices, and Opportunities*. Cambridge, MA: MIT Press, 2004, 455–481.

Melnick, R. Shep. "Administrative Law and Bureaucratic Rationality." *Administrative Law Review*, 28 (Spring 1992), 245–259.

Metzenbaum, Shelley H. "Measurement That Matters: Cleaning Up the Charles River." In Donald F. Kettl, ed., *Environmental Governance: A Report on the Next Generation of Environmental Policy*. Washington, DC: Brookings Institution, 2002, 58–117.

Mol, Arthur P. J., Volkmar Lauber, and Duncan Liefferink, eds. *The Voluntary Approach to Environmental Policy: Joint Environmental Approach to Environmental Policy Making in Europe.* Oxford: Oxford University Press, 2000.

Nash, Jennifer. "Tiered Environmental Regulation: Lessons from the StarTrack Program." In Theo de Bruijn and Vicki Norberg-Bohm, eds. *Industrial Transformation: Environmental Policy Innovation in the United States and Europe.* Cambridge, MA: MIT Press, 2005, 253–278.

Nash, Jennifer and John Ehrenfeld. "Codes of Environmental Management Practice: Assessing Their Potential as Tools for Change." *Annual Review of Energy and the Environment,* 22 (1997), 487–535.

National Academy of Public Administration. *Setting Priorities, Getting Results: A New Direction for the Environmental Protection Agency.* Washington, DC: NAPA, 1995.

National Academy of Public Administration. *Resolving the Paradox of Environmental Protection: An Agenda for Congress, EPA, and the States.* Washington, DC: NAPA, 1997.

National Academy of Public Administration. *environment.gov: Transforming Environmental Protection in the 21ˢᵗ Century.* Washington, DC: NAPA, 2000.

National Academy of Public Administration. *A Breath of Fresh Air: Reviving the New Source Review Program.* Washington, DC: NAPA, 2003.

National Research Council. *New Tools for Environmental Protection: Education, Information, and Voluntary Measures.* Washington, DC: National Academy Press, 2002.

Ochsner, Michele. "Pollution Prevention: An Overview of Regulatory Incentives and Barriers." *New York University Environmental Law Journal,* 3 (1998), 586–617.

O'Leary, Rosemary and Susan Summers Raines. "Lessons Learned from Two Decades of Dispute Resolution at the U.S. Environmental Protection Agency." *Public Administration Review,* 61 (November/December 2001), 682–692.

O'Leary, Rosemary, Robert F. Durant, Daniel J. Fiorino, and Paul S. Weiland. *Managing for the Environment: Understanding the Legal, Organizational, and Policy Challenges.* San Francisco: Jossey-Bass, 1999.

O'Leary, Rosemary, Tina Nabatchi, and Lisa Bingham. "Environmental Conflict Resolution." In Robert F. Durant, Daniel J. Fiorino, and Rosemary O'Leary, eds., *Environmental Governance Reconsidered: Challenges, Choices, and Opportunities.* Cambridge, MA: MIT Press, 2004, 323–354.

Organization for Economic Co-operation and Development. *Voluntary Approaches for Environmental Policy: An Assessment.* Paris: OECD, 1999.

Organization for Economic Co-operation and Development. *Voluntary Approaches in Environmental Policy: Environmental Effectiveness, Efficiency, and Usage in Policy Mixes.* Paris: OECD, Draft Final Report, 2002.

Orts, Eric. "Reflexive Environmental Law." *Northwestern University Law Review,* 89 (1995) 1227–1340.

Peters, B. Guy and John Pierre. "Governance Without Government? Rethinking Public Administration." *Journal of Public Administration Research and Theory,* 8 (1998), 223–243.

Porter, Michael. *Competitive Advantage.* New York: Free Press, 1985.

Porter, Michael and Claas van der Linde. "Green and Competitive: Ending the Stalemate." *Harvard Business Review,* 73 (September–October, 1995), 120–134.

Porter, Michael and Claas van der Linde. "Toward a New Conception of the Environment-Competitiveness Relationship." *Journal of Economic Perspectives,* 9 (1995), 119–132.

Portney, Paul R. and Robert N. Stavins, eds. *Public Policies for Environmental Protection,* 2nd ed. Washington, DC: Resources for the Future, 2000.

Potoski, Matthew and Aseem Prakash. "Covenant with Weak Swords: ISO 14001 and Firms' Environmental Performance." *Journal of Policy Analysis and Management,* 49 (2005), 745–769.

Potoski, Matthew and Aseem Prakash. "Green Clubs and Voluntary Compliance: ISO 14001 and Firms' Regulatory Performance." *American Journal of Political Science,* 49 (2005), 235–248.

Prakash, Aseem. *Greening the Firm: The Politics of Corporate Environmentalism.* Cambridge: Cambridge University Press, 2000.

President's Council for Sustainable Development. *Sustainable America: A New Consensus for Prosperity, Opportunity, and a Healthy Environmental for the Future.* Washington, DC: PCSD, 1996.

Press, Daniel and Daniel A. Mazmanian. "The Greening of Industry: Combining Government Regulation and Voluntary Strategies." In Norman J. Vig and Michael E. Kraft, eds., *Environmental Policy: New Directions for the Twenty-First Century,* 6th ed. Washington, DC: CQ Press, 2006, 264–87.

Putnam, Robert D. *Making Democracy Work: Civic Traditions in Modern Italy.* Princeton, NJ: Princeton University Press, 1993.

Rabe, Barry. "Integrated Environmental Permitting: Experience and Innovation at the State Level." *State and Local Government Review,* 27 (Fall 1995), 209–220.

Rabe, Barry. "Federalism and Entrepreneurship: Explaining American and Canadian Innovation in Pollution Prevention and Regulatory Innovation." *Policy Studies Journal,* 27 (1999), 288–306.

Rabe, Barry. "Power to the States: The Promise and Pitfalls of Decentralization." In Norman J. Vig and Michael E. Kraft, eds., *Environmental Policy: New Directions for the Twenty-First Century,* 6th ed. Washington, DC: CQ Press, 2006, 34–56.

Rajeski, David W. and James Salzman. "Changes in Pollution and the Implications for Public Policy." In National Research Council, *New Tools for Environmental Protection: Education, Information, and Voluntary Measures.* Washington, DC: National Academy Press, 2002, 17–42.

Rees, Joseph. "The Development of Industry Self-Regulation in the Chemical Industry." *Law and Policy*, 19 (1997), 447–528.

Regens, James L., Barry L. Seldon, and Euel Elliot. "Modeling Compliance to Environmental Regulations: Evidence from Manufacturing Industries." *Journal of Policy Modeling*, 19 (1997), 683–696.

Reinhardt, Forest. *Down to Earth: Applying Business Principles to Environmental Management.* Cambridge: Harvard University Press, 2000.

Ringquist, Evan. *Environmental Protection at the State Level: Politics and Progress in Controlling Pollution.* Armonk, NY: M.E. Sharp, 1993.

Roome, Nigel, ed. *Sustainability Strategies for Industry: The Future of Corporate Practice.* Washington, DC: Island Press, 1998.

Rose, Richard. *Lesson-Drawing in Public Policy: A Guide to Learning Across Time and Space.* Chatham, NJ: Chatham House, 1993.

Rosenbaum, Walter A. "Escaping the 'Battered Agency Syndrome': EPA's Gamble with Regulatory Reinvention." In Norman J. Vig and Michael E. Kraft, eds., *Environmental Policy: New Directions for the Twenty-First Century*, 4th ed. Washington, DC: CQ Press, 2000, 165–189.

Rothenburg, Lawrence S. *Environmental Choices: Policy Responses to Green Demands.* Washington, DC: CQ Press, 2002.

Ruckelshaus, William D. "Stepping Stones." *Environmental Forum*, 15 (1998), 30–36.

Scheberle, Denise. *Federalism and Environmental Policy: Trust and the Politics of Implementation.* Washington, DC: Georgetown University Press, 1997.

Scheberle, Denise. "Moving Toward Community-Based Environmental Management: Wetland Protection in Door County." *American Behavioral Scientist*, 44 (December 2000), 565–579.

Scheberle, Denise. "Devolution." In Robert F. Durant, Daniel J. Fiorino, and Rosemary O'Leary, eds., *Environmental Governance Reconsidered: Challenges, Choices, and Opportunities.* Cambridge, MA: MIT Press, 2004, 363–392.

Schmidheiny, Stephan. *Changing Course: A Global Business Perspective on Development and the Environment.* Cambridge, MA: MIT Press, 1997.

Schmidheiny, Stephan and Federico Zorraquin. *Financing Change: The Financial Community, Eco-Efficiency, and Sustainable Development.* Cambridge, MA: MIT Press, 1996.

Shaman, David and David Wheeler. "Controlling Industrial Pollution in the Developing World." *Environmental Quality Management*, 69 (1998), 69–75.

Speir, Jerry. "EMS and Tiered Regulation: Getting the Deal Right." In Cary Coglianese and Jennifer Nash, eds., *Regulating from the Inside: Can Environmental Management Systems Achieve Policy Goals?* Washington, DC: Resources for the Future, 2001, 198–219.

Spence, David B. "Paradox Lost: Logic, Morality, and the Foundations of Environmental Law in the 21st Century." *Columbia Journal of Environmental Law,* 20 (1995), 145–182.

Spence, David B. and Lehka Gopalakrishnan. "Bargaining Theory and Regulatory Reform: The Political Logic of Inefficient Regulation." *Vanderbilt Law Review,* 53 (March 2000), 599–652.

Stephan, Mark. "Environmental Information Dislosure Programs: They Work, But Why?" *Social Science Quarterly,* 83 (2002), 190–205.

Stephan, Mark, Michael E. Kraft, and Troy Abel. "Information Politics and Environmental Performance: The Impact of the Toxics Release Inventory on Corporate Decision Making." Paper presented at the annual meeting of the American Political Science Association, Washington, DC, September 1–4, 2005.

Stewart, Richard. "United States Environmental Regulation: A Failing Paradigm." *Journal of Law and Commerce,* 15 (1996), 585–596.

Sunstein, Cass. *After the Rights Revolution: Reconceiving the Regulatory State.* Cambridge, MA: Harvard University Press, 1990.

Sunstein, Cass R. "Paradoxes of the Regulatory State." *University of Chicago Law Review,* 57 (1990), 407–441.

Teubner, Gunther. "Substantive and Reflexive Elements in Modern Law." *Law and Society Review,* 17 (1983), 239–285.

Teubner, Gunther, Lindsay Farmer, and Declan Murphy, eds., *Environmental Law and Ecological Responsibility: The Concept and Practice of Ecological Responsibility.* New York: Wiley & Sons, 1994.

University of North Carolina at Chapel Hill. *Environmental Management Systems: Do They Improve Performance?* Project Final Report: Executive Summary (January 30, 2003).

U.S. Environmental Protection Agency. *Aiming for Excellence: Actions to Encourage Stewardship and Accelerate Environmental Progress.* Washington, DC: EPA, 1999.

U.S. Environmental Protection Agency. *Unfinished Business: A Comparative Assessment of Environmental Problems, Overview Report.* Washington, DC: EPA, Science Advisory Board, 1987.

U.S. Environmental Protection Agency. *Reducing Risk: Setting Priorities and Strategies for Environmental Protection.* Washington, DC: EPA, Science Advisory Board, 1990.

U.S. Environmental Protection Agency. *The Benefits and Costs of the Clean Air Act: 1970–1990.* Washington, DC: EPA, 1997.

U.S. Environmental Protection Agency. *The Common Sense Initiative: Lessons Learned About Protecting the Environment in Common Sense, Cost-Effective Ways.* Washington, DC: EPA, Office of Reinvention, 1998.

U.S. Environmental Protection Agency. *Green Dividends? The Relationship Between Firms' Environmental Performance and Financial Performance.* Washington, DC: EPA, 2000.

U.S. Environmental Protection Agency. *The United States Experience with Economic Incentives for Protecting the Environment.* Washington, DC: EPA, 2001.

U.S. Environmental Protection Agency. *Draft Report on the Environment 2003.* Washington, DC: EPA, 2003.

U.S. Environmental Protection Agency. *Fiscal Year 2004 Annual Report.* Washington, DC: EPA, Office of the Chief Financial Officer, 2004.

U.S. Environmental Protection Agency. *Innovating for Better Environmental Results: A Report on Progress from the Innovation Action Council.* Washington, DC: EPA, 2004.

U.S. Environmental Protection Agency. *Evaluation of Implementation Experiences with Innovative Air Permits.* Washington, DC: EPA Office of Air Quality Planning and Standards and Office of Policy, Economics, and Innovation, 2004.

U.S. General Accountability Office. *Environmental Protection: Overcoming Obstacles to Innovative State Regulatory Programs.* Washington, DC: GAO, 2002.

Van Muijen, Marie-Louise. "The Netherlands: Ambitious on Goals–Ambivalent on Action." In William M. Lafferty and James Meadowcroft, eds., *Implementing Sustainable Development: Strategies and Initiatives in High-Consumption Societies.* Oxford: Oxford University Press, 2000, 142–173.

Veljanovski, Cento G. "The Economics of Regulatory Enforcement." In Keith Hawkins and John M. Thomas, eds. *Enforcing Regulation.* Boston: Kluwer-Nijhoff, 1984, 171–188.

Vig, Norman J. and Michael E. Kraft, eds. *Environmental Policy: New Directions for the Twenty-First Century.* 4th ed. Washington, DC: CQ Press, 2000.

Vig, Norman J. and Michael E. Kraft, eds. *Environmental Policy: New Directions for the Twenty-First Century*, 5th ed. Washington, DC: CQ Press, 2003.

Vig, Norman J. and Michael E. Kraft, eds. *Environmental Policy: New Directions for the Twenty-First Century*, 6th ed. Washington, DC: CQ Press, 2006.

Vogel, David. *National Styles of Regulation: Environmental Policy in Great Britain and the United States.* Ithaca, NY: Cornell University Press, 1986.

Wallace, David. *Environmental Policy and Industrial Innovation: Strategies in Europe, the US, and Japan.* London: Earthscan, 1995.

Weber, Edward P. *Pluralism by the Rules: Conflict and Cooperation in Environmental Regulation.* Washington, DC: Georgetown University Press, 1998.

Welch, Eric and A. Hibiki. "Japanese Voluntary Agreements: Bargaining Power and Reciprocity as Contributors to Effectiveness." *Policy Sciences*, 35 (2002), 491–424.

Wilson, Woodrow. "The Study of Public Administration." In Louis C. Gawthrop, ed. *The Administrative Process and Democratic Theory*. New York: Houghton-Mifflin, 1970, 77–85.

Yosie, Terry. "Responsible Care at Fifteen Years." *Environmental Science and Technology* (November 1, 2003), 401A–406A.

Index

the new environmental regulation

DANIEL J. FIORINO

Environmental regulation in the United States has succeeded, to a certain extent, in solving the problems it was designed to address; air, water, and land are indisputably cleaner and in better condition than they would be without the environmental controls put in place since 1970. But Daniel Fiorino argues in *The New Environmental Regulation* that—given recent environmental, economic, and social changes—it is time for a new, more effective model of environmental problem solving. Fiorino provides a comprehensive but concise overview of U.S. environmental regulation—its history, its rationale, and its application—and offers recommendations for a more collaborative, flexible, and performance-based alternative.

Traditional environmental regulation was based on the increasingly outdated assumption that environmental protection and business are irreversibly at odds. The new environmental regulation Fiorino describes is based on performance rather than on a narrow definition of compliance and uses such policy instruments as market incentives and performance measurement. It takes into consideration differences in the willingness and capabilities of different firms to meet their environmental obligations, and it encourages innovation by allowing regulated industries, especially the better performers, more flexibility in how they achieve environmental goals. Fiorino points to specific programs—including the 33/50 Program, innovative permitting, and the use of covenants as environmental policy instruments in the Netherlands—that have successfully pioneered these new strategies. By bringing together such a wide range of research and real world examples, Fiorino has created an invaluable resource for practitioners and scholars and an engaging text for environmental policy courses.

DANIEL J. FIORINO has extensive experience in federal regulation and innovation programs. He is coeditor of *Environmental Governance Reconsidered: Challenges, Choices, and Opportunities* (MIT Press, 2004) and teaches environmental and public policy at American University and Johns Hopkins University.

"As *The New Environmental Regulation* makes clear, it's high time for a refined and improved approach to environmental protection. Dan Fiorino blazes a path toward the future, showing how we might diversify our policy tools, focus on performance, build in flexibility, and engage the business world."
—Daniel C. Esty, Hillhouse Professor of Environmental Law and Policy, Yale University

"Fiorino's book provides a cogent explanation of how environmental policy got where it is, our successes and our failures. It offers critical insight into the task of crafting a new array of policy tools to tackle the formidable environmental challenges we face today."
—William K. Reilly, Administrator, U.S. Environmental Protection Agency, 1989–93

"This is one of the most important books on U.S. environmental policy to appear in the past twenty years. Fiorino offers a convincing analysis of the strengths and weaknesses of existing approaches and points the way towards a new style of regulation appropriate to the challenges of the twenty-first century."
—James Meadowcroft, Canada Research Chair in Governance for Sustainable Development, Carleton University, Canada

The MIT Press
Massachusetts Institute of Technology
Cambridge, Massachusetts 02142
http://mitpress.mit.edu

0-262-56218-9
978-0-262-56218-8

90000

9 780262 562188